Advance Praise for
WriterSpeaker.com

"If a writer and speaker could only have one book on the Internet, this is it! Personable and readable, *WriterSpeaker.com* provides comprehensive coverage of how and why the Internet works. Reading this book is almost like consulting a trusted friend—who also happens to be an Internet expert. Add in the remarkable collection of site addresses, and you have a resource all writers and speakers should have on their bookshelves."

—MARY WESTHEIMER, CEO of BookZone.com,
the Internet's largest publishing company

"With this book, writing books just became faster, easier, cheaper, and a lot more fun. Carmen Leal reveals where to find what you need in the world's largest library: the Web. This book is a treasury of information for writers and speakers."

—DAN POYNTER, *The Self-Publishing Manual,* http://www.parapub.com

"Technology and the Internet are changing the book-publishing industry with lightning speed. In *WriterSpeaker.com,* Leal gives writers and speakers exactly what they need to succeed in this new and dynamic environment."

—JENNIFER BASYE SANDER, coauthor of
The Complete Idiot's Guide to Getting Published

"Whether novice or professional, every writer and speaker can learn something from this book. It is packed with solid research related in a user-friendly style."

—W. TERRY WHALIN, author of more than fifty books,
www.terrywhalin.com

"As I train and encourage speakers, I tell them that if they wish to be a success today they must be computer literate and Internet savvy. *WriterSpeaker.com* is THE resource for speakers and writers."

—MARITA LITTAUER, President of CLASServices, Inc.,
and author of ten books, including *Personality Puzzle*
and *Talking So People Will Listen*

"Hate spending hours looking for all that 'good stuff' you've been told is on the information superhighway? This book is guaranteed to save you literally hundreds of hours of hunting via search engines. *WriterSpeaker.com* must be on every computer desk—right next to your style manual and dictionary. And it just may become your favorite Internet reference book of all time because of Leal's unique Living Links system for updating."

—ELAINE WRIGHT COLVIN, director, Writers Information Network;
editor, WIN-INFORMER, http://www.bluejaypub.com/win

"If you can't find what you need to know about the Internet in *Writer-Speaker.com*, you probably don't need it. It is the most user-friendly and comprehensive guide I've ever read on the subject. Writers and speakers who do not have a copy of this resource are wasting vast amounts of time gathering expertise and information that Leal has put at their fingertips."

—SANDY BROOKS, director, Christian Writers Fellowship International

"I hate starting out on a trip without a well-marked map to guide me. When I entered the information superhighway, there was no such map to be found. Now Carmen Leal's *WriterSpeaker.com* not only provides detailed guidance and instruction along this often-frightening and frustrating road, it gives you the feeling that you're traveling with a friend who's been down this road before."

—SALLY E. STUART, *Christian Writers' Market Guide*

WriterSpeaker.com

Internet Research and Marketing for Writers and Speakers

| CARMEN LEAL

SHAW

WATERBROOK
PRESS

WriterSpeaker.com
A SHAW BOOK
PUBLISHED BY WATERBROOK PRESS
2375 Telstar Drive, Suite 160
Colorado Springs, Colorado 80920
A division of Random House, Inc.

ISBN 0-87788-876-0

Library of Congress Cataloging-in-Publication Data
Leal, Carmen, 1954-
    Writerspeaker.com : Internet research and marketing for writers and speakers / Carmen Leal.
        p. cm.
    ISBN 0-87788-876-0 (paper)
        1. Authorship—Computer network resources. 2. Public speaking—Computer network resources. 3. Electronic publishing—Computer network resources I. Title.

    PN142.5.L43 2000
    025.04—dc21

                                                            00-055663

Printed in the United States of America
2000—First Edition

10 9 8 7 6 5 4 3 2 1

*Thanks to the many talented and supportive writers and speakers
I have met through CWFI, CWG, CLASS, and other online groups
who have blessed me with their friendship, prayers,
and answers to countless questions.*

CONTENTS

Part 4: Putting Yourself on the Road Map

ACKNOWLEDGMENTS

No published book, including *WriterSpeaker.com,* was ever completed by just one person. Thank you to my editor, Joan Guest, at Shaw Publishers, who besides being a wonderful editor is a delightful person of great integrity. Thank you for your efforts in helping make this a book to be proud of.

I'd also like to thank my dear friend JoAnn Zarling, a marvelous editor who helped me through the first edits of the book. Her friendship means even more to me than her professional ability.

Writing a book on a technical topic, even one geared for the nontechnical reader, was a challenge for someone who has never even taken a computer course. My thanks to talented Webmaster Gary Scott, who has an inordinate amount of patience when it comes to explaining terms and unraveling the mysteries of the Web. I wish he had time to create a Web site for every one of you like the one he created for me.

Finally, I wish to thank the many people from various chat rooms, forums, and mailing lists who answered questions, identified what needed to be included in this book, and in the process, became special people in my life.

Success is not a destination: It is a journey. The happiest people I know are those who are busy working toward specific objectives. The most bored and miserable people I know are those who are drifting along with no worthwhile objectives in mind.—ZIG ZIGLAR

In 1943, IBM chairman Thomas Watson announced, "I think there is a world market for maybe five computers."

A 1949 *Popular Mechanics* article stated that computers in the future would probably weigh "no more than 15 tons."

And in 1968, an engineer at the Advanced Computing Systems Division of IBM commented on the microchip: "But what is it good for?"

As late as 1977, Ken Olson, president and founder of Digital Equipment Corporation, said there was "no reason anyone would want a computer in their home."

But my favorite quote about the future of the computer was made in 1981 by Bill Gates, self-proclaimed king of the nerds and the richest man in the universe, who asserted that "640K ought to be enough for anybody."

We chuckle over those statements now. Less than twenty years after Gates made his remark, ten times that amount of memory is standard, and hard drives come in gigabytes. Computers in small businesses and private homes are increasingly commonplace. And the world market for computers is a bit more than the five predicted in 1943. A September 1999 report released by internationally renowned Internet consulting and development company Nua *(http://www.nua.com)* reported there are currently over 201 million Internet users worldwide. A report by the same research group four years earlier had found a mere 26 million worldwide users. Clearly the Internet has been at least one of the driving forces behind computer sales over the last several years.

Paid for by U.S. tax dollars, the Internet was developed in the late 1960s as a tool to enable government researchers working on military projects to share computer files. Undocumented stories credit nuclear war survival as the catalyst for its creation; whether or not the stories are true—whatever the reasons at the time—the tax dollars used to create the Internet infrastructure were money well spent.

In 1993, after universities had been using the Internet for nearly twenty-five years, the media finally grabbed hold of the idea of cyberspace, touting its advantages as well as making dire predictions about how it would affect us in the future. Around 1994, the average American began to see the benefits—very tangible benefits—of learning more about this "cyber" stuff; in typical capitalistic fashion, people began to find ways to make money online. No one ever looked back.

About the time America began learning how to navigate the information superhighway, my husband was diagnosed with Huntington's Disease, an incurable neurological disorder. In my search for information about the condition, I found short paragraphs in medical books about the disease itself—but little about how my husband and I were supposed to get through each day. Learning that he was incurably ill was hard enough. Not having access to specialists, support groups, and information made the diagnosis even worse.

I remembered that months earlier I had heard a speaker wax enthusiastically about cyber communities, online shopping, and the World Wide Web. At the time, I'd scoffed at what I was hearing and wondered what kind of person led such an empty life that she had to turn to a computer to satisfy her needs. But with Huntington's Disease taking over our family life, I knew I had found a reason to get on the highway that speaker had talked about. All of a sudden, when things got personal, my computer became my new best friend.

After finding an online support group, I discovered first of all that I was not alone. People from around the world felt as uninformed and inadequate to cope with this disease as I did. There was nothing available for those of us who were struggling simply to get through another day. Someone, I decided, needed to write a book. Eventually, as no one else seemed willing to give a voice and a face to Huntington's Disease, I realized I would have to do it myself.

The Internet proved invaluable in the writing, editing, publishing, and selling of *Faces of Huntington's*. It was, in fact, the perfect school for me to learn not only how to write a book, but how to self-publish and market a book to thousands of people around the world. Ideas and submissions came from online support group members from California to the Netherlands and hundreds of places in between. An editor from Guam and an illustrator from North Carolina lent their talents to the book. A wonderful friend even e-mailed an offer of an interest-free loan!

Chapters were edited entirely by e-mail—and communication with my publisher was simplified thanks to being online. At this point, my Web page and my interactions with potential readers through e-mail lists and chat rooms have been responsible for at least 60 percent of total sales.

Since publishing *Faces of Huntington's,* I have begun speaking about Huntington's Disease and other topics throughout the United States. My Web page has been an information source for and a point of contact with members of the medical profession, support groups, churches, and other interested parties.

Even now that my husband is in a long-term care facility, I am finding the Internet tremendously helpful. As Dave continues to decline—he can no longer walk, talk, feed himself, or care for any of his physical needs—I find myself continually doing Internet research so I can teach the staff the best ways to care for him. The information superhighway has made me an expert.

Marita Littauer, author, speaker, and founder of CLASS (Christian Leaders, Authors and Speakers Services), maintains, "If you have something worth speaking about, you have something worth writing about. If you are a speaker, you can be a writer."

That is my own experience; I was a speaker long before I began putting my words down on paper. At some point, after many in my audiences began asking for copies of the stories I told in my presentations in order to share them with others, I started writing down those stories and making copies to have on hand to give away.

As I've said, about the time it became obvious that I needed at least to consider the idea of writing a book about Huntington's Disease, I discovered the Internet. Through trial and error, I learned almost everything I needed to know about the writing and publishing process—and about navigating the World Wide Web. With this book, I pass my discoveries on to you.

Littauer hits the mark when she says, "Speaking and writing are like a hand in a glove." As a writer and speaker myself, I know this, and I wanted to write a book that would be helpful for both endeavors, a book that would simplify the Internet for professional writers *and* speakers—and help them get the most out of their experience with it.

On the surface, much of the book may seem geared toward writers rather than speakers. There's a reason for that: While there are exhaustive numbers of Web sites for writers on the Net, there are fewer for speakers. The information required for researching, networking, "chatting," and using mailing lists and newsgroups, however, is the same for both. With the information presented in *WriterSpeaker.com,* you'll know how to find what you need and use it for your own unique purposes.

Simply put, the Internet is the world's largest computer network—a system that connects computers all over the world so they can share information. Writers, for instance, might use the Internet to send information such as articles, book chapters, submissions, and queries to publishers or directly to readers. They might also send graphic files such as an author's photo for the back of a book jacket. Speakers might use the Internet to post portions of their presentations or to host Internet conferences.

Is it hard to imagine yourself using the Internet in those ways? I'll be honest: Friends and family who have known me for a while can't believe that I visit cyberspace every day. After all, I never learned to type, and I've been banned from using any office equipment at every job I've ever had. There were even signs posted over the copier and paper shredder prohibiting me from touching them, since repairmen routinely earned a living wage by fixing what I broke. When I began giving workshops for writers about the Internet, my sons laughed hysterically at the idea of their mom teaching anything the least bit technical. But now that I have two books out, their publication and sales due almost entirely to the Internet, the kids have stopped laughing and are asking instead to be included in profit sharing!

Years ago I was a sales rep for a news, talk, and sports radio station. Before that job, sports interested me little. When I learned I could make money by knowing the teams and the odds and speaking the language, however, I quickly became an expert! Soon I knew the names of all the major players and could quote their stats. Every morning began with a quick look at the sports page. I cheered for the home team to make the playoffs—because it meant more opportunities to sell air time. But when I left that job, I no longer had a reason to follow the various teams—and I didn't!

That's how I view the Internet. I don't know a lot about computers, and I never really wanted to become well-informed about them. But when I found a way to use the Internet to meet my goals, I began to learn enough to take advantage of the technology.

It was an illness that got me started. For you it might be research, online learning, or keeping in touch with family and friends. No matter the reason, the Internet is a tool, and like any tool, it helps to understand how it works.

HOW TO USE THIS BOOK

Remember your driver's education class? First, the instructor made sure you buckled your seat belt, checked the mirror, and looked both ways. Only then were you allowed to turn the key and start driving. That's the purpose of *Writer-Speaker.com:* preparing you for travel on the information superhighway. If you're smart, before you travel any road—especially one with as many twists and turns and on-ramps as the Internet—you study a good map, and you take it with you. So before you begin your tour of cyberspace, let me explain the features of this "map" I've written for you.

WriterSpeaker.com has four sections, each building on the previous one. No matter your level of computer, Internet, writing, or speaking expertise, every section is a helpful guide for your journey.

Section 1 provides an educational foundation with a brief Internet history and a tutorial on using e-mail, chat, mailing lists, and newsgroups, as well as search engines and the Web. If you are well versed on the Internet, you might consider skipping this section. On the other hand, no matter how long you've been navigating the information superhighway, you may be surprised at how much there is to learn, even for old-timers.

Section 2 includes tips for using the Internet to find and use online courses, critique groups, grammar sites, bulletin boards, and newsgroups to help you perfect your craft. You will also explore the business of writing through listings of publishers' Web sites, online writer and speaker associations, and sites explaining copyright laws. The section ends with a compilation of top Web sites for various genres, such as fiction, romance, and inspirational.

The third section is filled with stories and ideas from actual writers and speakers who regularly use the Internet for submitting queries, proposals, and manuscripts and for booking speaking engagements. I've also included a number of suggestions for using the Internet for online support and networking with other professionals.

The fourth section contains samples and suggestions about how to create author and speaker Web sites, including marketing on the Internet. Listed are online resources for self-publishing, including e-zines, e-books, and other forms of electronic publishing. An appendix, glossary, and index complete the book.

WriterSpeaker.com is not filled with techno-jargon. It's reader friendly and fun. I have found, in my years as a speaker and writer, that people love stories. You'll find them here. You'll also find many ideas about how to use the Internet—an important focus of this book. Ultimately, knowing how to access information on the Internet will be more useful than simply having a list of Web sites, as valuable as that might be. My intent is that *WriterSpeaker.com* be more than just a glorified list of bookmarks for Web sites relevant to writers and speakers.

When a new car is driven off the lot, it's already obsolete. Automobile designers continually strive for better gas mileage, enhanced safety features, or simply more driver conveniences. Because the same is true of computers and the Internet, you may find slightly outdated information in this book—perhaps out-of-date Web sites or new technology that is not mentioned. The fact is that while Internet resources change daily, the basic Internet information and ideas for writers and speakers included in these pages remain relevant.

To make *WriterSpeaker.com* as helpful as possible, a Web site with links to all the resources listed in the book is available to readers. This service, called Living Links, is unique to *WriterSpeaker.com* and is not available through any other similar book for writers or speakers. The Web site is written in HTML format so that it is accessible from any Web browser on any computer where it's stored. Rather than having to type the URLs *(Universal Record Locators)* into your browser for each Web site you want to visit, you only have to click on the address and follow the links. When you are online, your computer takes you to the actual Web site. If you'd like a free copy of Living Links, go to the Web site listed at the end of this chapter. The ISBN number of this book acts as your password to enter the site, and anyone who registers will receive quarterly updates. (All links are checked periodically, and dead Web sites are eliminated. New Web sites come with brief descriptions.)

In choosing the sites to be featured in *WriterSpeaker.com,* I used several qualifiers. Knowing the site was informative and easy to follow certainly was important, but potential longevity was also a determining factor since I wanted sites that will be active for years to come. Rather than list every site in every category, I've tried to give you those that are regarded as the best or those that have become almost super writing-speaking sites because they link to so many others. Some sites simply give information while others have chat rooms, mailing lists, or forums.

It was also important that I not include sites that could be considered offensive to anyone. Each site selected for inclusion met that requirement; however, I have no control over what happens to these sites afterward. Sites change, and sometimes sites that were wholesome add unwholesome material or change their focus altogether. Further, I have no control over any links you may find as a result of surfing through various sites. If you stumble upon an inappropriate location, please accept my apologies and click to a different site.

If you have questions or would like to recommend sites for future editions of this book, a companion Web site for *WriterSpeaker.com* has constant updates and articles. You will also find at this location a subscription form for the *WriterSpeaker.com* newsletter and Living Links.

➤ Living Links at *http://www.writerspeaker.com/LL.html*

➤ WriterSpeaker.com at *http://www.WriterSpeaker.com*

Navigating the information superhighway can be like bouncing about in a clunker on a poorly maintained country road after a severe winter or like driving down a newly paved highway in a luxury car. The more you know about this incredible tool, the smoother and more fulfilling the ride will be.

To paraphrase a well-known quote: "Buckle your seat belts; you're in for an amazing ride!"

PART ONE

The Journey Begins

ONE

Getting on the Road

Decide what you want. Decide what you are willing to exchange for it.
Establish your priorities. Go to work.—H. L. HUNT

In an interview with CNN's Wolf Blitzer on March 9, 1999, Al Gore made a startling announcement: "During my service in the United States Congress, I took the initiative in creating the Internet." An outcry from around the virtual world ensued at the notion that any one person, even the vice president of the United States, had created the Internet, and a plethora of sometimes outraged, often derisive comments followed. The best one, in my opinion, allegedly came from former Vice President Dan Quayle, who quipped, "If Al Gore invented the Internet, I invented the spell checker." According to *Wired News,* when the Department of Defense started the system that ultimately became the Internet, "Gore was twenty-one years old at the time. He wasn't even done with law school at Vanderbilt University."

To give him his due, credit does go to Gore for coining the term *information superhighway* in the early 1990s. Often the simplest way to explain a complicated idea is by the use of metaphors. The popular use of Gore's term for the Internet helps make a complex technology easily understood.

Information superhighway is an appropriate metaphor; the automobile changed the world more profoundly than anything else in the twentieth century, and the Internet may very well do the same for the twenty-first.

Let me make a point right here. People incorrectly use the terms "Internet" and "World Wide Web" interchangeably. They are not the same. The Internet, or the information superhighway, is the infrastructure that includes the World Wide Web, along with e-mail, "chat" options, Usenet newsgroups, and more. The World Wide Web, also known simply as the Web, is the part of the Internet that allows users to travel between linked documents (Web pages). It's composed of Web servers that provide access to Web sites and Web documents.

Whether you are a writer, a speaker, or both, this book is designed to help you get the most out of the Internet. If you are embarking on this journey down the information superhighway for the first time, this book will, I hope, provide you with a rudimentary map to guide your travels. And if you've been down this road before, you'll find in these pages new and wonderful side roads to explore.

Whether navigating the interstate highway system or the information superhighway, the first requirement is a vehicle of some sort. There are many transportation modes for traveling the first, but for the latter a computer is the means of transit needed to cruise the cyber version of Route 66 and beyond.

I am frequently asked questions like, "Which computer is best for using the Internet?" Well, just as there is no "best" automobile for cruising the highways, there is no "best" computer for cruising the Internet. Sufficient memory to run the programs needed to take full advantage of Internet tools is one essential though. These days, using anything below a Pentium is a little like using a moped or a bicycle on the freeway. You will also need enough hard drive space to store the programs and whatever else you download. Beyond that, only your budget limits the possibilities.

The PC and Apple/MacIntosh war continues to rage, with PC currently well ahead, dominating almost 90 percent of the market. With the advent of Microsoft Windows, both systems are user-friendly. I use a MacIntosh, not necessarily because it's better, although I do prefer it. I switched from a PC to a Mac when Mac was the industry standard in graphics for those in advertising, publishing, and marketing. Now, with thousands of dollars invested in software and an intimate knowledge of the system, it makes sense for me to stick with the Mac. Macintosh hardware is generally more expensive, however, and Mac-compiled software less available—although for the average writer or speaker, there is more than enough excellent software out there.

Now that Apple has cloned its operating system and presented its own trendy new iMac "PC," marketed specifically to the Internet user, the popularity gap between the two companies is narrowing. According to PC Data, a computer hardware and software point-of-sales data reporting and analysis firm, the iMac closed 1998 as the best-selling PC on the market, selling more than eight hundred thousand units.[1] PC Data also reported that the iMac accounted for 7.1 percent of all PC sales in 1998[2] and brought Apple's market share from under 5 percent to over 10 percent. Thirty-two percent of iMac's purchasers were first-time computer buyers, and 13 percent were Windows converts.

Check out the many excellent books and Web sites designed to help you choose a computer to fit your needs and budget. Public libraries and schools often provide Internet access for those who want to do online research before investing in a computer. You'll even find information about various ways to buy equipment online.

THE MODEM: YOUR "WHEELS"

A computer without a modem might just as well be up on blocks, like a car without wheels. You can't do much cruising with either.

Modem is shorthand for "modulator demodulator," a device that allows a computer to receive and transmit data over standard telephone lines. A modem both converts digital data to analog signals and analog signals back to digital data. Computers purchased in the last few years, and definitely those available today, usually come with an internal modem and preloaded software to make the modem work. External modems can be added for use with older models that don't have an internal modem. The minimum speed sold with new computers is 56K, but slower models still work. Owners of older models need not madly rush out to purchase a faster model.

While Web TV, cable, and DSL connections are available in many areas, connecting via a computer modem is still the most popular and affordable option and the one we will discuss here. But be aware that it's only a matter of time till those other connection methods become more readily available and affordable.

INTERNET SERVICE PROVIDERS: ACCESS TO THE HIGHWAY

Once a computer is equipped with a modem, internal or external, the big decision is the selection of an *Internet Service Provider* (ISP). An ISP works like a highway on-ramp, giving you access to the Internet when your modem dials into its computers. ISPs typically charge a monthly fee and in return provide a dial-up telephone number, at least one e-mail address, and limited technical assistance. Many ISPs also provide space for a Web page.

When I first went online, I had to make certain an ISP had Mac software available. Surprisingly, there are still companies that offer PC-only start-up kits. The majority of ISPs do support both platforms, but it's always wise to check before getting started.

How Much Should I Pay?

When Internet use exploded in the midnineties, price was one of the major determining factors in choosing a provider. Back then, "unlimited" applied to the number of busy signals received and rarely to the amount of hours available for the monthly fee! ISPs rationed time, and the charge for time spent on the Internet beyond their set number of hours was as much as $2.95 an hour. Taking advantage of all the Internet had to offer could be costly.

Things have changed, and unlimited access to the Internet is now the norm. Whether you connect for one hour a month or stay online for every waking hour of every day, the cost is still the same. Until recently, $19.95 for unlimited use was considered excellent pricing. That's still not bad, but it's possible to pay as little as $14.95 or less for unlimited service. By paying for a year in advance, referring new users to the ISP, and taking advantage of other promotions, the cost of Internet service is constantly shrinking.

Many ISPs offer new customers a free month to evaluate their service. Even if it's not advertised, it's a good idea to ask if a free month is available. This gives a potential user time to evaluate the level of service and the company's responsiveness. Even a free service is worthless if it's next to impossible to log on to the Internet.

How Can I Get Service for Free?

Because money is often an issue for writers and speakers, you may want to consider getting free Internet access. While $19.95 a month may not sound like a lot, it can pay for a second phone line each month or stamps for mailing those SASEs when you're sending out manuscripts and queries.

If you've been online for any length of time, you've probably figured out that advertising is the gimmick behind free Internet access. If you're not bothered by banner ads on each page and you don't mind receiving lots of unwanted e-mail (generally known as spam), a free ISP is worth looking into. I've listed several links to help you find the right free service for your area. Remember to make sure the number you dial to access the Internet is not a long-distance or toll call.

➤ About.com offers an excellent set of links about free ISP services and also, in some cases, free computers. To access the list go to *http://www.about.com* and type "free ISP" in the search box.

➤ Aid4 Free ISPs *(http://www.y4i.com/freeaccess2.html)* features a list of free ISPs from around the world.

➤ BlueLight.com *(http://www.bluelight.com)* is a free ISP from Kmart. According to their site, 96 percent of the United States has local coverage.

➤ Giant search engine AltaVista *(http://www.freealtavista.com/)* now offers free service.

➤ Freei.Net *(http://www.freeinternet.com)* offers free nationwide Internet access.

➤ FreePPP *(http://www.freeppp.com)* is a free ISP for the Macintosh.

➤ WorldSpy.com *(http://www.worldspy.com/freeisp/free-isp-nav.asp)* is actually an online shopping service that also offers free Internet service.

Why Bother with a Commercial Online Service?

Imagine you're cruising the highway, out to discover new things and garner more information for your excursions. You take an exit off the highway, go through a series of turns, and eventually stop before an ornate gate. Glimpsing the perfectly manicured lawns and stately homes within, you ease the car into drive with intentions of investigating this new territory. Just then, a uniformed guard with clipboard in hand approaches. After a cursory glance at his list, he denies you entrance. As others freely glide through the open gate, you explain, to no avail, that you know someone inside. The guard insists that without being a resident, you can't get in, no matter whom you know. Finally, aware that no amount of cajoling or whining will get you onto the restricted grounds, you make a U-turn and, frustrated, head back onto the highway, where all drivers are allowed.

Welcome to America Online, CompuServe, Prodigy, or any other commercial online service. These specialized ISPs are the "gated communities" of the Internet. Restricted to those who have joined and paid a monthly fee, commercial online services bill themselves as user-friendly with easy-to-navigate icons. Each ISP community also provides an array of services and special interest forums for members only.

Until the last few years, providers like AOL made it next to impossible for nonmembers to navigate beyond their borders. The browsers available through commercial online services were considerably less than user-friendly, and subscribers to one service could rarely take advantage of the opportunities available through other commercial online services or ISPs. Yes, there were great meeting boards, libraries, chat rooms, shopping malls, and more on the Internet, but except through e-mail, only people using the same service could interact with each other.

Now the major browsers, such as Netscape and Microsoft's Internet Explorer, are free to anyone who retrieves ("downloads") a copy of the file from another computer using a modem or computer network. Today, a member of any online service can use the Internet with ease. Still, unless an Internet user joins a particular online service, the proprietary content of that ISP is still off-limits to him or her.

For writers and speakers, unique networking opportunities, message boards, libraries, chat rooms, résumé postings, genre forums, and more are available only by signing up for a commercial service such as America Online. For some, these extras are enough to keep them on a specific service, even when they can get Internet access for less or even for free.

While service through commercial ISPs is coming down in price, the average commercial online service price is as much as three or four dollars per month more expensive than an ISP. In areas with a large number of subscribers, getting online happens only after several frustrating busy signals. AOL users specifically have complained about the time it takes to get online, though the situation has greatly improved over the last few years. In my opinion, subscribing to a commercial online service is no longer the only or even the best way to get access to online writer and speaker resources; there are an ever-increasing number of forums and chat groups outside the commercial online services that are easy to find and use.

Should I Go National or Local?

ISPs, of which there are countless numbers, are either national or local providers. There are reasons to choose one over the other, depending upon your specific needs, location, and other factors.

National providers sometimes have faster, more advanced Internet connections, and they're likely to be around tomorrow and for years to come. While a local company may seem accessible, there is no guarantee it will stay in business over time.

For writers and speakers who travel, a national service provider that travels with you can meet some specific needs. Sign-up usually includes local dial-up phone numbers for connecting to the service from locations all over the country. While national ISPs also have toll-free numbers, be forewarned that a surcharge may be added when you use it instead of the local access number. Ask about the company policy regarding this issue before signing up with an ISP so that you don't find unwelcome surprise charges on your credit card. The ability to check and send e-mail while on the road without incurring long-distance phone charges is, for some, the deciding factor when choosing between national and local providers.

There are advantages to using local providers, too. They are often the first to debut new services such as cable modems and satellite and wireless access. As members of the local community, they may also offer promotions like featured Web sites and online newsletters that profile their customers. If you write or speak locally, this could be a great marketing opportunity for you.

Today, national ISPs have enough *points of presence* (PoPs) spread across the United States to let most people connect by making a local telephone call. Just because an ISP boasts a lot of PoPs doesn't mean that every area in your state is covered. You may live or travel where the "local access" number is actually a toll call. Yes, that call might be only twenty-five cents to dial in for unlimited time, but logging on only four times a day would cost thirty dollars a month in addition to your Internet service. Once you have the local access number for your ISP, check with the telephone company to make sure the call is really free.

What About the "Bad Stuff" Out There on the Web?

Many people who use their computers at home for writing and research, especially those with children in the home, have concerns about certain online content. Having access to the Internet can be great, but there are also negatives—the possibility you or your loved ones might stumble onto pornographic sites, for instance, or sites that promote racism, violence, and other destructive ideas and beliefs.

Filtering software that screens access to undesirable online content is available, and for many this is sufficient. The software is not foolproof, however. Anyone, including a child, who has some computer smarts can beat the system. The best software solution should include filtering, an audit-trail function, and the ability to block out search engines that are not family friendly. Without access to these search engines, undesirable sites are more difficult to find.

In some cases—for instance, when you are accessing Web sites containing medical information—you may wish to bypass the filtering system; most of the software available allows for this. (The classic example for why you might want to bypass a filtering program: AOL, trying to make the Internet family friendly, at one point chose to filter out the word *breast*. While that succeeded in keeping thousands of pornographic sites off AOL, it also filtered out information about breast cancer.)

Others find a filtered ISP—a server that screens content before it reaches your computer—is more reliable than filtering software, since the function cannot be erased or circumvented. There is also no software to update. ISPs eliminate millions of specific Web sites, keywords contained within URL addresses, specific keyword searches, and known pornography-hosting Web sites, newsgroups, chat rooms, e-mail, and messaging programs. Some of these ISPs also generate Internet activity reports that allow a parent to see how often family members are online and where they have gone.

Another solution to the problem might be an ISP provider that doesn't block sites but instead searches the Internet for allowable sites. This means that their crawler looks for what's *good* online versus screening out the bad. If it's not on their "good" list, it's not allowed. While that may be fine for children, it can severely limit research options for writers and speakers.

The choice to use a filter or to sign up with a filtered ISP is a personal one. Though local access numbers are growing in number, these ISPs are not available in every area or even in every state. Also, their monthly fees are often more costly that the larger national ISPs. I've listed some Web sites for several companies that provide filtering software and also for a number of filtered ISPs.

Filtering Software

- CyberPatrol at *http://www.cyberpatrol.com*
- Cyber Sitter at *http://www.solidoak.com/cysitter.htm*
- Net Nanny at *http://www.netnanny.com/netnanny*

Filtered ISPs

- CleanWeb at *http://home.cleanWeb.net*
- ClearSail at *http://www.clearsail.net*
- DotSafe at *http://www.dotsafe.net/staticindex.html*
- Family.Net at *http://www.family.net*
- Integrity Online at *http://www.integrityonline.com*
- Mayberry at *http://www.mayberryusa.net*

What Else Should I Look For?

Besides price, location, and content, there are other determining factors in choosing an ISP. Knowing when to change the oil and rotate an automobile's tires is about as far as most drivers go when it comes to understanding their car. There are comparatively few auto wizards out there, and if you're like most people, you are not, and have no desire to be, a computer or Internet techno-wizard, either. Things like ease of initial setup and access to technical support are as important to consider as other factors.

Easy Setup

Easy setup is an absolute must when it comes to an ISP. Once an ISP is selected, the CD or the download file, if one's available, should install everything you need to get started. A browser (usually Netscape or Microsoft's Internet Explorer), a stand-alone e-mail program (often Eudora or Pegasus), and a newsgroup client (program) should be part of any ISP setup. All the setup work, such as entering the ISP or server address, should already be done, leaving you simply to install and configure your mail and news accounts.

My provider, EarthLink, has one of the best new-member packages available. A few days after signup they send an excellent booklet called *Getting the Most Out of the Internet* by EarthLink founder, Sky Dalton. Know what I, as a writer, really like about the booklet? The actual writers receive credit—as does the entire team, including the editor and even the proofreader!

➤ EarthLink at *http://www.earthlink.net*

Technical Support

At a minimum, an ISP should offer toll-free telephone support. Most national providers have twenty-four-hour telephone and online support, where local providers often are available for fewer support hours. An e-mail support option should also be available.

E-Mail

E-mail is often quoted as the primary reason for a person going online. If this is so for you, be sure to check out the limit on the number of e-mail addresses you have available per account when choosing an ISP. AOL offers up to five mailboxes per account. If having a variety of e-mail addresses sounds helpful, this may be your deciding point. Most ISPs still offer only one mailbox, but some make additional addresses available for a small fee.

Web-Page Space and Tools

A Web page can be a wonderful marketing tool for writers and speakers. Most ISPs provide free Web-page space with each account. The amount of space can vary from three to ten megabytes (MB). In most ISP agreements, free Web space is for personal use only, though enforcement is quite lax. Publishing tools and links to help you create a Web page should also be considered, though these are available online by doing a little research.

Referral Credit

While not a big factor in choosing an ISP, some people might want to choose a provider that gives them credit for referring new users. For example, Earth-Link is among the ISPs that give incentives to their subscribers for referring others who ultimately sign up for their service.

What Questions Should I Ask?

Asking questions will always help you decide which ISP is right for you. Even then, remember it's always wise to request a free month to help you evaluate a particular provider's service. Here are some questions to ask prospective ISPs:

- *What is your installation fee? Can you waive the fee if I'm switching from another provider?*
- *What are your rates?*
- *Do you provide an 800-number for dialing in?*
- *What are your local calling areas?*
- *Do you have preconfigured software for your customers?*
- *What are the hours for your technical support and help desk?*
- *If I cancel service, will I be charged for the entire month? Do I need to cancel in writing?*
- *What is the user-to-modem ratio? (8 to 1 is the minimum for no busy signals when dialing in.)*
- *What are your privacy and security policies?*
- *Do you have any automatic cutoff features?*
- *What modem types and modem speed connections do you support?*
- *Do you charge for disk space? If so, how much?*
- *Do you provide an informational customer Web page or newsletter?*

Depending on whom you quote, there are three to five thousand ISPs nationwide, and the list is growing. Choosing the right provider is essential. It is becoming increasingly "smart" and very often required for writers and speakers to have an e-mail address and a Web site. Imagine the hassle, if you choose the wrong one, of reprinting business cards and stationary, forwarding e-mail—if your provider even does that—and redirecting traffic each time you change providers. Here are several excellent Web sites that list ISPs by area code, country code, or even by price.

➤ ISPcheck at *http://Webpedia.ispcheck.com*
➤ ISPs.com at *http://www.isps.com*
➤ The List at *http://thelist.internet.com/ internet.com* (bills itself as the "definitive buyer's guide to Internet Service Providers")
➤ The Ultimate Web ISP List at *http://Webisplist.internetlist.com*

The following ISPs offer local access POP numbers in all fifty states:

➤ America Online at *http://www.aol.com*
➤ A+Net at *http://www.aplus.net*
➤ CompuServe at *http://www.compuserve.com*
➤ EarthLink at *http://www.earthlink.com* *
➤ MindSpring at *http://www.mindspring.net* *
➤ Prodigy at *http://www.prodigy.com*

* *In September 1999, EarthLink and MindSpring combined to create the nation's second-largest Internet access provider after AOL.*

In summary, the primary requirements for going online are having access to a computer and modem and getting connected through an ISP. If you need more information in either of these areas, several of the books and Web sites listed in the appendix will help. But if you're ready, let's get on the road!

Exploring the Neighborhood

E-mail, Lists, Chatting, Forums, and Newsgroups

Enthusiasm is one of the most powerful engines of success. When you do a thing, do it with your might. Put your whole soul into it. Stamp it with your own personality. Be active, be energetic, be enthusiastic and faithful, and you will accomplish your object. Nothing great was ever achieved without enthusiasm.—RALPH WALDO EMERSON

In the not-too-distant past, communicating with other writers and speakers, not to mention making all our other business and social contacts, meant using the telephone or the postal services. While both methods are still in use, they are not now the most efficient, nor are they the most affordable.

According to a General Accounting Office (GAO) report delivered to the House Subcommittee on the Postal Service in late October 1999, the amount of first-class mail handled by the United States Postal Service is expected to begin declining by 2003, thanks in large part to e-mail and electronic bill paying. USPS projections are that the Internet could wipe out $17 billion in postal service revenues.

These are interesting facts for taxpayers' consideration, but what does the USPS's losing money have to do with writers and speakers using the Internet? Quite a bit, actually. It's not only bill payers who use fewer stamps these days. E-mail, chat rooms, and other online resources are communication tools to which more and more of us are turning for more and more reasons. We don't need to stand in line at the post office; we don't need to buy stamps.

For those of you not quite ready to give up the postal service, two companies, Estamp.com and Stamps.com, now provide Internet postage service with the approval of the USPS. Users can purchase, download, and print postage directly from their personal computers onto envelopes, labels, or documents using standard laser or inkjet printers.

➤ Estamp.com at *http://www.estamp.com*

➤ Stamps.com at *http://www.stamps.com*

Whether you continue to buy stamps the conventional way, on the Internet, or not at all, the purpose of this book is to help you learn to use the Internet for researching, networking, submitting queries, marketing, and other writing- and speaking-related activities.

As wonderful as the Internet is, incorrect usage of any of the tools it provides us can lead to disaster. E-mail, mailing lists, the various chat options, and newsgroups each have their own version of netiquette. Reading these brief overviews and following the tips will go a long way toward making the Internet work successfully for you.

A friend told me a story about her daughter, who was learning the Lord's Prayer. Night after night they practiced together until finally the little girl decided she could recite it perfectly. She did fine until the end of the prayer. "Lead us not into temptation," she prayed, "but deliver us some e-mail. Amen." With that not-too-subtle segue, we'll begin with a discussion about e-mail.

E - M A I L

"E-mail Now Primary Reason People Go Online" was the headline from a Reuters story in October 1999 in response to a survey by Price Waterhouse Coopers. The pollsters found that 48 percent of U.S. Internet users who responded to their survey said they went online for e-mail while 28 percent said they went online to do research. A year earlier, the identical numbers had been reversed.[1]

It may not have animated graphics, blaring music, or any of the ever-growing collection of cybernetic bells and whistles, but e-mail is the most used feature of the Internet—and with good reason. One advantage over regular mail is that you can get e-mail from virtually anywhere in the world almost instantly. Once you contact your mail server, you can immediately download your messages. For the same reason, e-mail has an advantage over the telephone, because differences in locations and time zones don't matter.

Types of E-Mail

Technically speaking, e-mail is an electronic message sent from one computer to another. The process can take seconds, allowing speedy communication with people around the world twenty-four hours a day. If you have an account through an ISP or an online service provider, you have an e-mail address and the ability to send and receive e-mail. Even without an account, it's now possible to have an e-mail address through a free e-mail service or a Web-based mail program.

Post Office Protocol (POP)

Most ISPs use *POP3* mail, which stores incoming mail on their *server,* or computer, until it is downloaded. Mail is downloaded into your PC or Mac using a stand-alone e-mail *client* or program, such as Eudora or Outlook Express. Browsers such as Netscape usually come with a mail client. These browsers and clients are either bundled with computer operating systems or are available free through an ISP starter kit or by downloading from one of the following Web sites. The benefit of POP3 mail is that these programs usually offer spell checkers, mail filters, and the ability to send and receive attachments.

➤ Eudora at *http://www.eudora.com*
➤ Netscape at *http://www.netscape.com*
➤ Outlook Express at *http://www.microsoft.com*

Free E-Mail

Juno is the largest of the free e-mail services, though they still do not support the Mac platform. Unfortunately, local access numbers are not yet offered in every area of the country, and while the mail is free, the access phone calls may be greater than the cost of traditional ISP service with e-mail included. Free e-mail services are supported by advertisers, and for some people that's reason enough not to use them. Free E-mail Address Directory has an international listing of more than one thousand free e-mail clients throughout the world.

➤ Free E-mail Address Directory at *http://www.e-mailaddresses.com*

➤ Juno at *http://www.juno.com*

Web-Based E-Mail

Browsers, search engines, and portals (gateways) are increasingly adding free Web-based mail to their menu of services. It's easy to implement and brings repeat visitors to their sites. Repeat visitors mean increased hits in an advertising-driven business, and more hits equal more dollars generated.

A Web-based e-mail provider stores e-mail messages, which a subscriber then retrieves using a user name and password. This type of service often lacks helpful frills like address books, spell checkers, and other services. Nevertheless, the price is attractive for anyone needing an additional mail account or wanting to check e-mail from any browser. Just remember that advertising banners and tag lines are included, and that can get annoying and, depending upon the service, offensive. Considerably less e-mail can be saved on Web-based mail servers than on POP3 servers. Web-based e-mail might not be the best option for people who anticipate receiving a large volume of incoming e-mail.

Free E-mail Address Directory has a listing of Web-based mail companies such as Hotmail, Microsoft's free Web-based e-mail provider. Web-based mail can be sent or received by anyone—including people who don't own a computer or who travel frequently—from any computer connected to the Internet.

➤ Free E-mail Address Directory at *http://www.e-mailaddresses.com*

➤ Hotmail at *http://www.hotmail.com*

Mail Retrieval

A mail retrieval service allows for the flexibility of checking or sending e-mail from your existing account from any browser. Using encryption software, this service goes to your ISP account and downloads the mail to the browser that you are currently using. The mail is also left on your mail server for future reference. Some services, like ThatWeb.com, even offer the ability to access your address book.

➤ ThatWeb.com at *http://www.thatweb.com*

E-mail Tips

I've listed a number of tips for using e-mail. Another good source for this type of information is the online version of the book *Netiquette* by Virginia Shea, published by Albion Books. Everything E-mail is a second comprehensive, well-written site to learn more about e-mail.

➤ Everything E-mail at *http://everythingemail.net*

➤ Netiquette at *http://www.albion.com/netiquette/book/index.html*

Identification

Most e-mail programs allow users to identify themselves by name in addition to their e-mail address. While I may not remember specific e-mail addresses, I do remember names, and those are the e-mails that I open and read first when I receive a batch. Using a nickname is not a good idea unless everyone knows you by that name.

Signatures

A *signature* is a block of text that appears at the end of each message you send. At a minimum, it usually contains contact information such as your name and e-mail and Web site addresses. E-mail programs typically have an automatic signature feature. This allows you to create a signature file, which is stored on your computer. Each time you start an e-mail message, the signature is added automatically, though you don't necessarily see it on the screen.

The use of signatures is also a great way to market yourself and your writing or speaking. I recently received an e-mail from a member of a mailing list who had seen my signature, which indicates my Web page has information on Huntington's Disease. It seems her neighbor's brother-in-law recently was diagnosed with this disease. She had never heard of it until then, but my signature prompted her to visit my Web site and buy my book and CD. She was writing to thank me for including the signature on each e-mail.

A word of caution: It is not a good idea to post private information such as your home address and phone number on an e-mail signature, especially on mailing lists. You really don't want everyone to have that information.

Signatures should be kept short and tasteful. No matter how funny or creative the message, people generally don't appreciate lengthy ones. For those individuals living in countries where they pay by bandwidth, long signatures can create financial burdens.

Subject Lines

Subject lines are essential in your e-mail. Be specific so that the recipient gets an idea of your message content. The word "information" won't mean anything to most people, whereas "information needed about recent fire" will. Also check the subject line to verify whether or not the same subject applies before responding. While this is especially important with mailing lists, it's also important for personal and business e-mail. Almost all e-mail programs have browse features to locate stored e-mail, and by including a relative subject line, you simplify the task of searching for and retrieving messages, both for the recipient and yourself.

Spell Checkers

Just about every e-mail client comes with a spell checker. E-mail messages should be checked for spelling and grammar the same as any manuscript sent out to the top New York publishing house. If your client doesn't have a spell checker, try using the e-mail client that is part of your browser. If you choose to continue with a program without this feature, type your message in a word-processing program first and then cut and paste it into the e-mail message.

Format

Short messages are well suited to the Internet. If you have a longer message to send, follow regular rules of proper writing by using paragraphs, etc., to make reading easier for your readers. Never type in all upper case except for emphasis. Even then, do so sparingly. Upper case is difficult to follow and, on the Internet, is reserved for yelling.

Attachments

In its infancy, e-mail was good only for short notes. With the advent of *Multipurpose Internet Mail Extension* (MIME) and other types of encoding methods, it's now possible to send or receive messages with attachments, such as pictures, formatted documents, and sound and video files. You can even send computer programs. But before sending an attachment, check with the recipients to determine that their software is capable of decoding it. To do otherwise is to risk frustrating the person on the other end. Some free and Web-based mail options don't accept attachments, and even when they do, not all computers or ISPs have the same capabilities or tolerance. Moreover, even if a user's program can accept attachments, it doesn't mean he or she will be able to open every file. As a courtesy, always ask first. Some people may not know if they can accept attachments or not. In this case, offer to send a trial attachment but have a backup plan just in case, such as pasting what you wanted to attach directly into the e-mail message.

If you are able to send an attachment, detail just how you created and saved the data. For example, I use Corel WordPerfect for word processing. Though I use a MacIntosh version, I am able to save my file in several different programs, such as Word or WordPerfect, which can be opened by a PC user. Telling the recipients which software and version I've saved the document in makes it easy for them to open the attachment. Some huge attachments take a long time to download. If you want to send a sound or graphic file you found on the Web, just include the URL and let your correspondent go there at leisure instead of bogging down his or her mail.

Replies

Whether it's e-mail from someone you write to on an ongoing basis or from a mailing list, it's irritating to see your entire message quoted back to you. Most e-mail programs have an option that allows users to include—or not—the entire letter in their response. In my opinion that feature should be turned off. Cut and paste into your reply only relevant sections from the original message to help the recipient place your reply in context, and use a visual indication as to what is quoted and what is new. Usually the marks << >> are used to begin and to end quoted passages. If it's necessary to include the entire text, you can cut and paste it all.

Carbon and Blind Copies

A carbon, or courtesy copy message, also called a CC, is a message sent to an individual who is not the primary addressee. If you're sending the same message to a group of people, the CC feature is invaluable. This saves a lot of time otherwise spent in creating and sending a number of identical e-mails.

With CCs, every recipient can see who else received the e-mail, while with the BCC (blind carbon/courtesy copy) the primary recipient sees no indication that someone else has also received the message. However, the others receiving the e-mail do see the primary name. Using the BCC function ensures your correspondents their privacy. CC or BCC functions also limit the time it takes to download the message because the computer does not need to retrieve a number of different names.

Forwarding Mail

Many people find the Internet a great source of humor, inspiration, and interesting facts. That doesn't mean everyone on your mailing lists wants to read that "adorable" story or view that "hysterical" graphic. Think carefully before sending a mass mailing, and when you do send something, consider cutting and pasting the item instead of using the forwarding function key. Using the "forward mail" function results in a ">" before each line, which makes it messy and difficult to read. Like the rings of a tree when cut open, you can tell how many times a piece has been forwarded by the number of brackets before the body of the e-mail.

Emoticons and "Internet Shorthand"

An *emoticon* (also known as a "smiley") is a kind of emotional shorthand composed of a few text characters that are used to add meaning to messages. Without clues like facial expressions and body language present in face-to-face conversation, sometimes messages are misinterpreted. For example, an emoticon may be used at the end of a comment to indicate that it was not seriously intended. Most emoticons are designed to be interpreted with the viewer's head tilted to the left. The most common smileys are probably :-) or :), denoting amusement. Another form of emoticons uses bracketed letters, like <G> or <GRIN>.

An "Internet shorthand" made up of abbreviations and acronyms has also sprung up over the last few years. Here are a few of the most common bracketed emoticons, acronyms, and abbreviations to get you started:

- *<S>—Smile*
- *LOL—Laughing Out Loud*
- *ROFL—Rolling On The Floor Laughing*
- *<G>—Grin*
- *WB—Welcome Back*
- *TY—Thank You*
- *YW—You're Welcome*
- *BTW—By The Way*
- *BRB—Be Right Back*
- *IMHO—In My Humble Opinion*
- *IRL—In "Real" Life*

MAILING LISTS

Interested in learning about gardening? No problem, there's a mailing list for you. Doing a presentation about nursing and want to get some stories and background for your talk? How about information on West African politics, French food, ballooning, or forestry? There's probably a list for those too, and if not, you can start one yourself. These lists are gold mines for writers and speakers who want to learn firsthand about a subject.

A mailing list is a group of e-mail addresses of people of like interests. When a subscriber sends a message, it goes to everyone. Anyone on the list can reply to the message, start a new discussion by sending a new message, or they can *lurk*. *Lurking* is a term given to someone who continually reads messages but doesn't respond. Instead of having to surf the Internet for information, messages are delivered to your mailbox, where you can read and respond to them at your leisure.

Internet mailing lists are often erroneously labeled as *Listservs*. Listserv is actually the name of one of the two most frequently used programs designed to automatically manage lists. The other popular Mailing List Manager (MLM) is Majordomo.

Mailing lists can be public or private, and there's usually no limit to the size of a list. In the beginning, mailing lists were usually hosted by universities. Now there are companies such as ONElist and eGroups, which merged and then were bought by Yahoo!, that have a multitude of groups already in progress. Like Web-based e-mail, these mailing lists are advertising driven and free to the user. They can simplify the task of starting your own mailing list, public or private, on any topic you desire. Of course, you have no control over the content of the advertisements that appear at the end of each message.

➤ Groups at *http://www.egroups.com*

➤ ONElist at *http://ONElist.com*

There are actually two types of lists. Announcement lists allow recipients to receive messages, but they cannot post anything to them. These lists are for information only. The more popular lists are the discussion lists, where everyone can participate.

Mailing lists are usually, but not always, free to subscribers. To subscribe to a list, send an e-mail to the automated list administrator. You'll receive a "welcome" e-mail in response, detailing any list rules and instructions about list participation and expected protocol by members. Then you'll start receiving mail from other list members. Keep the instructions; it's considered rude to ask list members how to unsubscribe later when you wish to do so.

Most lists have a digest version. Instead of receiving dozens, or even hundreds of messages each day, digests provide a periodic summary of the messages. Some digests are even archived on the Web so you can access them with your Web browser. This is wonderful for research as these archives can be searched by topic.

Finding the Right Mailing List

➤ CataList *(http://www.listserv.net/lists/listref.html)* is the "official catalogue of Listserv lists," with a database of 27,838 public lists out of 148,102 Listserv lists.

➤ The Directory of Publicly Accessible Mailing Lists *(http://paml.alastra. com)* says that they're "not the biggest, but we personally guarantee that our listings are the most accurate."

➤ Internet for Christians Newsletter *(http://www.gospelcom.net/ifc/mail/ view/?ifc)* has a search engine for those wishing to find Christian mailing lists. They have more than 300 lists with links to search for additional lists.

➤ The Liszt *(http://www.liszt.com)* is a directory of Internet discussion groups. There are over 90,000 lists in their searchable directory, and finding a list is as simple as typing in keywords, searching through the results and the line description, and choosing the right one for you.

➤ National Institute for Computer-Assisted Reporting (NICAR) and Investigative Reporters and Editors, Inc. (IRE) *(http://www.ire.org/ membership/listserv.html)* offer several opportunities for members and even nonmembers to exchange ideas, information, techniques, and war stories.

➤ Tile.net *(http://tile.net/lists)* is a search engine for Internet discussion and information lists. Featured on the site is subscription information for free e-mail lists hosted by Lyris.Net *(http://www.Lyris.net)*.

The same courtesies outlined in the section on e-mail should be observed with mailing lists. A few additional tips will help make your experience on a list both productive and enjoyable.

Mailing-List Tips

- *Keep your questions and comments relevant to the focus of the discussion group.*
- *Send an e-mail only to an individual when the response is not appropriate for the entire list. For example, congratulating a list member for a recent sale is wonderful but only to the person who made the sale. Watch where your personal messages are going. It can be embarrassing if you post a personal message intended for an individual to the entire discussion group.*
- *For others to write to you personally, in your signature add a mailto: followed by your e-mail address without a space. The address would look like this: mailto:Carmen@writerspeaker.com. By doing this, the recipient of your mail (in most e-mail programs) can simply click on your address and an e-mail box will be created, ready to use, addressed to only that address and not the entire list.*

- *A flame is an angry or rude e-mail message, often posted as a public response on a discussion group. The best way to handle a flamer is to ignore the post. Responding could easily result in a flame war with hurt feelings and people signing off the list.*
- *As writers and speakers, we are passionate about our subjects and what we do. Particularly if you frequent a list for information, be sensitive when posting. Lurk for a while to get the tone of the list. Definitely do not advertise.*
- *When going away for a week or more, unsubscribe or suspend mail from mailing lists.*

Mailing-List Resources

➤ Emily Post News *(http://www.templetons.com/brad/emily.html)* is a must-read for anyone wanting a satirical look at Internet mailing lists.

➤ Webcom.com *(http://www.webcom.com/impulse/list.html)* offers more information about mailing lists, including list commands and additional resources for finding lists.

"CHAT" OPTIONS

Chatting is ideal for communicators who excel at using the written word. Chatting allows two or more people to "converse" by typing messages in a text window in real-time online sessions.

One reason so many people stay with AOL and Compuserve is for the forums and chat rooms that are open only to their subscribers. However, for others who want to chat online, there are several different venues for chatting available, with more opportunities appearing every day via search engines and portals.

Internet Relay Chat

Probably the most frequented venues for online chatting are *Internet Relay Chat* (IRC) channels. IRC is the oldest text chat system on the Internet. To chat on IRC, you use a program such as mIRC for the PC or Ircle for the Mac. After downloading and installing the program, you log in to an IRC server through a direct Internet connection.

➢ Ircle at *http://www.ircle.com*

➢ mIRC at *http://www.mirc.com*

MOOs

Multi-Object Oriented (MOOs) provide another chat option. MOOs are text based and, in some cases, are multimedia virtual reality worlds. Like IRC, they require special software that you can download to your computer for free. For Macintosh users there's Savitar, and for the PC platform, Pueblo. MOOs have a greater learning curve than IRCs, and I mention them primarily because through them you can access a number of online writing courses sponsored by various universities.

➢ Pueblo at *http://www.chaco.com/pueblo*

➢ Savitar at *http://www.heynow.com/Savitar*

Chat Rooms

Chat rooms are now Web-based and available through search engines and portals such as Yahoo! and The Liszt. They are easier to use than IRCs and MOOs, as there are no commands to learn. Beseen's The Chat Zone offers a huge variety of chat topics, and LookSmart includes an impressive calendar of author chats.

All text chat systems are similar. Chatters must first choose a user name, which is the name that everyone else in the chat room will see. You can use your real name, or you can choose a nickname or "handle." When I chat in the Huntington's Disease room, I use my own name because I'm known to the Huntington's community as the author of *Faces of Huntington's.* I have been asked on more than one occasion, because chatters recognized my name, if I wrote "that book." The discussions I have in this room, answering disease-related questions, often result in book sales and speaking opportunities for me. In other rooms I go by a nickname. There is no limit to the names you can choose, and there are some bizarre names out there, but you can't choose a name that is already in use by someone else in that room.

Some chats are moderated, while others are not. A moderated chat room has a set of predetermined rules and a "room mother" who enforces them. Some of the more common rules include not using profanity or overt sexual innuendoes and keeping comments relevant to the current discussion topic. Breaking the rules can result in being ejected from the room for a period of time, and frequent abuse of the rules can get a chatter banned.

When chatting, common sense and courtesy are a must. Private information such as addresses and phone numbers should never be given out in an open chat session or stored in the profile section of the room. A feeling of camaraderie and closeness develops quickly in chat rooms, but as in all of life, not everyone is as they portray themselves to be. Use proper caution.

It's important to consider that you are not talking to other computers when you are chatting. You are talking to real, live people who happen to be communicating via computers. Not everyone is chatting in the same time zone, nor are they all from the same country as you, but they do have feelings, moods, and interests.

For example, I frequent various Huntington's Disease chat rooms, and one of the first things I like to determine is where others are living. As a caregiver, I spend much of my time cutting through Medicaid and Medicare red tape. While my experiences might be of great benefit to those in the United States, chatters from other countries, particularly those with socialized medicine, face a different set of challenges.

In a chat room, people are basically true to life. Some people will be rude or offensive online, while others will hog the conversation. Humor works better at diffusing potential problems than anger does. Ignoring them works even better.

As previously discussed, plain text often does not express the tone of a comment. Use emoticons, abbreviations, and acronyms to your—and other chatters'—advantage. As you spend more time chatting, you'll learn more and start using them more freely yourself.

➤ The Chat Zone at *http://www.beseen.com/chat/topics.html*
➤ The Liszt at *http://www.liszt.com/chat*
➤ LookSmart at *http://looksmart.yack.com/categories/Books*
➤ Yahoo! at *http://chat.yahoo.com*

Instant Messengers

Not patient enough to wait for someone online to contact you? Don't worry, instant gratification has reached the Internet. It started with AOL's *Buddy List,* or messaging system, but has now moved on to other services. *Instant messengers* help you to keep track of all your online friends, send and receive messages, and even chat with one or more friends in real time.

While you have to be on AOL to use their Buddy List, you don't have to be an America Online member to use AOL Instant Messenger. This program allows Internet users to send and receive private text messages. According to CNET, over 85 million 'Netizens' use Instant Messenger or the number-one ranked ICQ ("I seek you"). Instant messaging can also be found through search sites such as Yahoo! and Excite.

➤ AOL Instant Messenger at *http://www.aol.com/aim*

➤ Excite at *http://www.excite.com/communities/pal/home*

➤ ICQ at *http://www.icq.com*

➤ Yahoo! at *http://messenger.yahoo.com*

FORUMS OR MESSAGE BOARDS

For some, they are Web forums; others dub them message boards. In either case, they offer a nonthreatening form of research for writers and speakers and an opportunity to post or read messages about a specific topic. In some cases, people will leave their e-mail address or a Web site, but in many cases you will receive an answer to a question without the option of reaching the individual who posted the information. Web forums tend to be less argumentative than mailing lists or newsgroups.

There is no one repository of message boards, but typing "message board + [any topic]" in a search engine will give you links to message boards on a specific subject. My earliest contact with others who knew anything about Huntington's Disease was through a message board at Massachusetts General Hospital.

➤ Research Forum *(http://writers-bbs.com/inkspot/threads.cgi?forum=research)* is a message board devoted to all aspects of research for writers.

➤ Speakers Place *(http://www.speakersplace.com/forum)* offers a message board where speakers can discuss every aspect of professional speaking.

NEWSGROUPS

Usenet, one of the dinosaurs of the Internet, dating from the late 1970s, is a worldwide discussion bulletin board on the Internet. Usenet is also known collectively as *newsgroups.* With more than twenty thousand specialized newsgroups, Usenet is a researcher's dream—if you are willing to invest the time.

Once you find a newsgroup of interest, you can read messages posted by others all over the world, or you can post your own message. To get to a newsgroup you need some software. Browsing through the list of all newsgroups supplied by your ISP is cumbersome, but there are ways to search for newsgroups that are of particular interest to you. Many of the regular search engines have added Usenet searching to their basic Web search capacity. In the past, one of the best ways to locate newsgroups on particular topics was a Web site called Deja News. The site has grown to include non-Usenet-related information, and those who want a more stripped down engine might want to try Deja Power Search.

With a news client, typically called a *newsreader,* you connect to your ISP's news servers, sift out spam (junk mail), and manage the multitude of messages. Newsgroups.com, a site about newsgroups and newsgroup software, is a great source to find a newsreader. There is no central organization or set rules for these groups, which can be initiated by any user and which come and go frequently.

Newsgroups are divided into subject areas called *hierarchies.* Most services will carry the following "Big Eight Hierarchies," along with others, including those of regional interest.

- *comp. = an extensive collection of computer-related topics*
- *humanities. = topics in the arts and humanities*
- *misc. = a catch-all category about anything and everything—sort of the Seinfeld of newsgroups*
- *news. = topics related to use and administration of USENET news*
- *rec. = recreational topics such as sports, hobbies, and movies*
- *sci. = scientific topics, including medicine*

- *soc. = social issues and support for issues such as divorce and depression*
- *talk. = newsgroups for discussion of current affairs, politics, and general debate*

Other popular subjects include biz. (business-oriented newsgroups) and alt. (an alternative hierarchy, a loosely arranged collection of newsgroups outside the Usenet mainstream).

If you are looking for a newsgroup for writers, misc.writing has a home page you may want to review. According to their page, "misc.writing ('mw') is a Usenet newsgroup that provides a forum for discussion of writing in all its forms—scholarly, technical, journalistic, artistic, and mere day-to-day communication. It is a venue for professional writers, would-be professionals, and all those who write to communicate."

Two other sites you'll want to review, both filled with information about newsgroups, are Usenet Info Center and Newsgroup Terminology.

- ➤ Deja News at *http://www.deja.com*
- ➤ Deja Power Search at *http://www.exit109.com/~jeremy/news/deja.html*
- ➤ misc.writing at *http://www.scalar.com/mw*
- ➤ Newsgroup Terminology at *http://www.newbie-u.com/news/terms.html*
- ➤ Newsgroups.com at *http://www.newsreaders.com/index.html*
- ➤ Usenet Info Center at *http://metalab.unc.edu/usenet-i/usenet-help.html*

Whether you are doing research or simply connecting with other writers and speakers, e-mail, chatting, mailing lists, forums, and newsgroups can make a significant difference in your time spent online. To really take advantage of the massive amount of information online, knowing how to search and evaluate the results is an absolute must.

THREE

Learning to Read the Road Maps

Search-Engine Basics

Writing is an exploration. You start from nothing
and learn as you go.—E. L. DOCTOROW

Some days miracles do happen. The other day, for instance, as I sat in the artificially bright waiting room of my son's oral surgeon's office, I found a magazine. From the current year! In fact—would you believe—it was only two weeks old! When I saw the bill for my son's dental work, I knew why it was costing the earth to have those three wisdom teeth extracted: magazine subscriptions.

Anyway, I flipped through the pages of this miracle periodical. One of the first ads showed a picture of a haystack under the following caption: "This is the Internet. You're looking for a needle." Below the picture were the words "Start Here," followed by a door featuring the Intel Pentium III processor.

As trite as the cliché is, I have to agree: Finding something on the Internet can be like looking for a needle in a haystack. While the latest processor may help speed up the search, knowing how and where to find information online is the real starting place.

Some writers argue that their best writing is not done on a computer but with a pencil and paper or a typewriter. Just as the computer is not a replacement for writing the old-fashioned way, the Internet is not a substitute for the library. While the Internet is convenient, and anyone with access to a personal computer, a modem, and an online service provider can find information in usable form, it can also be frustrating. You'd think that with millions of Web sites, and more cropping up every minute of every day, the Internet would be comprehensive. Well, it's simply not so. Neither is it well indexed.

Imagine a massive library, a plethora of information within its walls. Now visualize darkness, no electricity, and the contents of the card catalogues strewn about. A tornado has ripped through the building; the cards have been scattered helter-skelter; everything is a chaotic mess.

Welcome to the research arm of the Internet.

The Internet is a great resource that offers you access to information from your hometown or around the world—if you know where and how to look for it. Wading through heaps of useless information while searching for an elusive fact can be daunting, though, and many eager Internet researchers have abandoned the quest in frustration.

Search engines and indexes are the virtual road maps of the information superhighway. Used properly, they can show you precisely where to find that elusive needle in the haystack—and take you directly to it.

THE SEARCH ENGINE'S ROLE

I got a joke from an e-mail humor list the other day that went something like this: "Why did Moses and his people wander around in the desert for forty years? Because the men in the group refused to ask for directions."

Some people are like that, whether cruising actual highways or the Internet. It's certainly possible to get to your land destination without directions, but it's usually a waste of time and gas. That also applies to the Internet. Yes, it's possible to find information without a search engine, but it wastes time and usually results in disappointingly small amounts of usable material. In either case, a road map is the answer. For the Internet, that means a search engine.

Search engines can also be described as the Web's automated card catalogues. Each search engine keeps huge electronic files with brief entries of millions of Web sites. Because no one has yet developed and implemented a "Dewey Decimal System" for the Web, the results are less than scientific.

Indexing, organizing, and often rating and reviewing Web sites—this is the role of the search engine. Different engines work in different ways—either as directories or as indexes. Some rely on people to maintain a catalogue of Web sites or pages; others use software to identify key information on sites across the Internet. Some use a combination of both. Consequently, the engine you select will determine, in part, the result of your search, and each will provide you its own particular outcome.

A directory groups its Web sites under similar categories of general information, displayed in a hierarchy of topics and subtopics. Beginning the search in a broad category, the user navigates the links identified by the engine, further refining the search until he or she zeros in on a particular site that is narrow enough to contain the desired information.

Web indexes use software programs called *spiders* or robots that scour the Web. URLs are collected and analyzed and eventually included in the index. Indexing is done by word rather than by category, so a search often turns up individual pages of a Web site that match the word, even if the site itself has nothing to do with the subject of the search.

Some search engines do not restrict their search to the Web but include the entire Internet. Results of using an index-search site often include information drawn from listservs, chat groups, newsgroups, and other areas of the Internet. You can sometimes find unexpected gems this way, but often you get lots of useless information, too.

With increasing competition and more search engines appearing almost daily, whether a search site is actually a directory or an index is subject to question. Yahoo! has a breakdown of search sites including directories, indexes, search engines, and more. Many sites offer information relating to specific topics. For example, Web Wombat is an Australian-based James Kirk Search Engine that bills itself as the engine that "seeks out content where no search engine has ever gone." Anyone writing for or about *Star Trek* may find that using this engine is preferable to searching on a general directory or index. Other specialized engines are listed later in this chapter.

> ➤ Web Wombat at *http://www.webwombat.com.au/trek*
> ➤ Yahoo! at *http://dir.yahoo.com/Computers_and_Internet/Internet/World_ Wide_Web/Searching_the_Web/Search*

SEARCH ENGINE RESOURCES

Many search engine resources are available, in all forms and sizes.

Major Search Sites

AltaVista, started in 1995, is one of the largest and most popular search engines on the Internet, with an index of more than 450 million Web pages and growing. In 1997, AltaVista put a translation program into its index so that people could read any Web page in English. In 1998, AltaVista teamed up with TheTrip.com to provide tourism information and Ask Jeeves, a service that allows users to ask questions about any topic and search for answers in plain English. AltaVista gets more than twenty-five million search requests each day and serves between fifteen and twenty million users each month.

Launched in 1995 by six students from Stanford University, Excite currently is one of the most popular search engines and is ranked second after Yahoo! Besides being a search engine, Excite is a network of sites that includes the WebCrawler search engine, the directory Magellan, and the tourist guide City.net. It also has different versions of the site for other countries, including Australia, Great Britain, France, Germany, Holland, Sweden, Italy, and Japan.

Infoseek is one of the top ten search engines and has the reputation for easy usability. Infoseek was started in 1994, and in 1998 Disney bought more than a 40 percent stake in the company. Since then, Infoseek has also created the Go Network. InfoSeek searches by keywords, including synonyms. It scans the information in its database and gives a score to your search results, returning the "best" matches to your query.

Lycos is another popular engine that was launched in 1994. In 1998, Lycos bought the Wired Digital Group, which gave them another search engine, Hotbot. Lycos has a section of their Web site devoted to finding the 5 percent most popular (frequently accessed) Web sites.

The Northern Light search engine is an indexing search engine but also offers some unique, advanced features. Northern Light automatically sifts the results of your search into customized folders based on type, similarity, location, and other criteria. Northern Light also indexes what they call *Special Collections*. These are large numbers of full-text documents that you have to pay a small fee (generally one to four dollars) to access. Much of the information available in these special collections is available nowhere else on the Web.

Yahoo! began with two hundred indexed sites in 1993 and today is the most visited site in the world. The Internet magazine *Yahoo! Internet Life* is the most popular Internet magazine around. Only a few months after starting the magazine, founders Jerry Yang and David Filio, students at Stanford University, were swamped with requests to be linked to the magazine site. Once initial categories of requests were filled, these categories were split into smaller ones. Yahoo! has never used computers to automate the categorizing process; over 80 percent of all Internet sites that ask to be listed are rejected. In other words, if one hundred people request their Web site listed on Yahoo!, only twenty will be accepted. Unlike other sites where computers process the requests, on Yahoo! human beings actually review all the requests. Yahoo! makes more than $200 million annually in advertising revenue. The search engine also has versions for twenty-one countries in three regions: Europe, the Pacific Rim, and the Americas.

➤ AltaVista at *http://www.altavista.com*

➤ Ask Jeeves at *http://www.askjeeves.com*

➤ City.net at *http://www.excite.com/travel*

➤ Excite at *http://www.excite.com*

➤ Go Network at *http://www.go.com*

➤ Hotbot at *http://www.hotbot.com*

➤ Infoseek at *http://www.infoseek.com*

➤ Lycos at *http://www.lycos.com*

➤ Magellan at *http://magellan.excite.com*

➤ Northern Light at *http://www.northernlight.com*

➤ TheTrip.com at *http://www.TheTrip.com*

➤ WebCrawler at *http://www.webcrawler.com*

➤ Yahoo! at *http://www.yahoo.com*

➤ Yahoo! Internet Life at *http://www.zdnet.com/yil/filters/channels/ netezuser.html*

Meta Sites

Another vehicle for searching the Internet is known as a *meta search engine*. These engines usually search several other search engines simultaneously instead of using their own indexes. A meta search queries multiple sites at a time and presents the results of all the engines in a unified format. Users see at a glance which particular search engine returned the best results for their query.

Meta search engines can be a quick place to start, but as they all use filters, the results will almost never be as comprehensive as the results from an individual search engine.

➤ Ask Jeeves *(http://www.askjeeves.com)* maintains its own index of Web sites and matches queries in its database of more than 7 million "answers" to common questions. This unique database lets you "Ask Jeeves" a question in plain English. Users are given "answers" from their database, followed by results from Excite, Infoseek, AltaVista, WebCrawler, and Yahoo!

➤ Beaucoup *(http://www.beaucoup.com)* is one of the new breeds of meta search engines, utilizing more than 2,000 search engines, indexes, and search directories.

➤ CNET's Search.com *(http://www.search.com)* can search the entire Web, or the user can limit the search to one of fourteen categories. CNET.com *(http://www.cnet.com)* is the parent of Search.com and is one of the best known, most respected sources for computers and technology.

➤ Dogpile *(http://www.dogpile.com)* searches twenty-six major search sites three sites at a time, beginning with a general index search. Results from each search engine are grouped together, with descriptions provided by each site. At the bottom of the results list is a button that continues your search with the next three search engines.

➤ Google *(http://www.google.com)* was founded in 1998 by two Stanford doctoral students. Google offers Web-site owners free basic search on their site.

➤ Inference Find *(http://www.InferenceFind.com)* searches WebCrawler, Yahoo!, Lycos, AltaVista, InfoSeek, and Excite and retrieves the maximum number of results each engine will allow. Some engines return hundreds of documents, some as few as ten. Inference Find clusters results into similar groups based on their types. Sites most closely matching the query will be grouped first, followed by clusters that include miscellaneous commercial, government, educational, and non-U.S. sites. Inference Find assembles the best results, then groups the related items together. Understandably, the number of sites retrieved can be enormous.

➤ Librarian's Index to the Internet *(http://sunsite.berkeley.edu/InternetIndex)* is a comprehensive search engine that features New This Week and Last Week links.

➤ Mamma *(http://www.mamma.com)* bills itself as "the mother of all search engines." Mamma searches ten major search sites and returns with the results in an easy-to-follow format. The search results are based on keyword frequency, site popularity, and other factors.

➤ With MetaCrawler *(http://www.metacrawler.com)*, duplicate results are eliminated once the queries from the major search engines and directories are combined into a single list.

Specialty Search Engines and Portals

Due to the information glut on the Web, it is often more effective to use smaller, specialized search engines than those listed above. Thousands of sites, some of them directories and indexes and some of them simply sites so large and packed with information that they serve the same function, are considered specialty engines. *Portals* also fall into this category.

Portals are designed to be gateways to the Internet and are sponsored by major search engine and browser providers. Like specialty engines, portals can offer a wealth of research information and contain links to a search engine, a subject directory, and services such as news, weather, entertainment information, and shopping. Many portal sites provide an option for users to customize the site according to their personal interests. They also offer free e-mail, Web pages, and chat capabilities.

Business, the arts, computers, education, government, health, parenting, religion, travel, and other topics all have specialty engines and portals. To find a comparison of portals, go to Traffick.com. The sites listed in the rest of this chapter are some of the best-known specialty engine and search sites.

➤ Traffick.com at *http://www.traffick.com*

Specialty Engines and Search Sites

➤ The Argus Clearinghouse *(http://www.clearinghouse.net)* is an online research library broken into thirteen topical categories.

➤ B.J. Pinchbeck's Homework Helper *(http://www.bjpinchbeck.com)* was created by a nine-year-old and his father so other students would not have to search the Web for good educational material. The site now has links to more than 570 other sites and is updated weekly. Even though it's designed for students doing homework, this site and Homework Central and TekMom:Resources for Students are great places to get quick, easy-to-find, and easy-to-understand information as a starting point for your Internet search.

➤ Ditto.com *(http://www.ditto.com)* is a unique search engine that allows you to search the Web using pictures instead of text. Users are directed to the Web site where the pictures are stored and are told to seek permission if they are planning on using them.

➤ FedWorld Information Network *(http://www.fedworld.gov)* is the brainchild of the National Technical Information Service (NTIS). They offer a comprehensive site packed with any and everything you've ever wanted to know about the federal government.

➤ HomeworkCentral *(http://www.homeworkcentral.com)* has an extensive database for students and is broken into sections for kids, teens, college students, and beyond.

➤ Inomics *(http://www.inomics.com)* is an Internet economics search engine.

➤ Internet Scout Project *(http://scout.cs.wisc.edu/index.html)* guides you to the best resources on the Internet. Librarians and educators read hundreds of announcements and bulletins each week before filtering them for the most valuable online resources to the education community.

➤ The Megasite Project *(http://www.lib.umich.edu/megasite)* compares health information megasites and search engines.

> Pilot-Search.com *(http://www.pilot-search.com)* is a free online search engine of literary links with access to over 10,000 searchable links in over 250 categories. Pilot finds sites about individual writers, book reviews, interviews, short story contests, and much more.

> Refdesk.com *(http://www.refdesk.com)* is a gold mine of information on the Internet. A great starting point for whatever you are looking for.

> Search Power *(http://www.searchpower.com)* is actually a search engine directory of more than 2,000 search sites, including categories such as government, media, references, and politics.

> TekMom: Resources for Students *(http://www.tekmom.com/students/index.html)* is actually a meta search engine of other family-friendly engines for students. This wonderful resource features a great layout and four main areas for students: search tools, technology buzzwords, citation guidelines, and computer ethics.

Encyclopedias

> The new Britannica.com site *(http://www.britannica.com)* is a fabulous resource that includes the complete, updated *Encyclopedia Britannica,* selected articles from more than 70 of the world's top magazines, the *Books in Print* database, and the *Britannica Internet Guide.*

> Encyclopedia.com *(http://www.encyclopedia.com)* features over 14,000 free articles from the *Concise Columbia Electronic Encyclopedia.*

People Locators

> 555-1212.com *(http://www.555-1212.com)* is a powerful Web search engine for locating businesses and individuals. The site includes a reverse lookup directory and international directories.

> AT&T Internet Directory *(http://www.att.com/directory/internet.html)* is the best place to start a search to locate people, businesses, etc. This page furnishes links to dozens of search sites.

> BigFoot *(http://www.bigfoot.com)* is a more advanced page to search for people online.

➤ Internet Address Finder *(http://www.iaf.net)* searches for e-mail addresses and includes a reverse directory to get the name of the person from the e-mail address.

➤ Telephone Directories on the Web *(http://www.teldir.com/eng)* is the most complete index of online phone books, with links to yellow pages, white pages, business directories, e-mail addresses, and fax number listings from more than 150 countries around the world.

➤ World E-mail Directory *(http://www.worlde-mail.com)* searches for e-mail addresses by continent.

Expert Links

➤ Ask An Expert *(http://www.askanexpert.com)* bills itself as a kid-friendly site where you can browse for an expert by category or do a keyword search. Most experts have links to their Web sites and many have a "frequently asked questions" (FAQ) page. If the user can't find information on the site, he or she can e-mail questions to the expert.

➤ Associations on the Net *(http://www.ipl.org/ref/AON)* is a collection of sites from over 1,100 professional and trade associations, cultural and art organizations, political parties and advocacy groups, labor unions, academic societies, and research institutions.

➤ The Dot.com Directory *(http://www.dotcomdirectory.com)* is one of the most comprehensive resources available to locate business information about companies that have a presence on the Web. Sometimes going directly to the business for a quote or a story does work, and this is a great way to find information and begin communication.

➤ Experts.com *(http://www.experts.com)* is a worldwide resource of experts who are authors, consultants, specialists, and experienced expert witnesses. The database can be searched by topic, keyword, or category.

➤ Profnet *(http://www.profnet.com)* is a free service linking over 6,000 public relations professionals on the Internet. This service is designed to give journalists and authors convenient access to expert sources. The links include news and information officers at colleges and universities, corporations, think tanks, national labs, medical centers, nonprofits, and PR agencies.

➤ YearbookNews.com *(http://www.YearbookNews.com)* is the online version of the Yearbook of Experts, Authorities & Spokespersons. Year-bookNews is an interactive guide to thousands of leading experts and sources.

Portals

MSN began as an ISP but has grown into more of an Internet portal. It isn't just a search engine; it's a database of Microsoft services like Expedia, a vacation and travel site, and CarPoint, a car-buying site. MSN has Microsoft links and the capability to search through the yellow pages and white pages. It also offers the Web-based mail server Hotmail.

➤ Car Point at *http://www.CarPoint.com*

➤ Expedia at *http://www.expedia.msn.com/*

➤ MSN at *http://www.msn.com*

➤ About.com *(http://www.about.com)*, formerly "The Mining Co.," is a network of over 650 sites, each overseen by a professional guide. Each site is devoted to a single topic, allowing the guide to focus on his or her expertise. Included are the Internet's best link directories, original content, and community features such as chat and free e-mail.

➤ Canada.Com *(http://www.canada.com)* calls itself Canada's "most comprehensive Internet network and portal." This Canadian portal has personalized information and services including Canadian and international news, financial data, online shopping, free e-mail, career postings, and a business and people directory. Canada.com has more than 2.3 million independent users per month.

➤ CNN *(http://www.cnn.com)* is the Cable News Network portal for news junkies. You can design your own personalized news page with the news topics of interest to you. CNN also offers free e-mail and chat.

➤ Crosswalk.com *(http://www.goshen.net)* is a Christian community with a directory bringing together the best Christian sites on the Internet. Crosswalk.com membership benefits include chat, forums, e-mail, free movie guides, and Web filtering.

➤ Search Engine Watch *(http://www.searchenginewatch.com)* is the best place to learn everything you need to know about search engines and how to search. This site includes search engine and Web tips, search engine listings, resources, news, and more.

➤ Gospelcom.net *(http://www.gospelcom.net)* is a strategic alliance of more than 230 evangelical Christian groups and still growing. According to the *Wall Street Journal,* "Gospelcom.net consistently ranks in the Media Metrix list of the 500 most-visited Web sites, which is otherwise short of religious sites."

➤ OnePlace *(http://www.oneplace.com)* bills itself as having everything for the Christian community. This portal has links to some of the prominent Christian sites and ministries on the Web.

➤ Snap.com *(http://www.snap.com)* is an offshoot of CNET, The Computer Network. Not satisfied with being a premier computer site, CNET began Snap.com. NBC eventually bought into Snap, bringing with it both cash and clout. Snap offers an easy to use, comprehensive Web directory. In addition to offering a search function, Snap.com has chat, E-cards (electronic greeting cards), and discussions.

➤ Suite101.com *(http://www.suite101.com)* is similar to About.com and bills itself as "real people helping real people." Suite101.com has over 785 topics and keeps a database of previously addressed issues, operating instructions, FAQs, and more. Like About.com, sites are devoted to a single topic, with an editor assigned to each who writes articles and maintains and rates links about the topic. Each site also offers chat rooms, bulletin boards, and more.

No single search engine, even a major one, keeps track of everything on the Internet. Your best bet is to try several engines to determine which one best fits your needs. If a search fails to produce the desired results, it doesn't necessarily mean the information you want isn't on the Internet. It may just mean you need to try another search engine.

In other words, if one map of the information superhighway doesn't show your destination, find one that does.

FOUR

Cruising the Information Superhighway

It takes most of us a long time to learn our craft. So keep at it. Don't give up.—JACQUELINE BRISKIN

I have a confession to make, and it isn't pretty. I'm directionally challenged. No matter the size of the city or whether I'm a newcomer or not—I can't get there from here. I get lost going to places I've been to countless times. Maps, to me, just look like colors and lines.

For years I lived in Hawaii, where directions are given exactly as directionally challenged people need them. Instead of using north, south, east, and west, which make no sense at all to me, Hawaiians use commonsense landmarks. In Honolulu, *makai* (ocean), *mauka* (mountain), *ewa* (toward the airport), and Diamond Head, the most famous landmark in Hawaii, helped to at least point me in the right direction. Life was simple with landmarks so large even I couldn't get lost.

Searching on the Internet is a little like that. In the beginning, deciding which search engine to use, like finding the right map for a road trip, was difficult for me. Somehow I never managed to find the information I needed. I quickly learned that simply typing in a word or two and expecting to find exactly what I wanted, without hundreds or thousands of other sites getting in the way, was like pointing to a spot on a map and expecting to magically arrive at my destination.

I have come to terms with being directionally challenged. Whenever possible, I get someone else to drive, or I search for detailed directions on the Internet. Hopefully the discussion that follows about how to search the Internet will be a bit like giving you your own *makai, mauka, ewa,* and Diamond Head as points of reference that even a directionally challenged person can use to get from "here" to "there."

RESEARCH ON THE WORLD WIDE WEB

The most basic kind of search, regardless of the type of engine you use, starts with typing a *keyword* (or words) into the box and pressing the search button. But with engines searching indexes of hundreds of millions of pages, it is also the most frustrating and inefficient way to search.

Personally, I do about as well with math as I do with driving. When it comes to searching on the Internet, though, math is a great help. The English mathematician George Boole developed an "algebra of logic" that has become the basis for computer database searches. *Boolean logic* uses three little words— AND, OR, and NOT—to make Internet searches easier. These words, which must appear in ALL CAPS with a space on each side in order to work, are enormously helpful when doing online searches.

For example, a friend of mine from an online writers' group sent me an e-mail asking for information about the world-famous spy Mata Hari. Typing in "Mata Hari" on Yahoo!, I turned up two Yahoo! sites and 1,791 Web page matches. However, the two Yahoo! matches were for furniture and gifts, and it wasn't until the eleventh Web page site that the Dutch courtesan was mentioned. Numbers one through ten included topics like yachts, houseboat charters, and crystal elephants, not to mention the search engine Mata Hari.

By typing "Mata Hari AND spy," the Web page matches shrank to only thirty-seven, with no Yahoo! matches. I hit pay dirt on the first Web page match; it was exactly what my friend needed. "Mata Hari AND spy AND war" brought the total number of matches down to twenty-four—considerably less than the 1,793 from the initial search.

By typing "Mata Hari OR WWI," I was able to review sites not only about the legendary spy, who was killed in 1917, but about Europe during that period. On another note, in my first search, without qualifiers, I noticed several adult-oriented sites were listed. My last search was "Mata Hari NOT exotic," and though there were restaurants, products from India, books, and play reviews, there were no exotic sites listed.

For some search sites, the much simpler +, -, and "" symbols to indicate words that must be included (+), excluded (-), or in phrases ("") can be used instead of spelling out the three little words.

Clicking the advanced search button on major search engines will take you to a brief online tutorial to help you understand how a specific engine works.

For more information on effective Internet search techniques, visit the Web site for Targeted Listings, an online marketing resource.

➤ Targeted Listings at *http://www.targetedlistings.com/tip8.html*

Conducting Your Research

Understanding how an engine works is a great beginning, but there's more to becoming an expert online researcher. When you're prepared and precise, your search will yield fewer sites, but they will be targeted more directly to the information you are seeking.

Narrow Your Search
When I first started searching for information about Huntington's Disease, I simply typed in the keyword "Huntington's." The initial sites I found were about various cities and counties with that name, then libraries, banks, and sports teams, and, finally, "Huntington's Disease."

I learned that computers are literal: They don't *read* what you type; they simply give you matches based on your input—which means you might get lists of sites that have nothing to do with your real topic of interest. By adding the word "disease" to my search, I immediately found relevant sites. Adding the words "caregiving," "at-risk," "gene test," and other specific phrases, I found even more pertinent facts about various aspects of Huntington's Disease and wasn't bombarded with links to useless sites. Following the Boolean rules narrowed my search to sites where I could learn about Huntington's Disease, caregiving, medication, support groups, and anything else that interested me.

Use the Appropriate Index

Whereas general indexes are useful for researching common topics, specialty search engines should find information on specialized topics more quickly. For example, if you're doing a story on charitable organizations, a specialty engine like Guide Star, with a searchable database of more than 620,000 nonprofit organizations in the United States, would be a great starting point. If Guide Star or a similar engine doesn't have what you need, then choosing a general index and using Boolean or advanced search techniques would be the next best bet.

> ➤ Guide Star at *http://www.guidestar.org*

Research from Different Angles

Recently I was writing a story about the death of the Chicago Bears running back Walter Payton. Payton died of a rare liver disease called primary sclerosing cholangitis, the same disease that had killed my brother two years previously. Because I'd met Payton on several occasions and had a personal interest in the disease that took his life, I decided to do a bit of research.

The sports angle, about Payton's as-yet-untouched rushing record in the National Football League and his role in leading the Bears to their one-and-only Super Bowl championship, was thoroughly covered in my initial search. But I wanted to write about Walter Payton the man, not Walter Payton the sports hero—about his disease and his response to it.

With that angle in mind, it was easy to use Boole's three little words to learn not just about Walter Payton but about primary sclerosing cholangitis and transplants. I gained new information about the disease, and I learned that in response to his diagnosis, Payton did public service announcements about being an organ donor. My personal interest, coupled with a fresh angle, made it a poignant story.

Organize Your Bookmarks

Both Netscape and Internet Explorer have a *bookmark* or *favorites* function that is invaluable in organization. As a site is bookmarked, get into the habit of immediately moving it to a folder that corresponds best to the site's topic.

Create themed folders with related subject folders inside as an efficient, easy system to keep your bookmarks current and useful. For example, my folder labeled *WriterSpeaker.com* is filled with a variety of topical subjects, such as E-zines, Quotations, Search Engines, Conferences, and Dictionaries.

If you've been on the computer for a while, you've probably had a hard drive crash or lost data in some other way. It's important to save your work to a zip drive or floppy disk, but don't forget to save your bookmarks and address book files too. Once wiped out, the file of Web sites you took months or even years to compile is impossible to reconstruct completely.

Leave an Electronic Trail

There is nothing worse than spending time finding sources then forgetting where and how you found them in the first place. Unfortunately, it's simple to do with paper resources and even easier with electronic ones. Using Netscape's bookmarks or Internet Explorer's favorites might seem the best way to mark your trail, but it really isn't. Unless you have an organized system in place, bookmarks or favorites can end up as a long string of hundreds of Web sites with no easy way to find the desired information.

Yes, there's a search function in most browsers, but remembering the exact words needed to find those lost sites is usually next to impossible and a waste of valuable hours. One idea is to create a paper or computer file folder for each project. As the Internet may not be your only resource, the folder could include not only a list and brief description of relevant Web sites, perhaps written on index cards, but printed pages from the Internet, magazine and newspaper articles, lists of related books, etc.

It's a good idea to write yourself a note on paper or even to e-mail yourself, outlining the history of your search for specific information. The benefits are these: First, writing it down reinforces the information and helps you master efficient research techniques; and second, when you see the same Web sites popping up over and over in a short period of time, you'll know to bookmark them for future use. For example, I use Amazon.com consistently both to check orders for my two books and to do research. I have two links to Amazon.com: one directly to my account and the other to the bookstore front page. They are at the top of my bookmarks in my frequent sites folder.

When I find a Web site I think I might want to use for a specific project, rather than bookmark it, I save it in a desktop folder labeled with the name of the current project or topic, along with other notes. When I'm ready to review the site again, all I need to do is drag the saved Web site icon off the desktop folder onto the browser icon and it opens. Depending on the operating system, double-clicking the icon will open it too. This method helps me remember exactly why I saved the link. If it turns out to be a site I will use again, I bookmark it. If not, I throw it in the trash.

Use the Right Address

It's next to impossible to locate a home or a business without a street address. It's also difficult to locate a specific Web site without a URL, the standardized address system used for locating Web sites and other resources over the Internet. Most but not all URLs start with "http://," which stands for *hypertext transfer protocol*. This grandiose phrase simply indicates the formatting method by which computers exchange information on the Web. The "www" in the address stands for World Wide Web and is followed by the name of the ISP or the organization where the server is located. The three-letter code used to designate the type of server or the location follows. The folder, followed by directories and a file name, completes the address.

Six three-letter codes are used to designate the type of server or domain.

- *.com = commercial*
- *.edu = educational*
- *.gov = government*
- *.net = network*
- *.org = nonprofit organization*
- *.mil = military*

Sites originating from other than the United States usually have a two letter code at the end of the server, such as .ca for Canada, .cz for the Czech Republic, and so forth.

To get to the site, URLs must be typed into the browser exactly. Depending on the server, addresses are often case sensitive, so if a letter is capitalized on a business card or in a newspaper ad, it needs to be capitalized in the Web address.

More and more, Web sites can be found on both Netscape and Internet Explorer without typing in http://www. before the rest of the address. For example, by simply typing in writersdigest.com, the browser goes directly to the *Writer's Digest* magazine site of http://www.writersdigest.com.

Domain names are increasingly the norm for companies, especially those with national or international recognition. If you're looking for a site on the Web, try the obvious first. It isn't always necessary to go through the search process to find a company. Typing in "http://www.<companyname>.com" will often get you directly to the desired site. That's why it's important to understand the three-letter code system. The American Red Cross has a Web site, but adding ".com" after "http://www.redcross" will result in a message that the site doesn't exist. Because it's a nonprofit organization, adding ".org" brings up the Web site. There are instances when a nonprofit organization uses a ".com" or ".net," but by starting with the obvious you can often save time.

If after typing in an address you're told that the site doesn't exist, try going backward and eliminating everything after the three-letter code to see if the home page exists. Often, the link you're looking for has ceased to exist or has been renamed, but the home page for the company or organization is still there.

Check Spellings

Proper names can be spelled in various ways. A different spelling than one that actually appears in a site can point you in the wrong direction. Yes, we all know that writers and speakers are perfect spellers! But that doesn't mean everyone else is. Not all people run their text through a spell checker before putting it online. If your search yields either the wrong site or no site at all, try a spelling variation.

Evaluating Results

The Internet is the proverbial "good news/bad news" medium. The good news is there are Web sites, articles, e-mail lists, and more devoted to every topic imaginable. That means there's no shortage of possible information sources. The bad news is that not everything posted on the Internet is reliable. When evaluating information you've gained through the Internet, ask yourself the same questions you ask about any source:

1. Who wrote it? Not only does no one own the Internet, but no one moderates it either. This means that anyone can post anything on any subject at any time. Before using information you have found on the Internet, find out more about the author and his or her credentials. I constantly get e-mails from writers researching Huntington's Disease, neurological disorders, and similar topics. In my responses, I always point out that I am not an expert or a medical doctor, merely someone who has learned more than I ever cared to know about this disease. I offer my comments as a layperson who has been thrust into the role of caregiver and spokesperson. I also send them other URLs and the contact information of medical doctors and researchers who can help them. It's then up to the one writing the article to use my comments appropriately.

2. Who posted the information and why? Everyone has a motive for writing what they write. If the purpose of the information is to educate the public, I look at that as potentially more reliable than information specifically designed to sell a product or an agenda.

3. When was it published or updated? For every new site on the Internet, there are countless old ones that have not been updated in months or even years. Look for a date when the page was created and last updated.

4. Are there links to other sites with related resources? By following the links provided, you can check the material presented on the original site.

5. Is it an urban legend? According to David Emery, About.com's guide to urban legends, "Urban legends are popular narratives alleged to be true, transmitted from person to person by oral or written communication. Said stories always involve some combination of outlandish, humiliating, humorous, terrifying, or supernatural events—events which always happened to someone else."

The Internet, e-mail specifically, is a prime breeding ground for urban legends, and it's essential to check the stories you hear this way to make sure they are true. The AFU and Urban Legends Archive is an excellent starting point.

A friend of mine was writing a piece for breast cancer awareness month and received an e-mail she wanted to incorporate into her article. The e-mail was from a respected friend, so she didn't doubt its veracity.

"The leading cause of breast cancer is the use of antiperspirant," the e-mail read. "Yes, ANTIPERSPIRANT. Most of the products out there are an antiperspirant/deodorant combination, so go home and check your labels. Deodorant is fine, antiperspirant is not."

The e-mail went on to explain what sounds like a rational argument. "The [body's] toxins are purged in the form of perspiration. Antiperspirant, as the name clearly indicates, prevents the body from perspiring, thereby inhibiting it from purging toxins from below the armpits. These toxins do not just magically disappear. Instead, the body deposits them in the lymph nodes below the arms since it cannot sweat them out. This causes a high concentration of toxins and leads to cell mutations: a.k.a. CANCER."

I've been on the receiving end of one too many urban legends delivered by e-mail, so I suggested she become an antiperspirant sleuth. I urged her to visit the American Cancer Society Web site and see what she could find on this topic. Thankfully she did and was saved from submitting an embarrassing and incorrect story. She went to the site, checked the archives, and found the myth, along with the American Cancer Society rebuttal.

➤ AFU and Urban Legends Archive at *http://www.urbanlegends.com*
➤ American Cancer Society at *http://www2.cancer.org/zine/dsp_StoryIndex. cfm?fn=001_05211999_0*

OTHER FORMS OF INTERNET RESEARCH

While there's enough information on the World Wide Web to keep even the most dedicated researcher busy, the Web is not the only way to conduct online research. Sometimes, it's not even the best way. As with encyclopedias and books, the information found on the Web is static. Someone produces an information-filled Web page; users read it and digest the information.

Hopefully, the content of each page is changed with greater frequency than books on the shelf of the local library, but that's not necessarily the case. I've visited Web pages that haven't been altered since their appearance online two, three, or even four years ago.

Other aspects of the Internet—the e-mail, mailing lists, chat rooms, newsgroups, and forums we talked about in chapter 2—are, by their very nature, fluid. Opportunities abound to communicate directly with real people via the Internet, versus simply reading the contents of a Web page. The information you find is current. What's more, you have direct access to its provider. These Internet tools provide creative ways for writers and speakers to research data and connect with each other.

"E-Exploring"

Eva Marie Everson, coauthor of the book *Pinches of Salt, Prisms of Light* (Essence, 1999), is an expert at Internet research. Having grown up in Georgia, she had firsthand knowledge of that location and lifestyle for her first novel, *Shadow Fall,* but she had no experience with other things she wanted to include in the book, such as real-estate brokers of New York City, upper-class hotel management and operations, Hell's Kitchen in 1975, New York's Upper West Side in 1995, the Hamptons, Paris, AIDS Foundation fund-raising.

Asked how she gathered her information, she replies, "I went online. I had a friend who had lived in Hell's Kitchen in 1975. I e-mailed him and asked for an interview, and he granted it."

That was the beginning. America Online proved to be an excellent source for Everson. Unlike some ISPs, commercial online services like AOL and CompuServe maintain member directories, which sometimes include members' city of residence and occupation. Through her AOL member directory, Everson interviewed Robert A. Marino, president of a New York City real-estate brokerage business, Marino Real Estate Consulting.

"From there I met Peter Wirth, a hotel developer who at one time managed the Waldorf Astoria," she says. "We scheduled a telephone interview. A young man named Stephane, who lives in Paris, helped me with proper French and beautifully described a Parisian café. He did it so well that when I used it as the setting for one of my scenes, a friend who read the manuscript insisted I must have visited that café since I described it so perfectly. Considering I've never been to Paris, I'd say my online research worked out well!"

It worked well in other ways, too. When she needed a reporter, she simply searched through her member directory and found one. She didn't abandon the Web in her research though. When she wanted to set a scene in a small town outside Paris, she "visited" the town from the comfort of her office chair, carefully studying the photographs provided in the town's Web site.

Everson's favorite experience was meeting a member of AOL who not only lives across from the American Museum of Natural History, but also is a retired research editor for *Glamour* magazine. Her tutelage and online friendship have proved priceless.

Everson is sold on using the Internet for her writing. *Shadow Fall* rings with authenticity. "I have my own name for this process," Everson says. "I call it E-exploring. It's so much cheaper than a round-the-world plane ticket, and I find that most people are willing to be of assistance. My only warning is that you must be able to determine if people really are who they say they are. Interviewing in detail will typically assure you of that."

Everson is only one writer who is going beyond the Web to find information and people to talk to for research purposes. Remember, credible sources lend veracity to writing that boosts a manuscript's salability.

Speakers, too, can benefit from frequenting chat rooms and mailing lists. Depending upon your topic, you can easily find first-person stories and anecdotes through others online, and the expert you need to verify statistics and information may be only a click away.

Surfing for Stories

Sometimes doing research simply involves finding the right stories to be used in the context of your project. Jennifer Basye Sander became an Internet sleuth for her book *The Gift of Miracles: Magical True Stories to Touch Your Family's Heart* (William Morrow, 1999). She and her coauthors, Jamie C. Miller and Laura Lewis, collected stories from many sources, including the Internet.

Surfing Web sites for ideas worked well for Jennifer—and for me! I had posted a Christmas story on a site called Afterhours Inspirational Stories. Jennifer saw it, contacted me, and a flurry of e-mails resulted in one of the easiest sales I've ever made. My story appeared in her book, and I can add a prestigious publisher to my writing résumé. My Walter Payton story, as a result of being posted on Heartwarmers4U, was published in the American Liver Foundation newsletter—and I was invited to submit several other stories to various upcoming Chicken Soup for the Soul books. It pays to have stories out there; editors and compilers are looking for them.

➤ Afterhours Inspirational Stories at *http://www.inspirationalstories.com*
➤ Chicken Soup for the Soul at *http://www.chickensoup.com*
➤ Heartwarmers4U at *http://www.heartwarmers4u.com*

E-mail Interviews

My friend and colleague, author JoAnn Wray, wrote an article on the effects of Polycystic Ovarian Disease (PCOD) and the infertility problems it produced. To get firsthand, unbiased information, she went to PCOD chat rooms for others' comments. "Not only did it help my article and give me insight to their problems," says Wray, "but it also helped my daughter, who suffers from PCOD. She realized she wasn't alone in this battle and that there was hope for her to one day have children."

Wray is also editor of the Fellowship of Christian Writers—Tulsa newsletter, *Ready Writer.* In her quest to write informative articles for her readers, she turned to the Internet. "I've begun to send magazine editors e-mail requests to do interviews with them on their publications and what they are looking for from writers. After only three weeks, I have already obtained extensive interviews and answers from three different magazine editors.

"It seems to me," Wray continues, "that people feel a certain 'cloak of anonymity' in e-mail and seem to open up more than they might normally. I approach it like a normal conversation for me. I am just up-front and honest and inject humor where appropriate, which helps. If I'm real with others in e-mail, then others are real with me."

Georgia Shaffer's book *A Gift of Mourning Glories: Restoring Your Life After Loss* (Servant Publications, 2000) contains more than seventy personal stories or quotes from people who have rebuilt their lives after devastating losses. Although not everyone she interviewed for the book had access to the Internet, those who did made Shaffer's work simpler, faster, and more economical. "I could e-mail them their written story as it appeared in the book for approval," she explains. "They could send me suggestions for corrections, and then I could e-mail them the updated text."

Of course, all the world isn't yet wired. For those who didn't have e-mail, she sent a hard copy of the chapter containing their story and a self-addressed, stamped envelope. "After reviewing what I had written, they mailed me their response with any corrections, and later I had to send the permission form required by the publisher with another SASE. This process was much more costly and tedious."

➤ Georgia Shaffer at *http://www.georgiashaffer.com*

➤ Ready Writer at *http://www.ilovejesus.com/lot/epistlewriter/TCWCpage.html*

Sharing Lives, Being Friends

The Huntington's Disease mailing list is the reason that *Faces of Huntington's* (Essence, 1998) even exists. I found the forum on a message board when I was stressed out and needed support. Little did I know I had also found dozens of individuals who were delighted to share their experiences and ultimately become part of a special book. Since then, the list and various chat rooms have been sources for speaking engagements, not to mention paying customers.

The Internet search is an art form that requires time to polish. Given their ability to communicate well with the written word, writers and speakers will find online resources a natural avenue. But keep in mind that communicating via the Internet does not convey emotions nearly as well as face-to-face or even telephone conversations, and it lacks vocal inflections, accents, diction, dialects, gestures, dress, and shared environments. People can have difficulty deciding if someone is serious or joking, angry or sad or frustrated. Sarcasm, at which wordsmiths often excel, is sometimes misunderstood or falls flat entirely online.

Lurking for a while to get a feeling for a particular mailing list or chat room can go a long way toward making you more comfortable with the "invisible" correspondence of the Internet. Online correspondents who start out as strangers can often come to feel like friends. Once you understand the nuances, you'll be surprised at just how rewarding and productive cruising the information superhighway can be.

PART TWO

Stops Along the Way

FIVE

Back to School

Web Sites to Help Perfect Your Craft

*It usually takes more than three weeks to prepare
a good impromptu speech.*—MARK TWAIN

In her book *Sally Stuart's Guide to Getting Published* (Harold Shaw, 1999), Sally Stuart writes candidly about her early writing years. "I was fortunate to sell the first things I ever wrote, but I realize now it was probably God's way of keeping me interested until I discovered writing was my calling." I can identify with her; the same thing happened to me when I began writing.

"It wasn't long," Stuart writes, "before I realized that I didn't know what I was doing right or wrong."[1] At that point, Stuart, like me and so many others, realized that she needed to hone her craft.

In recent history we've seen continual advances in cyber-technology that have greatly simplified that task. But back then, Stuart didn't have the Internet filled with online writing resources, hers for the taking. Today, countless Web sites, mailing lists, newsgroups, and chat rooms exist for those interested in style and grammar, along with online classes and workshops and critique groups. Sometimes simply finding a list of frequently asked questions (FAQs) about writing can be a gold mine of information. This chapter is filled with excellent online learning opportunities. Make sure to take time to explore each site and to link to additional Web sites I haven't mentioned.

ONLINE WRITING RESOURCES

No matter how creative your idea for a novel or how compelling the need for your nonfiction book, if your writing is sloppy and your grammar usage unacceptable, your manuscript is not publishable. Even an article intended for posting on your Web site should be error free and sparkling.

The Internet has truly helped to level the playing field when it comes to learning how to write. The following sites will help you create a polished manuscript.

Grammar and Usage

> ➤ Common Errors in English *(http://www.wsu.edu:8080/~brians/
> errors/index.html)* is a fun alphabetical listing of common errors and also
> perceived errors that are actually correct. Click on the word or phrase to
> see the accurate use or the history of the misuse that has become
> accepted English. An example is the phrase "You've got another thing
> coming." According to Paul Brians, professor of English at Washington
> State University, "The original expression is the last part of a deliberately
> ungrammatical joke: 'If that's what you think, you've got another think
> coming.'"

> ➤ Copy Editor: Language News for the Publishing Profession *(http://www.
> copyeditor.com)* is an award-winning newsletter published in New York
> City. It is only available as a subscription print newsletter at this time,
> but a companion Web site features copyeditor links and workshops.
> About 2,500 publishing companies subscribe to *Copy Editor,* which
> focuses on American English, with features such as updates on usage
> and style, answers to sticky copyediting questions, new words, and
> excerpts from house stylebooks. Some of the links include the *Chicago
> Manual of Style* FAQ, discussions and information about copyediting
> matters pertaining to the Internet from the editors of *Wired Style,* the
> newsgroupalt.usage.english FAQ, several online dictionaries, and the
> Editors' Association of Canada.

➤ The 1918 edition of *Elements of Style* is online courtesy of Columbia University at the Bartleby Library of Great Books Online *(http://www. bartleby.com)*. There are dozens of classics from 1776 to 1921 at this site, complete with search engine.

➤ The English Grammar Clinic *(http://www.lydbury.co.uk/grammar)*, out of Lydbury English Centre, is a conference and chat room for the discussion of the English language. To post and chat you need to register for a free membership.

➤ The Grammar Hotline *(http://www.tc.cc.va.us/writcent/gh/hotlino1.htm)* is a project of Tidewater Community College in Virginia Beach, Virginia. This alphabetical listing features universities in the United States and Canada where the Grammar Hotlines are located. Short questions about writing may be asked by telephone or e-mail.

➤ The Grammar Lady Online *(http://www.grammarlady.com)* is a one-woman, free service offering a hotline number to ask about grammar questions. There is also a Q&A message board, or you can send e-mails with specific questions.

➤ Guide to Grammar and Writing *(http://webster.commnet.edu/HP/pages/ darling/original.htm)* is an impressive grammar site complete with a large question-and-answer section. You may also submit questions to experts.

➤ The Slot *(http://www.theslot.com)* is the brainchild of the *Washington Times'* copy desk chief, Bill Walsh. Walsh began The Slot in August 1995 as the Crusty Old Slot Man's CopyEditing Peeve Page. This site is designed to supplement the AP Style Guide.

➤ The Writing Center at Rensselaer Polytechnic Institute in Troy, New York, has compiled an array of grammar helps *(http://www.rpi. edu/dept/llc/writecenter/web/handouts.html)*. The site also includes a section on preparing a presentation that speakers will find helpful.

Word Power

➤ Cliché Finder *(http://www.westegg.com/cliche)* is a searchable cliché database.

➤ Jesse's Word of the Day *(http://www.randomhouse.com/wotd)* explains the meaning and origin of common words. There is also an extensive archive.

➤ The Phrase Finder *(http://www.shu.ac.uk/web-admin/phrases/go.html)* is a large collection of English phrases and sayings. This site is great as a phrase thesaurus, to find the meanings of English phrases and sayings or to use as a reference for the origin of phrases.

➤ The Roget's Thesaurus site *(http://humanities.uchicago.edu/forms_ unrest/ROGET.html)* has a search engine and is based at the University of Chicago.

Quotable Quotes

The following quotation search sites are excellent resources for those of you needing quotations for your speaking or writing:

➤ Link Bank's Quotation Links at *http://www.linkbank.net/get_ links/ default/quotes/8*

➤ The Quotations Archive at *http://www.aphids.com/quotes/index.shtml*

➤ The Quotations Page at *http://www.starlingtech.com/quotes*

➤ Quoteland at *http://www.quoteland.com*

➤ Quotez at *http://business.virgin.net/mark.fryer/intro.html*

Dictionaries

➤ OneLook Dictionaries *(http://www.onelook.com)* looks for the definition of a word by searching, at last count, 2,655,106 words indexed from 580 dictionaries. The site also has the OneLook Best Price Search engine to find the best prices on books, CDs, computers, software, and more.

➤ WWWebster Dictionary *(http://www.m-w.com/netdict.htm)* is a dictionary and thesaurus search engine from Merriam Webster Dictionary. The site also includes links to Word of the Day, Word Game, Words from the Lighter Side, and Language Info Zone.

➤ YourDictionary.com *(http://www.yourdictionary.com)* is a service of Bucknell University. In addition to an English dictionary search engine, the site includes foreign language and multilingual dictionaries, specialized English dictionaries, thesauruses and other vocabulary aids, language identifiers and guessers, an index of online dictionaries, a Web of online grammars and a Web of linguistic fun.

Other Resources

- The Arrow *(http://www.wport.com/~cawilcox/mainpath/page1.htm)* is an outlining tool for writers. The site helps you "find your voice, organize your thoughts, untangle kinked prose, unstick your frozen brain, and stir your creative juices."
- Encyberpedia *(http://encyberpedia.com/glossary.htm)* calls itself a living encyclopedia and offers dictionaries, encyclopedias, glossaries, language dictionaries and translators, and thesauruses. This site is a gold mine on a huge variety of topics.
- The University of Wisconsin, Madison Memorial Library has an out-standing Web page for citing electronic sources in research papers and bibliographies *(http://www.library.wisc.edu/libraries/Memorial/citing.ht)*. Organized by style, most of the sites include formats and/or examples of citations. Style guides include the APA (American Psychological Association), CBE (Council of Biology Editors), *Chicago Manual of Style,* MLA (Modern Language Association), and others.
- The Word Detective on the Web *(http://www.word-detective.com)* is the online version of "The Word Detective" newspaper column. Evan Morris has an archive of past questions posed by readers and will accept your question about words via e-mail.

ONLINE WRITING CLASSES

Wish you could take a writing class but none are available in your rural area? Your busy work schedule prevents you from taking the time to learn how to create believable characters?

Online writing classes from universities and other organizations offer an excellent way for busy or isolated writers to learn. One of their biggest selling points is flexibility. Another is that oftentimes the classes are either free or much less expensive than traditional courses.

Classes consist of lectures and lessons, which are usually posted on a Web site. Some classes are conducted entirely via e-mail: You turn assignments in and receive them back from your instructor, graded, by e-mail. Some classes offer e-mail or bulletin-board discussions or even chats.

Susan Letham of the Wordweave Creative Writing Lab *(http://welcome. to/wordweave)* has a passion for online learning. Says Letham, "Online learning is…very important, and will probably become…more so in the future as people are required to fit things into…their busy lives. It's also a vital step in overcoming isolation, both location and interest based." Wordweave offers a variety of courses and workshops, including one for beginners or blocked writers called Outset: An Introduction to Creative Writing Techniques.

Regardless of your level of expertise or your genre, online classes you can take from the privacy of your own home, on your own schedule, are all over the Web. The following list is just the beginning.

Free Online Learning

- ➤ F2K *(http://fiction.4-writers.com/creative-writing-classes.shtml)* has a free introduction to fiction-writing courses. The site has mentors, discussion boards, chats, and study groups to help in the weekly lessons.
- ➤ Recently purchased by electronic-publishing giant Xlibris, Inkspot *(http://www.inkspot.com/craft/courses.html)* wins my Grand Prix Award as the best of the best. This site is packed with its own FAQs, articles, a newsletter, and forums. The comprehensive and well-organized set of writing links takes you all over the Internet to sites focused on grammar, style, critique groups, writing courses, and even a Beginning Writer's FAQ.
- ➤ Literature Unbound *(http://www.wordcircuits.com/literature/workshop. htm)* has a nice list of online free and fee-based poetry workshops.
- ➤ Simple Steps to Landing Profitable Assignments *(http://members. aol.com/bugsley/doug.htm)* is a free, self-directed course for aspiring writers. According to author Doug Schmidt, "The material was highlighted in the New and Noted section of *Writer's Digest* magazine and has been

getting great reviews by people who have gone through the self-directed course (and landed high-paying assignments)."

➤ Universities are excellent places to get training, and many now offer online writing labs (OWLs). Many OWLs use a MOO real-time communication environment that gives writers a chance to chat with other writers, take college-level writing courses, share their writing, and meet with tutors. Although primarily for registered students, some sites do accept questions from nonstudents via e-mail as well as provide handouts and other information that writers may find helpful. Colgate University's Web site *(http://departments.colgate.edu/diw/NWCAOWLS.html)* includes a comprehensive alphabetical list of OWLs. This site also has a link for handouts, online tutoring, and other great resources.

➤ The online writing lab at Purdue University *(http://owl.english.purdue. edu/writers/#guides)* has over 120 documents available for writers, with a summary of each included.

➤ Wordweave Creative Writing Lab *(http://www.welcome.to/wordweave)* is a well-put-together site from Susan Letham. Letham's workshops, two or four weeks in length, change often and are usually seasonally linked. Other classes include Introduction to Creative Writing, Basic Poetry, and Writing from Life, as well as an advanced level Collabowrite! course, which explores the possibilities of various forms of collaborative writing. Wordweave offers a discussion list and a small and highly focused ongoing group of writers called Themeweavers. According to Letham, "Wordweave is a labor of love and is in no way commercially oriented."

➤ The Write Life *(http://welcome.to/thewritelife)* calls itself "the creative writing Web haven." Beginning and confident beginner classes are featured. The site also includes a mentoring program, an e-mail discussion group and message board, and several creative-writing exercises.

Fee-Based Online Learning

➤ Sponsored by 4-Writers.Com *(http://4-writers.com)*, Writers' Village University offers over 130 writing courses. To take the free classes, you must subscribe to the online publication. Still, once you have subscribed, you can take unlimited classes.

➤ Coffee House for Writers *(http://www.coffeehouse4writers.com)* has a series of four-week workshops covering fiction, poetry, nonfiction, and the basics. The site offers a weekly motivational mailing for writers, a free newsletter, a novelist critique group, monthly contests, and a monthly grammar test.

➤ Diversity University *(http://www.du.org/duSvcs/teachers.htm* and *http://www.explorationsu.com)* is a fee-based opportunity for educators to learn how to teach effectively in virtual reality. The site provides training, tools, and services to enable you to bring your own classes online.

➤ Fiction Writer's Connection *(http://www.fictionwriters.com)* offers an e-mail fiction writing course. You can become a member for a modest fee and receive a 10 percent discount on all classes, a free newsletter, critiquing, and consultations.

➤ Gotham Writers' Workshop *(http://www.writingclasses.com/online/courses. html)* is the online version of the largest private creative writing school in New York City. Four thousand students a year attend classes for adults in Fiction Writing, Screenwriting, Playwriting, Nonfiction Writing, Novel Writing, Children's Book Writing, Memoir Writing, Poetry Writing, Comedy Writing, TV Writing, and four-hour workshops on Selling Your Writing. The school also has creative writing classes for teens.

➤ The Institute for Children's Literature *(http://www.institutechildrenslit. com)* is a popular home-study writing course for those interested in writing for children.

➤ Novel Craft *(http://www.noveladvice.com/craft/index.html)* has a variety of online classes, including Elements of Fiction, Writing Dialogue, Science Fiction and Fantasy, and Mystery Writing.

➤ Online Course Centre *(http://www.accesstv.ab.ca/courses.html)* offers a wide variety of courses, including many for writers of various genres. The center also features chat and forum capabilities.

➤ Painted Rock Writers and Readers Colony *(http://www.paintedrock.com/ conference/wrtclass.htm)* has classes taught by authors published in a wide variety of genres. The site also includes author home-page links, message boards, and mailing lists.

➤ Poynter Online *(http://www.poynter.org/class/q1-2000sked.htm)* offers dozens of journalism classes on a huge array of topics online.

➤ A list of electronic screenwriting classes is available through the Screenwriters and Playwrights page *(http://www.teleport.com/~cdeemer/Distance. html* or *http://www.writerspage.com).* Some of these classes require software such as StoryCraft.

➤ Scribe and Quill Mailing List *(http://come.to/ScribeQuill)* has comprehensive writing workshops facilitated by published professionals.

➤ Word Museum *(http://www.wordmuseum.com/classes.htm)* is the brainchild of author Lori Soard. In addition to more traditional classes, Lori also features a class on how to design your own Web page.

➤ With more than fifty courses and growing all the time, Writers Club University is part of the iUniverse Web site *(http://www.iuniverse.com).* Online sessions consisting of e-mailed readings, homework, and special message boards start every two months. Some courses even have informal chats.

➤ Writers.com *(http://www.writers.com)* has been offering online writing classes, tutoring, and writing instruction via e-mail in all genres since 1995. The site has free writers' groups and a free monthly newsletter, writing tips, information on contests, and an online bookstore. Tutoring is available for an additional cost.

➤ Writing Unlimited *(http://www.writing-unlimited.com)* is an online writing workshop offering separate material by e-mail for the intermediate and advanced writer. Each student is assigned a teacher who reads, evaluates, and comments on the writing assignments over a semester. The site offers a thirty-day writing skills development booklet, including a journal-writing plan and vocabulary exercises.

WRITING CRITIQUE GROUPS

It's been said so often it's almost a cliché—writing is a lonely business. Writing is something you have to do by yourself, and isolation can become a problem. Online critique groups are an easy way to meet other writers and, hopefully, have others review and make helpful suggestions about your work.

Critique groups vary in size, but the goal is usually the same as face-to-face groups: to provide a safe and supportive environment for members to polish their manuscripts and gain overall writing skills. Like online classes, members use e-mail to submit and comment upon manuscripts.

Writer Gail Welborn believes that being a part of Kingdom Writers, a Christian critique group, has definitely helped her writing. Two of the members are journalism majors, which Welborn says gives them a strength others may lack. All but one writer in her group are published; the majority are novelists. The group critiques for story lines, transitions, and passive writing and generally works together to help the members polish their manuscripts.

"I am a strong advocate of e-mail critique groups, but small ones work best," says Welborn. "When you send [a piece] into a large group, you never know if or when the piece will be looked at. Because of the size of our group, most things are turned in [back to the writer] within forty-eight hours, and if there's a push because of a deadline, we all put extra effort into it."

Wanting a smaller group, fellow Kingdom Writers member Tracey Bateman contacted three other members and asked about forming a smaller critique group. Welborn was one of those asked to join the new group, Ready Writers.

Welborn insists that her e-mail group has been more responsive than the face-to-face group where she lives. "I hold other writers in high esteem and value their opinions and the time they generously share with me. I am a better writer today because of them."

Part of that may be the flexibility and anonymity the Internet presents, as well as the lack of idle conversation that is prevalent in real-life gatherings. Whatever the reason, others agree with Welborn, and you may too once you give it a try.

The listings below represent only a small portion of what's available online. If you don't see a group that meets your needs, start your own. Either way, a critique group makes good sense for improving your writing skills and feeling less alone.

> ➤ Amy Foundation *(http://www.amyfound.org/onlinecwg.html)* is a small
>   Christian e-mail discussion and critique forum primarily used for Letters
>   to the Editor critiques.
> ➤ Coffee House for Writers *(http://www.coffeehouse4writers.com)* has a free
>   e-mail critique group for novelists.

➤ *Writer's Digest* magazine says that the science fiction writers' group Critters Workshop *(http://brain-of-pooh.tech-soft.com/users/critters)* is "well run and quite stable." Critters is for serious writers and also has a chat section and market helps for writers who want to break into the genre.

➤ Fictech for Novelists' Inner Circle Writers Club *(http://www.geocities. com/SoHo/Lofts/1498/circlefaq.htm)* is an international club and critique group of over 1,500 writers. Several biweekly subscription newsletters are also available.

➤ Internet Writer's Fantasy List *(http://www.fantasytoday.com)* is the home of the Internet Fantasy Writers Association. You must be a list member to join the critique group, but you will find research information, market information, sites for writers, and more.

➤ IRC #Undernet Writers Site *(http://www.getset.com/writers)* has a variety of critique opportunities, including romance, religious, mystery, fiction, short story, science fiction, fantasy, and freelance. They also have a chat room, newsletter, and other resources for writers.

➤ Kingdom Writers *(http://www.angelfire.com/ks/kingwrit)* is an e-mail critique group and fellowship for Christian writers. This list is for beginning and professional writers and offers both critique and the discussion of writing topics. All subscribers are required to submit a short biography before being added to the list.

➤ Local Writers Workshop *(http://www.elanworks.com/lww.html)* is a community of writers who meet and discuss ideas, problems, and works in progress. You must become a member before posting anything for critique on the forum. The group also discusses writing-related topics.

➤ Misc. Writing Mailing Lists *(http://www.scalar.com/mw/pages/mwmlist. shtml)* is a compilation of mailing lists for those wishing to be in an online critique group. Instructions for joining all lists are included. Some of the topics covered are mystery, technical, romance, fiction, nonfiction, novel, writing for children, scriptwriters, and poetry.

➤ Preditors & Editors *(http://www.sfwa.org/prededitors/pubwork.htm* or *http://www.sfwa.org/links/workshops.htm)* is part of the Science Fiction and Fantasy Writers of America, Inc. Web site. This page has links to workshops, critique groups, and other online learning opportunities for many different genres.

➤ The Six Foot Ferret Writers' Group *(http://pages.cthome.net/6ft_f errets/index.html)* is for serious science fiction and fantasy writers.

➤ Write Links *(http://www.writelinks.com/critgroup/critgroupa.htm)* has three experience-based, peer-critique groups. These moderated e-mail groups are limited in size, and new applicants often wait several months before a place becomes available. The writers in these groups need to be very committed. A monthly e-zine for writers is also available.

➤ The Writers Write Web site *(http://www.writerswrite.com/groups.htm)* has a large database of online groups. Many of those listed have critique options.

➤ Young Writer's Clubhouse *(http://www.realkids.com/critique.htm)* is an e-mail critique group for young writers sponsored by the *Real Kids* adventure TV series.

The learning sites, critique listings, and other helps listed are invaluable for those who want to get to the next level with their writing and speaking. Whether you're looking for the perfect word, the genesis of a phrase, or a critique group, you may find the perfect place online.

SIX

Business Calls

Online Conferences, Agents, Contract and Copyright Information, Speakers' Bureaus, and More

The beautiful part of writing is that you don't have to get it right the first time, unlike, say, a brain surgeon. You can always do it better, find the exact word, the apt phrase, the leaping simile.—ROBERT CORMIER

Shortly after college I joined the Peace Corps. I was assigned to one of the poorest countries in the world, Mali, West Africa. Teaching English as a foreign language to high school students, I spent my first year in the capital, but the second year was spent in the Sahara Desert in the city of Gao. Although Gao is an underdeveloped country, my desert home boasted all the creature comforts I needed, including mud construction, an indoor bathroom, and running water. Of course, only the first was guaranteed, since we had water for just thirty minutes daily, usually at 4:00 A.M.

Never having spent time in any desert, I was unaware that it doesn't just rain there. No, it pours. Man, it pours! Unlike many houses in Gao, my house did not have the popular corrugated tin roof. Mine was simply a flat mud covering. Not only had no one educated me about the torrential downpours that fell virtually without warning, but no one had advised me of something called the life span of mud houses: They last about five years unless they are maintained by adding more mud, straw, and dung to keep them intact. The weight of the water on a five-year-old, nonmaintained roof can cause a collapse, and since it seems my house was five years old, that's exactly what happened when the first downpour came—the roof fell on my face. Literally. I was covered in mud, straw, and dung as the rain continued. Now I can laugh, but then, being wet and smelly in the midst of a downpour did not make me happy.

In the case of the collapsing roof, it would have taken only a few dollars, some readily available supplies, and time to make sure my house stayed intact. Similarly, whether you're a veteran writer or speaker or a novice waiting for that break, you also need to do routine maintenance.

Writers' conferences, agents, speakers' bureaus, and other associations all have costs attached, but they are how writers and speakers hone their skills and keep up-to-date. This chapter is filled with "routine maintenance" Web sites for writers and speakers so you won't find yourself embarrassed, covered in mud, and unable to make a move. The good news is, thanks to the Internet, much of what you need to keep your career on target is now free.

WRITERS' CONFERENCES: ONLINE RESOURCES

Writers want to be published. The vast majority of us feel we have an important message that needs to be heard. Letters to the editor, writing for the PTA, and even sending out our annual Christmas letters allow others to hear us. Most writers, however, eventually would like to be heard on a larger scale.

Everyone, it seems, has a story to tell and a computer to simplify the process of telling it. Competition is fierce, whether we are writing the great American novel or a series of articles on parenting for the hometown paper.

Perfecting our craft is only part of the picture. We can read every book out there on writing, study the markets, ask for samples and publishers' guidelines, write and rewrite manuscripts, send professional query letters, format our manuscripts precisely—and we still aren't guaranteed a contract.

At a time when more and more publishing houses aren't even looking at unsolicited or unagented manuscripts, one way to get your manuscript noticed is to personally meet the acquisition editors. But you live in Nebraska and your book is a perfect fit for a certain New York publisher. What can you do?

A writers' conference is one answer. Conference organizers work hard to present a variety of ways for writers to introduce their work to editors. Publishing houses also use conferences to their benefit, sending their editors in the hopes they will discover hot new talents rising in the métier. Besides attending workshops and presentations, meeting with editors, and networking with other writers, conference goers can pick up dividends like catalogues, magazines, and current submission guidelines.

Wendy Lawton, premier doll-maker-turned-writer, has this to say about attending conferences: "I found the manuscript submission opportunity a big plus. I received excellent feedback and appreciated the impromptu opportunities to meet the editors at mealtimes. I was able to chat with each of the editors I had hoped to meet in a natural, comfortable setting."

Evidently it was also the perfect setting for her. While at Sandy Cove Christian Writers' Conference, Lawton submitted her middle-reader biographical fiction series proposal to Julie Ieron of Moody Press. It must have been a memorable proposal, because when Ieron left Moody, she passed it on to the editorial director, who took it to a committee.

"After I submitted a revised proposal," Lawton says, "it was taken back to committee, and I was offered a two-book contract with an option for the series."

Lawton, who has managed to combine her doll making and writing, has plans to create a line of dolls based on her books. "I choose unforgettable girl protagonists—they not only make the best fiction heroines; they make the most compelling subjects for dolls."

Not everyone who attends a conference gets a book contract, but many people do sell articles or make invaluable contacts for the future. Linda Gilden has reason to be enthusiastic about conferences. "I was scared to death at the first one I ever attended in 1990," she remembers. "But it didn't take me long to understand their immeasurable value. I believe every time I have attended it has resulted in a sale or in a lead that led to a sale. The encouragement factor from editors who show an interest in your work is wonderfully motivating."

Writers' conferences come in all sizes and cover many genres, so it's important to choose one that fits your needs. Consider the length of the conference and its location, size, and cost. The following list of Web sites is a great place to start looking for conferences that provide education, networking opportunities, and the rare chance to meet with editors who are actually there to spend time with writers.

> American Christian Writers (ACW) *(http://www.ecpa.org/acw/schedule.html)* hosts dozens of annual one-, two-, and three-day writers' conferences throughout the United States. ACW even offers an annual cruise conference for those wanting to combine the business of writing with a vacation.

> Authorlink! *(http://www.authorlink.com/confren.html)* includes listings of national and regional events and contests.

> Inkspot *(http://www.inkspot.com/tk/network/conf.html)* lists a few additional conferences not featured on the larger compilations.

> National Institute for Computer-Assisted Reporting (NICAR) and Investigative Reporters and Editors, Inc. (IRE) *(http://www.ire.org/training),* both a part of the same organization, offer national conferences and regional workshops, week-long boot camps, and on-site newsroom training.

> Sally Stuart's Christian Writers' Market Guide *(http://www.stuartmarket.com)* has an extensive listing of Christian conferences updated in conjunction with her annual guide.

> Screenwriters Online Guide to Writers' Conferences *(http://www.screenwriter.com/insider/WritersCalendar.html)* is an extensive compilation of conferences for both screenwriting and other genres. The listings are by state, with a few Canadian and international conferences.

> Shaw Guides *(http://www.shawguides.com/writing)* and Writer's Digest *(http://www.writersdigest.com/conferences/index.htm)* both offer a listing of the Shaw Guide to Writers' Conferences.

> Writers' Conferences and Festivals *(http://www.gmu.edu/departments/awp/wcf/wcfmembers.html)* was founded in 1990 for directors of writers' conferences. Their mission is to support and promote literary conferences and festivals. They offer an extensive listing of conferences that includes dates, faculty, cost, and a short description of the program. Web sites are linked as available.

> Writers Information Network *(http://www.bluejaypub.com/win/conferences.htm)* has a listing of Christian conferences.

➤ YWAM Woodcrest *(http://www.ywamwoodcrest.com)* is part of the Christian organization Youth With A Mission. Their school of writing has five-day workshops.

THE BUSINESS OF WRITING: ONLINE RESOURCES

If you ask writers if they'd rather write or take care of the business side of writing, you probably won't be surprised by the answer. However, unless writers learn at least the basics of the industry, their chances of success will be greatly diminished.

Do all writers have or need an agent? Are contracts negotiable? What needs to be done to make sure your work is protected by copyright laws? Whether you're looking for representation as a speaker or wondering what deductions to take on your taxes, the Internet is a great source for answers.

Finding an Agent

Publishers are increasingly requiring writers to submit their manuscripts through an agent. Yet agents usually won't talk to an unpublished writer. This is one of the biggest conundrums in the publishing industry. Becoming aware of how agents work won't change that, but it will help you make wise decisions and hopefully find an agent who is right for you.

A literary agent markets your work and negotiates your contracts. Good agents accept only clients in whom they believe and whose writing they honestly think they can market. Their commission is usually a percentage of your advance and royalties.

W. Terry Whalin is a prolific writer. His articles have appeared in more than fifty publications, and he has authored fifty-five books, including *Lessons From the Pit* (Broadman and Holman, 1999). I met Whalin on an Internet writers' list, and I appreciate his permission to reproduce some of his advice here.[1] A member of the American Society of Journalists and Authors (ASJA), Whalin is a believer in agents, with one caveat: "I believe all too often writers don't [use] necessary diligence before they get an agent. A part of being a professional writer is to act like a professional—that is, to move with caution and cover all the bases."

With slush piles getting larger and publishers taking longer to accept or reject manuscripts, Whalin sees another advantage to having an agent. "Agents simultaneously submit my material [submit to more than one publisher at the same time], and the industry expects such action. A number of editors have told me that agented material is usually read quicker—because of their respect for the agent and because they know it is usually simultaneously submitted."

Because there is no literary agent degree or certification process, anyone can call himself or herself an agent, just as anyone can call himself or herself a writer. If you feel the urge to be an agent, you can simply hang up your shingle. Qualified agents who do know what they're about are plentiful, but writers need to put some effort into finding out who they are. All too often that isn't the case. Frustrated writers may sign a contract with an agent who speaks well of their work without ever checking his or her credentials.

The following sites will help you learn more about what agents do, how to find one, what to beware of, and even whether or not you need one.

➤ Agent Research and Evaluation *(http://www.agentresearch.com)* is a consulting service designed to help writers find effective literary representation in the United States, Canada, and the United Kingdom. AR&E offers free agent-verification assistance, but they also have several fee-based services, such as a newsletter and a new-agent list.

➤ The Association of Authors' Representatives, Inc. (AAR) *(http://www. publishersweekly.com/AAR/Topics.html)* is a not-for-profit organization of independent literary and dramatic agents. Their site, hosted by *Publishers Weekly,* offers invaluable information on selecting an agent. The site includes an excellent set of questions to ask prospective agents and a list of member agencies.

➤ Authorlink! *(http://www.authorlink.com)* has a free database of agents for access by Authorlink! authors. Agents are listed in a private directory and may view Authorlink! manuscripts.

➤ Inkspot *(http://www.inkspot.com/market/agents.html)* has several links to information and articles regarding agents.

➤ LiteraryAgent.com *(http://www.literaryagent.com/index.html)* is a joint venture of the Mesa Group and Proteus Design, developed to help authors meet agents. The site offers a search engine that allows authors to search for an agent by agency name, city, state, country, or genre.

➤ Preditors & Editors *(http://www.sfwa.org/prededitors/peala.htm)* has an excellent listing of literary agents. The words "not recommended" and "charges fee" appear as warnings to writers. The site also has helpful information for writers at Writer Beware *(http://www.sfwa.org/beware/)*.

➤ Writers.net *(http://www.writers.net/agents.html)* offers a search engine of literary agents. The site also has a link to FAQs and a discussion board.

➤ Writing.org *(http://www.writing.org/html/a_agents.htm)* has a four-part series on literary agents. There are also links to other agent sites.

Negotiating Contracts

The National Writers Union defines a contract as "any agreement between you and another party regarding the use or sale of your writing. It may be written or oral; it may be with a publisher, agent, work-for-hire client, website or other party; it may concern a book, article, research report, short story, computer manual, screenplay or what-have-you."

Writing and selling your book or article takes an enormous amount of time and energy. If you're like most authors, when a contract finally comes, you want to leap for joy, screeching, "They like me! They really, really like me!" With that excitement comes the compelling urge to sign the contract and get down to the business of seeing your name in print.

My first two books were self-published. The experience helped me learn enough about the publishing business to know I needed help in negotiating my contracts. When I received the contract for *WriterSpeaker.com,* I had a moment of panic. "If I tell them I want some things changed, will they call me ungrateful and tell me to forget it?"

After I calmed down, I realized this simply would not be the case. By the time a publisher offers you a contract, time and resources have already been invested in you and your project. They really do want you, or you wouldn't have the contract in hand. Whether you negotiate your own contract or work through a literary agent or attorney, publishers can and do make contract changes for reasonable requests.

The question is, what's "reasonable"? As with any area of writing and publishing, you should familiarize yourself with contracts. Then you can judge what's reasonable and what's not. Excellent books on the subject and an ever-increasing number of Web sites with contract information from reputable sources exist. Terry Whalin helped me find an excellent literary attorney from a law clinic for writers. The clinic charged me a realistic amount to review and negotiate my contract.

Whalin was quick to point out, "I reviewed many of my own contracts for years and didn't use such a service on several of my books with an agent. Looking back, I think I was too trusting and generally not protected."

If you have an agent, why would you need the services of a literary attorney? "The contracts are getting more and more complex," Whalin explains. "The slight phrase means a great deal, and someone has to interpret such matters for you as the writer. One of my last contracts was about eighteen legal pages single-spaced. Talk about legalese! The key with using a literary attorney is that they represent you and only you. [Agents have] other clients and their own bias and I believe a literary attorney is less biased."

According to Whalin, "The time to get contract advice from a literary attorney or an agent is before you give your final assent orally or in writing to the publisher (or their representative). The purpose of such a review is to be sure that you receive or try to receive the best possible contractual terms."

Getting the best possible terms is not mercenary; it is good business sense. The following Web sites are excellent starting points to learn more about contracts.

➤ The American Society of Journalists and Authors *(http://www.asja.org/resource.htm)* has a number of helpful links about contracts. The site also offers a free electronic newsletter from the Contracts Committee of the American Society of Journalists and Authors *(http://www.asja.org/cwpage.htm)*.

➤ The Freelance Editorial Association's Code of Fair Practice *(http://www.tiac.net/users/freelanc/Code.html)* defines ethical standards and contract guidelines for editorial freelancers and clients. Nonmembers may purchase a hard-copy version of the code from the association.

➤ Ivan Hoffman, J.D. has an informative essay called "The Ten Negotiating Key Points in an Author-Publisher Agreement" *(http://home. earthlink.net/~ivanlove/points.html).*

➤ The National Writers Union offers its members contract advice *(http://www.nwu.org/grv/grvcont.htm)* and also has an informational site with tips for a better work-for-hire contract *(http://www.nwu. org/bite/tipswfh.htm).*

➤ The Publishing Law Center *(http://www.publaw.com)* is primarily for publishers, but writers can also learn more about contracts, book publishing, multimedia, magazine or newsletter publishing, copyright, trademark, subsidiary rights, electronic rights, licensing, and other intellectual property issues.

➤ Science Fiction Writers of America *(http://www.sfwa.org/contracts/index. htm)* has contract information, including position papers on electronic publishing.

➤ Tom Brosnahan offers contract information geared toward guidebook writers at *http://www.infoexchange.com/Author%20Table%20Pages/ Contracts.html.*

➤ The Writers Union of Canada *(http://www.writersunion.ca)* has a variety of contract services for both members and nonmembers.

Understanding Copyright Laws

Every writer, even those who have an agent or an attorney, should be knowledgeable about copyright law. A wealth of Web sites exists to help you learn all you need on the subject.

I have also included music-related sites in this section. Songwriters need to know about copyrights. As a writer-speaker-singer, it amazes me how little writers know about the legality of quoting songs in their work. Writers, speakers, and singers ought to know that when they wish to use songs or portions of songs in their work, permission to do so is almost always necessary. Usually there are fees involved. The sites at the end of this section will guide you to music publishers and help you understand the process of permissions, as well as how to protect yourself as a writer using copyrighted material.

➤ Books A to Z Copyright Basics *(http://www.booksatoz.com/copyrigh/whatis.htm)* has a list of easy-to-understand answers to the most common copyright questions.

➤ Copyright Clearance Center *(http://www.copyright.com)* provides licensing systems for the reproduction and distribution of copyrighted materials in print and electronic formats throughout the world.

➤ The Copyright Law site *(http://www.duq.edu/Technology/copy/copylaw1.html)* has an impressive collection of links including copyright law and basics, multimedia fair-use guidelines and production, educational fair use, intellectual property, copyright permission/registration, and much more.

➤ Intellectual Property Law *(http://www.intelproplaw.com)* includes information on copyrights, trademarks, patents, and even jobs. Besides many legal links, the site has links to the intellectual-property discussion mailing list.

➤ Ivan Hoffman, J.D. *(http://www.ivanhoffman.com)* has written and compiled a collection of articles and links for writers and publishers, songwriters, Web-site designers and owners, and others. Copyright issues about the Internet and electronic rights and articles about trademark are also featured.

➤ O'Reilly and Associates *(http://www.oreilly.com/oreilly/author/permission)* has an extensive list of permission guidelines from their book *So You Want to Write a Book.* Although aimed at those wishing to write computer books, this is an excellent resource for all authors. The site includes resources, checklists, and sample forms.

➤ Stanford University Libraries, Council on Library Resources, and Find-Law Internet Legal Resources have created this site *(http://fairuse.stanford.edu)* filled with copyright information.

➤ "Ten Big Myths About Copyright Explained" is an essay by Internet publisher Brad Templeton at *http://www.templetons.com/brad/copymyths.html.*

➤ The U.S. Copyright Office *(http://lcweb.loc.gov/copyright)* offers information on copyright law.

➤ Writers Write *(http://www.writerswrite.com/journal/dec97/cew3.htm)* has an informative article called "A Novice Writer's Guide to Rights."

Music Copyright Issues

> The American Society of Composers, Authors and Publishers (ASCAP) *(http://www.ascap.com/ascap.html)* has a membership association of over 80,000 composers, songwriters, lyricists, and music publishers. ASCAP's function is to protect the rights of its members by licensing and paying royalties for the public performances of their members' copyrighted works. The organization collects money from those who use music in their writing or other venues and then pays that money as royalties to the composers and publishers.

> Christian Copyright Licensing Information (CCLI) *(http://www.ccli.com)* exists to help individuals, churches, and organizations in the area of worship by offering information, services, and products. The organization offers a "permission of use" concept, whereby churches can obtain blanket permission for specific copying activities that are labeled "noncommercial." This international organization was founded as a way to "educate the church about copyright laws, to protect the church from the consequences of copyright infringements and to encourage greater utilization of copyrights in church services."

> The Harry Fox Agency, Inc. (HFA) *(http://www.nmpa.org/hfa.html)* provides an information source, clearinghouse, and monitoring service for licensing musical copyrights.

> Sesac, Inc. *(http://www.sesac.com)* is a performing-rights organization.

Finding Speaking Venues

A number of online resources, including speakers' bureaus and fee-based search engines, exist to help speakers find venues. Visiting the Web sites of trade associations and unions such as those listed at the end of this chapter may also lead speakers to engagements.

Speakers' Bureaus

Speakers' bureaus work in much the same way for speakers as agents do for authors, assisting them in creating promotional materials and obtaining bookings. While some speakers do have agents, as a professional speaker, you should know that meeting planners, corporations, nonprofit organizations, churches, and other groups and individuals will often consult a bureau to find the "perfect" speaker for their event.

Some bureaus work only with high-profile speakers, while others use fee structure, topic, location, or other parameters to determine if a speaker is right for their list. The bureau's job is to negotiate for you, make arrangements, and collect the fee. Like an agent, they are paid a percentage of your earnings.

Also like agents, any organization can call itself a speakers' bureau. Speakers wishing to find representation should do careful research before signing any contract. The following list of bureau Web sites is a good starting point to learn more.

> ➤ Ambassador Speakers Bureau *(http://www.ambassadoragency.com)* is an agency specializing in speakers for Christian and religious programs nationwide. Their speakers are leaders in their respective areas of expertise.

> ➤ Christian Leaders, Authors and Speakers Services (CLASS) *(http://www.classervices.com)* is a complete service agency for both the established and aspiring Christian speaker, author, and publisher. Focusing on the Christian community, CLASS finds, trains, develops, educates, and nurtures raw talent and launches it through their speakers' service. The organization also offers publishing assistance.

> ➤ International Speakers Bureau *(http://www.internationalspeakers. com/speak.htm)* represents more than five hundred speakers. The site features an online questionnaire.

> ➤ Leading Authorities, Inc. *(http://www.leadingauthorities.com)* is one of the nation's largest and fastest-growing speakers' and entertainment bureaus. Their presenters include leading authors, athletes, academicians, executives, journalists, television personalities, and former officeholders.

> ➤ Professional Woman Speakers Bureau *(http://www.protrain.net)* is a private, international network of certified Professional Development Trainers. These independent consultants and trainers are available to present workshops, seminars, and keynote speeches.

> ➤ Speakers.com *(http://speakers.com)* has links to some of the top speakers' bureaus in the nation.

➤ Speakers Spotlight *(http://www.speakers.ca)* is a Canadian Speakers Bureau.

➤ Walters Speakers Services *(http://www.walters-intl.com)* is the source for information on speakers and speaking, seminar leaders, humorists, and experts. The site includes articles for professional speakers from their newsletter, *Sharing Ideas.*

Fee-Based Search Engines for Speakers

➤ Christian Speakers International *(http://www.journeypubs.com/csi)* has local, regional, or international listings of Christian speakers. The search engine can be used to find a speaker by ministry or location.

➤ Speakers.com *(http://speakers.com)* charges listing fees for speakers wishing to be added to their database.

➤ Women's Ministry Network *(http://www.womensministry.net)* calls itself "the premiere site" for women's ministry leaders and organizations. They offer a basic free listing to speakers and musicians and a charge a fee for more detailed information. The site has a newsletter, chat room, and other helpful tools.

TRADE ASSOCIATION AND GOVERNMENT SITES

The Internet is a great place for both writers and speakers, but nothing can replace the valuable face-to-face contact that takes place through trade associations and union meetings. These organizations usually have a governing board, annual or even regional conventions, educational opportunities, insurance plans, and more.

I've listed not only the traditional writer and speaker sites but others like the American Marketing Association and Public Relations Society of America. Writing and speaking take different forms, and each association listed offers the potential for learning better skills and making valuable contacts.

I've also included a list of government sites on which you might find helpful information about tax laws, especially as they relate to writers and speakers. And just in case you ever need the postal service again, the USPS and Canada Post Web sites are listed too!

Trade Association Web Sites

> ➤ The American Advertising Federation (AAF) *(http://www.aaf.org)* is a professional advertising association for corporate advertisers, agencies, media companies, suppliers, and academia.

> ➤ The American Christian Romance Writers *(http://ordinarywoman. com/acrw.html)* is a membership organization of writers of Christian romance and women's fiction. Their site includes online workshops, member and related links, and a membership application.

> ➤ The American Crimewriter's League *(http://members.aol.com/theACWL)* is an organization for crime and suspense writers.

> ➤ The American Marketing Association (AMA) *(http://www.ama.org)* is an international society of marketing professionals.

> ➤ The American Society of Journalists and Authors (ASJA) *(http://www. asja.org)* is the nation's leading organization of independent nonfiction writers, with more than 1,000 members.

> ➤ The Association of American Publishers (AAP) *(http://www.publishers. org/home/index.htm)* is the principal trade association of the book-publishing industry.

> ➤ Associations on the Net (AON) *(http://www.ipl.org/ref/AON)* is a collection of over 1,100 Internet sites from the Internet Public Library and provides information about a wide variety of professional and trade associations, cultural and art organizations, political parties and advocacy groups, labor unions, academic societies, and research institutions.

> ➤ Authors Guild Online *(http://www.authorsguild.org/welcome.html)* is a society of published authors devoted to fair compensation, free speech, and copyright protection.

> ➤ The Business Marketing Association (BMA) *(http://www.marketing.org)* is an organization devoted to business-to-business marketing and marketing communications.

> ➤ The Children's Book Council (CBC) *(http://www.cbcbooks.org)* is a non-profit trade organization dedicated to encouraging literacy and the use and enjoyment of children's books. Since 1996, CBC has also included

children's book packagers and producers of book-related multimedia products for children.

➤ Christian Writers Fellowship International (CWFI) *(http://www. cwfi-online.org)* is a multiservice ministry for Christians in publishing.

➤ Crime Writers of Canada *(http://www.crimewriterscanada.com)* is the national association for professional practitioners of the crime-writing genre in Canada.

➤ The Direct Marketing Association (DMA) *(http://www.the-dma.org)* is comprised of those in the direct-marketing industry, including cataloguers, list companies, ad agencies, consultants, and industry suppliers.

➤ Founded in 1970, the Editorial Freelancers Association *(http://www. the-efa.org/main.html)* is a national, nonprofit, professional organization of self-employed workers in the publishing and communications industries. Members are editors, writers, indexers, proofreaders, researchers, desktop publishers, translators, and others who offer a broad range of skills and specialties.

➤ The Evangelical Christian Publishers Association *(http://www.ecpa.org)* is an international, nonprofit, trade organization for those engaged in the Christian publishing industry.

➤ Evangelical Press Association *(http://www.gospelcom.net/epa/aboutepa.htm)* is an organization of over 375 periodicals, organizations, and individual members.

➤ The Freelance Editorial Association *(http://www.tiac.net/users/freelanc)* is a nonprofit organization of freelance editors, illustrators, indexers, production specialists, proofreaders, translators, and writers.

➤ InScribe Christian Writers' Fellowship in Canada (CWF) *(http://www. inscribe.org)* is a Canada-wide organization. Their purpose is to stimulate, encourage, and support Christians across Canada. They have critique groups, a newsletter, conferences, and more.

➤ Investigative Reporters and Editors, Inc. (IRE) *(http://www.ire.org)* is a grassroots nonprofit organization dedicated to improving the quality of investigative reporting within the field of journalism.

➤ Mystery Writers of America, Inc. *(http://www.mysterywriters.net)* is the premier organization for mystery writers and other professionals in the mystery field.

➤ The National Speakers Association (NSA) *(http://www.nsaspeaker.org)* is an organization for experts who speak professionally.

➤ The National Writers Union (NWU) *(http://www.nwu.org/nwutoc.htm)* is the trade union for freelance writers of all genres who work for American publishers or employers. They offer their members grievance resolution, contract assistance, health insurance, a national job hot line, and more.

➤ The Public Relations Society of America (PRSA) *(http://www.prsa.org)* is the world's largest professional organization for public relations practitioners.

➤ Publisher's Marketing Association *(http://www.pma-online.org)* is the largest nonprofit trade association representing independent publishers of books, audio, video, and CDs.

➤ Romance Writers of America *(http://www.rwanational.com)* is a national, nonprofit association for writers of the romance genre.

➤ Sales and Marketing Executives International (SME) *(http://www.smei.org)* is the world's largest association of sales and marketing managers. The site offers an extensive marketing library with over 200,000 searchable articles covering all areas of sales and marketing.

➤ Science Fiction and Fantasy Writers of America *(http://www.sfwa.org)* is an organization for writers of science fiction and fantasy. However, there is a wealth of information on the site that is relevant to writers of other genres. Membership requires "the professional publication (acceptance and payment) of three short stories or one full-length fiction book or a dramatic script."

➤ The Small Publishers, Artists and Writers Network (SPAWN) *(http://www.spawn.org)* is a membership organization for writers, artists, and small publishers. It provides education, information, and resources for anyone interested in publishing.

➤ The Society for Technical Communication (STC) *(http://stc.org)* includes writers, editors, illustrators, printers, publishers, educators, students, engineers, and scientists employed in a variety of technological fields. STC is the largest professional organization serving the technical-communication profession.

➤ The Society of Children's Book Writers and Illustrators (SCBWI) *(http://www.scbwi.org)* is dedicated to serving the people who write, illustrate, or share a vital interest in children's literature. The monthly *SCBWI Bulletin* is available through this site.

➤ The Society of Professional Journalists *(http://spj.org/spjhome.htm)* is the nation's largest and most broad-based journalism organization.

➤ Toastmasters International *(http://www.toastmasters.org)* is an international organization comprised of local chapters. Toastmasters is a mix of professionals and others who desire to enhance their public-speaking abilities.

➤ Writers Guild of America, West (WGAW) *(http://www.wga.org)* is a union representing writers in the motion picture, broadcast, cable, and news-media industries.

➤ Writers Information Network (WIN) *(http://www.bluejaypub.com/win)* was organized in 1983 to provide a much-needed link between writers and editors and publishers in the religious publishing industry.

➤ The Writers Union of Canada *(http://www.writersunion.ca)* is a national organization of professional writers of books for the general public.

Government Web Sites

➤ Canada Post *(http://www.canadapost.ca)* is the Canadian postal service.

➤ The Internal Revenue Service (IRS) *(http://www.irs.treas.gov)* is a helpful, well-written site.

➤ Revenue Canada *(http://www.ccra-adrc.gc.ca/menu-e.html)* is the Canadian equivalent of the IRS.

➤ Stamps Online *(http://www.stampsonline.com)* is a feature from the United States Post Office. All orders are shipped priority mail for only $1.00. Orders arrive in five to seven business days.

➤ TaxPlanet *(http://www.taxplanet.com)* is edited by syndicated tax columnist Gary Klott. TaxPlanet includes information about changes in tax laws, a library of downloadable forms, and more.

➤ The United States Postal Service Web site *(http://www.usps.com)* is a great resource, complete with a zip-code finder, rate calculator, tracking capabilities, and all sorts of tools to keep those manuscripts circulating.

➤ The Writer's Pocket Tax Guide *(http://foolscap-quill.com/wptg2000.html)* is a free guide about writers and taxes that's updated annually.

Sometimes the task of connecting with all the right people and learning the business side of writing and speaking seems daunting. The Internet, with its wealth of Web sites, has made those less-than-enjoyable tasks easier to handle. We're in a competitive business, and knowing where to find information to help locate the right association, negotiate a contract, or get a speaking engagement can make a difference.

SEVEN

Side Trips Worth Exploring

Writer and Speaker Web Sites

Writing is rewriting. A writer must learn to deepen characters, trim writing, intensify scenes. To fall in love with a first draft to the point where one cannot change it is to greatly enhance the prospects of never publishing.—RICHARD NORTH PATTERSON

As a young girl, my dream was to travel. Anywhere. I thought no place could possibly be as boring as Topeka, Kansas. I didn't care where I traveled—as long as it was out of the state. My mother's claim that our trips to visit friends in Kansas City, Missouri, were actually trips to a different state didn't wash. No matter what they said, Kansas City was just a bigger Topeka.

When I was seventeen, my mother decided to take us on a grand adventure. It was to be our first real vacation. The arrival of eight children in twelve years may have had something to do with the fact that our previous summers had been spent primarily in our front yard, playing with children from other large families. But this summer, my mother was determined to take her children to visit relatives and to see some of our country along the way.

Somehow, Mom found the money—how, I don't know—to make our vacation a reality. Loading seven of her eight children, ages ten to twenty, into a bright red, rented station wagon, off she drove. We were on our way to meet our cousins in Seattle! From that trip, our one-and-only family vacation, came many great memories that we tell and retell at family gatherings. The cramped conditions, the smelly socks, and the usual big-family cacophony are forgotten. Instead, we talk about the amazing sights we saw and the people we met. We go through the litany of games we played and songs we sang to keep the driver awake. We also remember the constant dual refrain from the twins, relegated to the most uncomfortable seats in the very back of the station wagon: "Are we there yet?"

I knew the answer to that question when I began this chapter: a resounding "No!" Even before I wrote the proposal for *WriterSpeaker.com*, I'd gathered a pretty impressive set of links. But not being a poet or a science fiction writer, my bookmarks reflected little relating to those and several other genres. I wasn't "there yet."

I knew that in order to make this book a valuable resource, I had to do two things for my readers. First, I had to introduce those who were Internet novices to Information Superhighway Map Reading 101. Second, I had to provide them with information on some great destinations—and directions for getting there.

Back in 1975, when that crazy woman packed up seven kids for a cross-country adventure, there were no electronic trip-planning devices or Internet sites to help map out the journey. My mother dutifully got a set of maps from AAA, and off we went.

Writing and publishing were different in 1975 too. Typewriters were as good as it got, and information about specific genres was found only in books—and few books at that. Today, thanks to the Internet, we have access to abundant information about every conceivable category of writing, along with tips on how to write it and how to sell it and everything in-between.

As we reached the Rocky Mountains on that family trip, I could finally see that, yes, Carmen, we weren't in Kansas anymore. During the rest of the trip I gained an appreciation for the diverseness and vastness of my country. The same thing happened as I spent time surfing the Internet. I confess to seeing some flat, boring landscapes, but I also found some incredibly helpful places for writers of all genres. There's no way to calculate the hours that went into creating all these sites, or the number of professionals who share their knowledge through them, but it's awesome to contemplate.

The summer of "the vacation," we managed to lose our way more than once. And each time we seemed hopelessly lost, we somehow came upon a jewel of a town, a great restaurant, or a group of wonderful people. Many of these unplanned side trips actually ranked among the highlights of the trip.

The same phenomenon is possible on your journey over the information superhighway. Sometimes when you use a link to travel from one site to another, you end up at an unplanned destination—possibly even more valuable than anything on your planned Internet itinerary. Yes, you can spend more time than prudent, so it's wise to watch a clock—especially when you find yourself doing more surfing than writing.

There was no way during our cross-country trip that summer that we could get to every city on the map between Topeka and Seattle. Neither could I possibly review, or even find, every writing and speaking site on the Internet for this book. But I have compiled lists of links for ten different writing genres and an additional list for speakers. As you take your own side trips on your Internet adventures and identify information sources that I haven't found, I'd love to hear about them and add them to my ever-growing database. E-mail your suggestions to me at *links@writerspeaker.com.*

In the first section, I've listed several informative writing sites of interest to every writer or speaker. Directly following these listings are sections with addresses for Web sites offering writing and publishing tips for specific genres. Some of the sites also offer networking opportunities in the form of chats, mailing lists, and forums.

Many of the sites listed under each category have crossover appeal as well. For example, even if you're not a working journalist, some of the sites listed under the journalism section are a must-visit for every writer.

Remember that question "Are we there yet"? With the explosive growth of information on the information superhighway—and no end in sight—the answer is clear: We're *not* there yet. We're never going to get there. There's always some place new to explore.

Enjoy the journey!

WRITING SITES

All sites listed include writer's tips, information on the business of writing and publishing, and a vast array of links. Some sites include chats, forums, newsletters, and mailing lists. You'll notice that specific links from most of these sites are mentioned elsewhere in this chapter under various other headings as they offer resources for particular genres. Put on your favorite CD, get some coffee or a cold drink, and settle down for a long surfing session.

➤ Absolute Write at *http://www.absolutewrite.com*

➤ Black on White at *http://www.bfree.on.ca/bow*

➤ Business Writer's Free Library at *http://www.mapnp.org/library/commskls/cmm_writ.htm*

➤ The Eclectic Writer at *http://www.eclectics.com/writing/writing.html*

➤ ForWriters.com at *http://www.forwriters.com*

➤ Inkspot at *http://www.inkspot.com*

➤ Universe at *http://www.iuniverse.com*

➤ John Hewitt's Writer's Resource Center at *http://www.poewar.com*

➤ Mom Writers at *http://www.momwriters.com*

➤ The Official Misc. Writing Website at *http://www.scalar.com/mw*

➤ Pure Fiction at *http://www.purefiction.com*

➤ SharpWriter.com at *http://www.sharpwriter.com*

➤ Tips for Writers at *http://www.tipsforwriters.com*

➤ Write Links at *http://www.writelinks.com*

➤ The Write Page at *http://www.writepage.com*

➤ Writercise at *http://www.writercise.net*

➤ The Writer's BBS at *http://www.writers-bbs.com/home.shtml*

➤ Writer's Digest at *http://www.writersdigest.com*

➤ Writer's Links from Bricolage at *http://bricolage.bel-epa.com/scripts/links.py?wo*

➤ Writer's Toolbox at *http://www.writerstoolbox.com*

➤ Writer's Tools at *http://www.writetools.com*

➤ Writers.com at *http://www.writers.com*

➤ Writers Write at *http://www.writerswrite.com*

➤ WritersNet at *http://www.writers.net*

➤ Writing Corner at *http://www.writingcorner.com*

➤ YouCanWrite at *http://YouCanWrite.com*

➤ Zuzu Petal's Literary Resources at *http://www.zuzu.com*

The Children's Market

"The internet has served as a most valuable resource [for me] to communicate with classes, teachers, parents, and anyone else interested in children's literature. It's great to be a part of classroom studies and have the Web page be so much a part of their study of authors. I travel all over the country and see my posters, illustrations, and even pictures [from our Web page] on the walls of the schools. Teachers are using these resources in many creative ways. My kids answer over fifty letters a day.... You can't get that kind of one-on-one any other way. It's great!"
—PATRICIA POLACCO, CHILDREN'S AUTHOR

➤ Visit Patricia Polacco's Web site *(http://www.patriciapolacco.com/h.html)* to see how one writer has put herself on the map of the information superhighway.

➤ The BookWire Index Publishing for Young Readers *(http://www.bookwire.com/index/publishing-for-young-rdrs.html)* has an impressive list of links for young readers, writers, and those who write for young people.

➤ The Children's Book Council (CBC Online) *(http://www.cbcbooks.org)* is the Web site of the Children's Book Council. The site features pages for publishers, teachers, librarians, booksellers, authors, and illustrators.

➤ Children's Book Publishers *(http://www.scils.rutgers.edu/special/kay/publish.html)* has links to various publishers of children's books.

➤ The Children's Literature Web Guide *(http://www.acs.ucalgary.ca/~dkbrown/index.html)* gathers Internet resources related to books for children and young adults for teachers, librarians, parents, writers, editors, booksellers, storytellers, and children. The site includes a discussion board, awards, recommended books and book reviews, resources for writers and illustrators, and research guides.

➤ The Children's Writing SuperSite *(http://www.write4kids.com/index.html)* is presented by *Children's Book Insider,* the newsletter for children's writers. The site is packed with FAQs, essays, and links.

➤ Cyberteens *(http://www.stonesoup.com)* includes writings, art, games, and links for teenagers by teenagers.

➤ Inkspot for Young Writers *(http://www.inkspot.com/young)* is an excellent place for writers under eighteen. Articles, tips, market news, and other encouragers are here, as well as several discussion forums.

➤ The Institute for Children's Literature *(http://www.institutechildrenslit. com)* is a popular home-study writing course for those interested in writing for children. The site includes information about the organization's writing classes, chat rooms, weekly scheduled interviews to learn about writing, a writer's support room, and writing tips.

➤ KidsWeb *(http://www.kidsvista.com/Arts/literature.html)* is devoted to children and writing with links to children's books and authors, electronic children's books, fairy tales and fables, poetry, theater, and science fiction.

➤ Kidword *(http://www.bconnex.net/~kidworld)* is another Web site for kids by kids. This site includes a writing contest.

➤ The Purple Crayon *(http://www.users.interport.net/~hdu/index.html)* has useful articles, mostly for writers and illustrators, and selected links to resources for writers, editors, teachers, librarians, parents, and others. The site also includes advice for children's writers and illustrators, a primer on agents, an article on writing multicultural books, interviews, a useful publishing glossary, and more.

➤ The Quill Society *(http://www.quill.net)* is a free online writing club dedicated to young writers. Included are activity centers, online publishing, critiquing forums, and other resources. Membership is restricted to those between twelve and twenty-four.

➤ The Society of Children's Book Writers and Illustrators (SCBWI) *(http://www.scbwi.org)* is the only professional organization dedicated to serving the people who write, illustrate, or share a vital interest in children's literature. Sections of this site include publications, grants and awards, members, and more.

➤ Stone Soup Magazine *(http://www.stonesoup.com)* is a magazine comprised entirely of stories and art by children for children.

➤ Verla Kay's Web site *(http://www.verlakay.com)* is an excellent example of an author's Web site. She not only showcases her work, but also offers writing tips, chats, book reviews, and a site just for kids. Her tips page has some great examples of what not to do to get published.

The Christian Market

"Too often in the Christian marketplace, we confuse the issue of working for God and being fairly compensated. It's necessary to 'pay your dues' in the Christian market and often work for minimum pay [in order] to build credibility in the industry. Even after that credibility is established, it's a struggle to be treated as a professional and fairly compensated—yet those well-paying opportunities where you can express your spirituality are out there. It simply takes persistence, continued professionalism and hard work to get there."—W. TERRY WHALIN

➤ Visit the Web site of multipublished author W. Terry Whalin *(http://www.terrywhalin.com)* for another example of ways to establish a presence on the Internet.

➤ American Christian Writers *(http://www.ecpa.org/acw/index.html)* is a ministry providing service to writers and speakers. The goal of ACW is to locate, educate, and motivate Christian writers and speakers. The organization provides writers' conferences and a monthly magazine geared exclusively to Christian writers and speakers *(http://www.acwpress.com/links.htm)*. The Web site includes links for Christian writers.

➤ The Amy Foundation *(http://www.amyfound.org)*, founded in 1976 by W. James Russell and his wife, Phyllis, was named after their daughter. The foundation is best known for its Amy Writing Awards, which is a call to present spiritual truth reinforced with biblical references in secular, nonreligious publications. Other programs of the foundation include the Church Writing Group effort, point-of-view columns, and book reviews in local newspapers.

➤ Christian Writers' Fellowship International (CWFI) *(http://www.cwfi-online.org)* is a multiservice organization for writers designed to instruct, equip, and encourage beginning writers to get started and experienced writers to become more effective. They offer a critique service, market consultation, and *Cross and Quill* newsletter.

➤ Christian Writers Group *(http://members.truepath.com/CWG)* has a page for Christian writers including links, writing tips, and member writings. CWG also has an e-mail discussion list for subscribers.

➤ Christian Writers Workshop *(http://www.billyates.com/cww/default.html)* brings together Christian writers of all genres and experience. The site offers weekly workshops in a chat venue, a superb list of Christian links, and a newsletter.

➤ Kingdom Writers *(http://www.angelfire.com/ks/kingwrit)* is primarily an e-mail critique group for Christian writers. The site also offers links to other Christian and secular writing sites.

➤ Write His Answers Ministries, Marlene Bagnull's Web site *(http://www. writehisanswer.com),* provides writing resources, teaching, and Bible studies for writers. Marlene teaches a series of seminars and is also the director for the Colorado and Greater Philadelphia Christian Writers Conference.

➤ Writers Information Network (WIN) *(http://www.bluejaypub.com/win)* is a professional association for Christian writers and is designed to provide a much-needed link between writers and editors and publishers of the religious publishing industry. Founded by Elaine Wright Colvin, WIN offers one of the best sources for market information, industry news, and trends. The bimonthly subscription magazine, *Win Informer,* is a must-read for anyone serious about Christian writing. The site also offers professional advice on marketing, ethics, contracts, editor relations, copyright, writing problems, and miscellaneous writing concerns. WIN offers a referral service to professionals seeking writers and speakers. The Web site has a chat room and message board.

Freelance Opportunities

"Several months ago, I set a personal goal of a query a day. The Internet has been a tremendous asset in accomplishing that goal. More publishers are accepting e-queries, and the turnaround rate has been reduced from weeks to days—in some instances even hours. I used to look forward to my daily trek to my mailbox, but it's my 'inbox' that delights me now."—T. SUZANNE ELLER

➤ T. Suzanne Eller *(http://www.intellex.com/~eller/tseller.html)* is one of the most versatile freelancers around. Visit her site and learn more about her creative ways of finding writing opportunities, including books, magazines, newspapers, and even electronic books.

- Ants.com *(http://www.ants.com/ants)* is an online community devoted to freelancers.
- Community Writers Association *(http://www.communitywriters. org/index.html)* is for self-employed, home-based professionals. The Web site includes opportunities for networking and a job bank.
- Creative Freelancers *(http://www.freelancers.com)* is primarily a job search Web site for freelancers.
- Freelance Editorial Association *(http://www.tiac.net/users/freelanc)* works to promote the interests of freelance editors, illustrators, indexers, production specialists, proofreaders, translators, and writers.
- Freelance Online *(http://www.FreelanceOnline.com/index2.html)* is a directory of resources for freelance writers. The site also has a free FAQs section.
- Freelance Success *(http://www.freelancesuccess.com)* offers a subscription magazine (electronic or print) for professional freelance nonfiction writers. They also offer a variety of fee-based classes.
- Freelance Writing.com *(http://www.freelancewriting.com)* is the Web site for today's working writers, including a newsletter, forums, and a writers' idea lab.
- NetRead *(http://www.netread.com/jobs/jobs)* is a searchable database of job listings in the publishing industry. The site includes the option to post résumés for public viewing.
- Sun Oasis Jobs *(http://www.sunoasis.com)* includes jobs for writers, editors, and copywriters. Visitors are able to search, by region, for freelance or online jobs and for new job postings.
- Writing Employment Center *(http://www.poewar.com/jobs.htm)* has several employment articles in addition to an extensive listing of writing and writing-related jobs.
- WritersWeekly.com *(http://www.writersweekly.com)* is a free e-mail newsletter of freelance job listings and new paying markets.

Opportunities for Journalists

"The Internet makes it easier than ever before for writers to publish and find an audience. Breaking into popular, established publications remains difficult. But

with a few days' study of basic Web-page creation techniques, even the newest writer can look like a million dollars on the Web. E-mail, discussion forums, and chat rooms give every writer the ability to find readers and develop a following. It took me five years to establish my freelance writing career, but I estimate I could do it in a year or less by using the Internet."—DOUG MILLISON

➤ Veteran journalist Doug Millison is writing online these days. His informative site *(http://www.online-journalist.com)* includes online journalism links and frequently asked questions.

➤ American Journalism Review has links and a search engine to newspapers worldwide *(http://ajr.newslink.org/news.html)*. They also have sites for magazines *(http://ajr.newslink.org/mag.html)*, television and radio *(http://ajr.newslink.org/broad.html)*, and other resources *(http://ajr.newslink.org/spec.html)*.

➤ The Newsroom Home Page at AssignmentEditor.com *(http://assignmenteditor.com)* was created by Jim Lichtenstein, managing editor at Chicago's WBBM-TV (CBS). Lichtenstein originally intended the AssignmentEditor.com site to be accessible only to professional journalists, but because of tremendous public response, he has made the site free and available to everyone. The site includes media links of all types, research and political sites, directories, and even fun stuff such as crossword-puzzle links.

➤ The Associated Press *(http://wire.ap.org)* is the news Web site of the AP and its member newspapers and broadcasters. This site has daily news stories and an engine to search their archives.

➤ Business and Science News *(http://www.businesswire.com)* is recognized as a leading source of news and information. The site offers a service called ExpertSource, developed in consultation with the nation's leading news organizations. Journalists submit queries, seeking experts for specific editorial projects. ExpertSource searches its proprietary database of thousands of academic and industry experts and quickly responds with a roster of prospective interview candidates.

➤ Executive's Toolbox *(http://ceoexpress.com)* has everything plus the kitchen sink. They say that they are a "site designed by a busy executive for busy executives." That may be the case, but it's also a resource-rich site for journalists or any other information junkie.

➤ FACSNET *(http://www.facsnet.org)* is a service for journalists provided by FACS in partnership with the San Diego Supercomputer Center. The site also offers an excellent search engine of journalists' links *(http://www.facsnet.org/left_preview.html)*.

➤ Guide to Electronic and Print Resources for Journalists *(http://www.cio. com/central/journalism.html)* is simply the best storehouse of information for journalists on the Net.

➤ JournalismJobs.com *(http://www.journalismjobs.com)* is a searchable database of jobs in the publishing industry.

➤ Monique's Newsjobs *(http://www.newsjobs.net)* is an impressive Web site of alphabetical job listings for journalists. The site includes information about job listings and job-hunting tips.

➤ National Institute for Computer-Assisted Reporting (NICAR) *(http://www.nicar.org)* is a program for Investigative Reporters and Editors, Inc. and the Missouri School of Journalism. Founded in 1989, NICAR has trained thousands of journalists in the practical skills of finding, prying loose, and analyzing electronic information.

➤ National Press Club Reporter's Internet Resources *(http://npc.press. org/what/library/reporter.htm)* for journalists around the world is compiled by the staff of the Eric Friedheim Library. The site includes a mailing list, job bank, and various links of interest to journalists.

➤ NewsDirectory.com *(http://www.newsd.com)* is a guide to English-language media online.

➤ Newstream.com *(http://www.newstream.com)* is an online journalists' source for free multimedia news. Registration is required for this site, which is a joint venture of Business Wire and Medialink.

➤ Poynter Online *(http://www.poynter.org* or *http://www.poynter.org/links)* has a number of excellent essays on journalism. The site also includes an impressive array of journalism links and journalism research sites.

➤ PubList.com *(http://www.publist.com)* is an Internet directory of publications with a database of over 150,000 magazines, journals, newsletters, and other periodicals.

➤ Reporter.org *(http://www.reporter.org)* provides a variety of resources for journalists, journalism educators, and the public at large via the Web.

They provide Web space, an e-mail address, and other services to members of Investigative Reporters & Editors. This site has many resources, including a search engine, current news, and the "beat page," a jumping-off point for journalism resources, organized by newsroom beats, or categories, including politics, healthcare, religion, and education.

➤ Reporter's Internet Guide *(http://www.crl.com/~jshenry/home.html)* is the most comprehensive guide to Internet resources for working journalists. This shareware ($25; see glossary) is part training guide, part reference work. RIG contains hundreds of links to data and information at all types of Internet sites.

➤ Scoop Cybersleuth's Internet Guide—Journalism Links *(http://www. courierpress.com/courier/scoop/journalism.html)* has a nice collection of journalism links.

➤ Ultimate Collection of News Links *(http://www.pppp.net/links/news)* is a categorized list of online newspaper links, searchable by nation or state.

Mystery and Suspense Genre

"Mystery writing requires more authentic detail than any other form of genre fiction. Anything you write about weapons, forensic medicine, or police procedure had better be correct in every particular. The Internet makes doing this extensive research a lot easier for crime writers."—KATE DERIE

➤ Mystery writer Kate Derie's ClueLass is a mystery lover's notebook. This well-arranged site *(http://www.cluelass.com)* has cleverly named features, such as Making Tracks: mystery conventions and conferences; Hanging Together: organizations for writers and readers; Just Rewards: awards for mystery fiction and related nonfiction; and lots more. The site also includes library collections and archives, author newsletters and Web sites, and various publishers. A must-visit is the page dedicated to real-world law enforcement, forensic medicine, legal machinations, and more *(http://www.cluelass.com/Cyber.html)*. If you can choose just one Web site to visit, this is it.

➤ Bibliomysteries *(http://www.bibliomysteries.com)* is a site created and maintained by author Marsha McCurley.

➤ Mystery Pages *(http://www.mysterypages.com)* is a Web site for mystery lovers of every kind.

➤ Crime Writers of Canada *(http://www.crimewriterscanada.com/links/mystery.htm)* is an excellent source for mystery and crime links.

➤ Hollywood Crimewriting Network *(http://crimewriters.com/Crime/index.html)* is hosted by crime writer Martin Roth. The site includes articles, interviews, and everything you need to get started. Some areas on this site are accessible only by fee-paying members.

Opportunities for Poets

"I was given a poem by my great-great-grandfather in 1998. He never published any of his poetry and the lone poem is all that survived. I was struck with the reality that there are many poets who have the ability to create beautiful poetry, who may never have the opportunity to share their work with others. It is my hope and prayer that Adoration *will become a prominent magazine in the Christian poetry market."*—KURT MCCULLUM

➤ Kurt McCullum is editor of the quarterly print magazine *Adoration: A Journal of Christian Poetry.* The related Web site *(http://www.mccullumsoftware.com/adoration)* has writers' guidelines, subscription information, and a request for a sample issue.

➤ The Academy of American Poets *(http://www.poets.org)* has a beautifully designed site featuring a poetry FAQ. The site also contains information on National Poetry Month, poetry awards, a search engine of featured poets, and sound clips of poetry being read.

➤ Aha! Poetry *(http://www.ahapoetry.com)* features an open mike for those who want to share their poetry. The site features poetry books, "The Bookrack" to help you promote your books, critiques, publisher links, contests, and more.

➤ AlienFlower *(http://www.sonic.net/web/albany/workshop)* is an interactive site where poets share ideas about poetry and its place in society. Poetry links, networking, workshops, essays, and classes are all available on this site.

➤ Christianity and the Arts is a quarterly arts magazine for Christians. The site *(http://www.christianarts.net/literature/literature.html)* features Web-only fiction and poetry. The e-zine also features its own poetry contest.

➤ The Electronic Poetry Center (EPC) *(http://wings.buffalo.edu/epc)* serves as a central gateway to resources in electronic poetry and poetics produced at the University of New York at Buffalo as well as elsewhere on the Internet. You'll find poetry in the EPC's author libraries, poetry and poetics resources, poetry events, and an electronic poetry journal.

➤ The Glossary of Poetic Terms *(http://shoga.wwa.com/~rgs/glossary.html)* features phonetic pronunciation, definitions, hyper-linked keywords and cross references, and poetic quotations.

➤ GreetingCardWriter *(http://www.greetingcardwriter.com)* is a new online publication, which premiered in 2000. It's an interactive guide to writing and selling greeting cards; writers can actually direct what they will receive by asking specific questions they'd like to have answered and by suggesting topics they would like to see addressed as articles. Otherwise, it covers the basics, as well as the more in-depth points of writing and selling cards.

➤ The Internet Poetry Archive *(http://metalab.unc.edu/ipa)* created by the University of North Carolina features a selection of poetry, audio clips of poets reading their work, and photos.

➤ Neile's Advice On How To Sell Poetry *(http://www.sff.net/people/neile/how.to.sell.poetry.htp)* is a great resource created by Neile Graham.

➤ The Online Writery *(http://web.missouri.edu/~writery)* is an online community of writers, complete with a poetry forum.

➤ Poets and Writers Online *(http://www.pw.org)* is part of the magazine by the same name. The Speakeasy Message Forum is available after registration. The site also includes information on workshops, conferences, and author home pages.

➤ Semantic Rhyming Dictionary *(http://www.link.cs.cmu.edu/dough/rhyme-doc.html)* is a handy tool for poets. You can find rhymes by matching sounds, syllables, consonants, meanings, and definitions. There is also an option to search for pictures and related words.

The Romance Genre

"The Internet is opening up new means of publication and promotion for authors like never before. Ten years ago, a writer had to make it or break it in the marketplace. Now, there is the opportunity to supplement slow periods in writing with teaching courses online or offering other services. For example, I offer Web design for authors through Word Museum. Not only do I get to work with some wonderfully talented people, but I also am able to supplement my income between royalty checks or article sales."—LORI SOARD

➤ Author Lori Soard *(http://www.wordmuseum.com)* has designed a visually appealing Web site with a special emphasis on romance. Features of the site include market news, a twenty-four-hour chat, contests, author pages, and great information.

➤ The Literary Times *(http://www.tlt.com/news/itiner.htm)* online edition allows authors to post their book-signing itineraries for free.

➤ Romance and Women's Fiction Exchange (RomEx) *(http://www. romex.dm.net)* is a community of writers and readers of romance and women's fiction. Chat, forums, newsgroups, tip sheets, and newsletters are just the beginning of this site. They also have access to the membership-only community called Dualing Modems.

➤ Romance Writer and Reader Retreat in Simegen.com *(http://www. simegen.com/romance/index.html)* has a full site with bulletin boards, reviews and guidelines, the Simegen.com writing school, writing articles, chats, and author spotlights.

➤ Romance Writers of America (RWA) *(http://www.rwanational.com)* exists to allow members to "share experiences with other writers, to gain insights into publishing as well as the art and craft of writing, and to meet industry professionals."

➤ Romancing the Web *(http://www.romanceweb.com/index5.cfm)* is a place where authors and readers of romantic fiction and nonfiction meet. In addition to a links section for writers, the site includes links to upcoming events. The Research Haven is a must-visit-and-revisit area of this Web site *(http://www.romanceweb.com/research.cfm)*.

The Science Fiction and Fantasy Market

"There was an absence of consolidated market information when I started The Market List. E-mail allowed immediate access to up-to-the-minute information from writers and editors about new publications, changes in pay rates, long response times, etc. More and more of this information is available online from a variety of sources. This trend toward instant dissemination means aspiring writers don't have to know someone on the inside...to find new markets, and don't have to waste postage mailing stories to closed ones."—CHRISTOPHER HOLLIDAY

> ➤ Science fiction writer Christopher Holliday has created an incredible site *(http://www.marketlist.com)* for science fiction and fantasy writers. The Market List features small press listings and online resources for writers, such as market news, guidelines, articles, interviews, and reviews.

> ➤ Critters Workshop *(http://brain-of-pooh.tech-soft.com/users/critters)* is an online workshop/critique group for serious writers of science fiction and fantasy.

> ➤ Internet Fantasy Writers Association *(http://www.fantasytoday.com)* has research and market information, classes and sites for writers, and more. They also have a chat room and e-mail discussion list.

> ➤ Moira Allen has done an incredible job of compiling not just links, but informative articles, market information, author interviews, and other valuable resources *(http://www.tipsforwriters.com/fantasy.shtml)*.

> ➤ Ralan's Webstravaganza *(http://www.ralan.com)* is a great site for information on science fiction markets. This site also has humor markets and hundreds of writing-related links.

> ➤ Science Fiction and Fantasy Writers *(http://www.sfwa.org)* of America has articles on writing and a bookstore selection of helpful works. Lots of links, research resources, magazines, member Web pages, and market reports are included.

> ➤ Science Fiction Resource Guide *(http://www2.lysator.liu.se/sf_archive/sf-texts/SF_resource_guide)* has links to chat channels, FAQs, clubs, bookstores, mailing lists, e-zines, Usenet groups, and more.

> ➤ The SF Site *(http://www.sfsite.com)* is an attractive site filled with interviews, links, publishers, e-zines, conventions, and author book lists for

the science fiction and fantasy writer. A database of authors is
included.

➤ SFRT on the Web *(http://www.sfrt.com/sfrt2.htm)* is one of the premier
sites on the Web for science fiction and fantasy writers. Excerpts from
new books, links to conventions and conferences, publishers' Web pages,
resources for writers, and the SFRT Mailing List are included.

➤ The Ultimate Science Fiction Web Guide *(http://www.magicdragon.
com/UltimateSF)* boasts almost 6,000 links to Web science fiction
resources.

Opportunities for Playwrights and Screenplay Writers

*"What the Internet has really done for screenwriters who can't live in Los Angeles is
break down the clubby world of closely held Hollywood insider information on how
to write and format screenplays and then get those scripts into the hands of producers who might actually make them [into movies]. Before the Internet, going to university film schools and hanging out in the LA or NY film industry party scene was
about the only way you could learn this."*—RICHARD TOSCAN

➤ Richard Toscan's exhaustive 230-page site, The Playwriting Seminars
(http://www.vcu.edu/artweb/playwriting/seminar.html), covers everything
from writing to selling (from both the creative and the business angle),
complete with quotes from over 400 playwrights and screenwriters.

➤ Act One Writing for Hollywood *(http://www.actoneprogram.com)* is a
month-long, writing-intensive program sponsored by Inter-Mission.
Its purpose is to prepare Christian screenwriters who have the talent
and professional skills to translate the Christian world-view to the
screen.

➤ The Dramatic Exchange *(http://www.dramex.org)* is a Web resource for
playwrights, producers, and anybody interested in plays. Playwrights can
make their plays available to producers and readers.

➤ Essays on the Craft of Dramatic Writing *(http://www.teleport.com/
~bjscript/index.htm)* explores the craft of writing dramatic stories. Bill
Johnson's essays are designed to help all writers, whether working on a
screenplay, book, or play.

➤ Fade In Through Fade Out *(http://members.aol.com/anniraff/contents.htm)* is the free text of a complete book on screenwriting.

➤ Hollywood Screenwriters Network *(http://hollywoodnet.com//scriptindex. html)* has forums, a newsgroup, lists, and chats. One of the most helpful parts of this site is a list of FAQs from over 100 industry professionals *(http://hollywoodnet.com/hosts.html).*

➤ Moviebytes.com *(http://www.moviebytes.com)* is an impressive site packed with information, including contests, screenwriting news, agency listings, postings from producers, a bulletin board, and a free e-mail newsletter.

➤ The Online Communicator Web site *(http://www.communicator. com/toppage.html)* has links to everything imaginable and a whole lot more. A must-visit if you're writing for film, television, or video.

➤ The Playwrights Union of Canada Web site *(http://www.puc.ca)* features industry and contract news and membership information.

➤ ScreenTalk *(http://www.screentalk.org)* is the online version of *ScreenTalk* magazine. The site includes actual movie scripts, interviews, and more.

➤ The Screenwriters Homepage *(http://home.earthlink.net/~scribbler)* has articles and interviews by screenwriting professionals. A list of agents, ideas, quotes, and other writing links rounds out the site.

➤ Screenwriters Online *(http://www.screenwriter.com/insider/main.html)* is the site of veteran screenwriter Lawrence Konner. This site features a chat room, interviews with writers, and articles from *The Screenwriter's Insider Report.* The site also features script analysis, *The InsiderReport Online* magazine, and more links.

➤ Screenwriters Utopia *(http://www.screenwritersutopia.com)* has links, chat, message boards, and other resources for screenwriters.

➤ TV Writer.com *(http://www.tvwriter.com)* calls itself "Larry Brody's Guide to Writing for the Medium Everyone Loves to Hate." The writer's search engine is a helpful feature of this site, as well as a writer's chat with transcripts, message board, TV Writer FAQs, reviews of scripting programs, and downloadable scripts to review.

➤ The Visual Writer, Ltd. *(http://visualwriter.com/descript.htm)* is a free, downloadable e-book that explains in detail how to write a movie screenplay, from planning an idea through developing a plot to finishing the play. The site also has an essay and links to "Twenty Most Common Problems and How to Fix Them."

➤ The Writers Guild of Canada *(http://www.writersguildofcanada.com)* represents over 1,500 freelance writers working in film, television, radio, and news-media production in Canada.

The Technical and Scientific Market

"At first, the Web had little impact on technical communications: [it was] just another online format with undefined standards and relatively crude output. However, continuing development of the technology, standardisation of user interface elements, and widespread adoption of the 'Net have made it a viable publishing option. The main selling point is its ubiquity: 'Write once, read anywhere' is possible at last."—GARY CONROY

➤ Technical writer Gary Conroy's Techwriting *(http://techwriting.about. com/arts/techwriting)* is the technical writing guide for About.com. According to Conroy, the Web site is packed with "product reviews, tutorials and articles, 'war stories,' case studies of actual writing projects, coverage of developments in electronic publishing, salary surveys, and anything else that shakes and bakes in the world of technical writing."

➤ Inkspot's Web page for science and technical writers *(http://www.inkspot. com/ss/genres/tech.html)* has links to associations, publications, and directories; informative essays and articles; newsgroups; and a mailing list.

➤ John December Technical Communication Information Sources *(http://www.december.com/john/study/techcomm/info.html)* has a tremendous quantity of information about technical communication.

➤ John Hewitt's Technical Writing Center *(http://www.poewar. com/links/technical.htm)* is filled with articles on technical writing and resources, dictionaries, employment leads, and more.

SPEAKER RESOURCES

"My next three print books will have a corresponding Web site, so I can be constantly updating statistics and information in the books. I'm also providing additional

Internet resources for topics in the books. That way I'm utilizing the best of both print and online resources."—JIM WATKINS

➤ Jim Watkins's Web site *(http://www2.fwi.com/~watkins/speak.htm)* is an easy-to-navigate Web site designed to introduce himself to the market-place. Watkins effectively uses sound files on his site so people can hear his message as well as read about his books, speaking topics, schedule, and other information.

➤ Canadian Association of Professional Speakers (CAPS) *(http://www. canadianspeakers.org)* is comprised of speakers, trainers, and presenters. CAPS is a part of the International Federation for Professional Speakers.

➤ Christian Leaders, Authors and Speakers Services (CLASS) *(http://www. classervices.com)* is a training organization for Christian speakers. CLASS also has a speakers' bureau and promotional department.

➤ Experts Who Speak *(http://www.ExpertsWhoSpeak.org)* is comprised of independent, professional speakers in the United States and Canada who are leading authorities in their fields. The Web site includes an application for speakers who would like to be added to their database.

➤ Great Speaking *(http://www.antion.com/ezinesubscribe.htm)* is an electronic magazine geared for those engaged in public speaking.

➤ The National Speakers Association (NSA) *(http://www.nsaspeaker.org)* is the premier organization for experts who speak professionally.

➤ The OnSpeakers.com Web site *(http://www.speaking.com)* features a chat room, message boards, and speaking-related articles.

➤ Presenters Online *(http://www.presentersonline.com)* features tips, tools, and techniques for successful presentations. This site has free downloads of clip art, sounds, templates, and lots of other essentials for creating dynamic presentations.

➤ SpeakerNet News *(http://www.SpeakerNetNews.com)* is a weekly e-mail newsletter sent to professional speakers, consultants, trainers, and authors.

➤ Speakers.com *(http://speakers.com/database/speakersonline.asp)* is an Internet supersite for speakers, trainers, consultants, and personalities.

➤ The Speakers Place *(http://www.speakersplace.com)* is a community for speakers and trainers.

> Speeches.com *(http://speeches.com/gentips.htm)* offers an excellent set of tips and resources for speakers. The site also offers speechwriting workshops.

> Toastmasters International *(http://www.toastmasters.org)* is an international organization comprised of local chapters.

> Voice Personality *(http://www.voicepersonality.com)* is the brainchild of radio personality Roy Hanschke. Available on his site is the ten-minute trainer tape series that helps speakers with their voice articulation, intonation, and inflection. Speakers can have their speaking voice professionally evaluated with the Speaking Voice Evaluation Kit and receive professional voice mentoring with the Mini Mentor.

The beauty of the Web is the plethora of information, much of it free and easy to access for anyone willing to spend time online. The sites I've listed are just the beginning. Each Web site has links, many not featured in this book, that offer learning opportunities about specific genres, as well as general writing and speaking information. Assignments can also be found by visiting message boards, reading e-zines, and networking with other writers and speakers.

PART THREE

Conversations in Transit

EIGHT

More Dignified Than Yelling Out the Window

Connecting with Editors and Meeting Planners

This manuscript of yours that has just come back from another editor is a precious package. Don't consider it rejected. Consider that you've addressed it "to the editor who can appreciate my work" and it has simply come back stamped "Not at this address." Just keep looking for the right address.—BARBARA KINGSOLVER

While doing research for this book the other day, I found a forum that posted writers' messages. It took only a quick glimpse to affirm what I already knew: Just about everyone who writes a book thinks he's written a bestseller and someone should publish it. What's more, he's often looking for an "easy" way to publication.

For example, one of the messages went something like this: "I'm a schoolteacher, and I tell my students lots of stories. They love them! Could someone tell me the best way to get my stories published? Once I start collecting royalties, I can quit work and stay at home with my own kids."

Here's another wannabe writer's desperate plea: "I have this great idea for a book. It's a bestseller for sure. Does anyone have an e-mail address for Stephen King? If I can just get the idea to him, I know he can make us both rich!"

If you're like me, at least once in your life you took a shortcut that went bad. You passed places you never knew existed as your gas gauge slowly moved toward the red marker. What began as a great idea to get wherever you wanted to go quickly turned into another excuse for your spouse's smirk and smug "I told you so."

While there are ways the Internet can help streamline the process of publication and definitely make it easier, there are no shortcuts either to getting published or becoming a professional speaker. Shortcuts—like the ones desired by the writers of those two posts I mentioned—usually lead to dead ends.

Eleanor Roosevelt said it all: "If you prepare yourself at every point as well as you can, with whatever means you have…you will be able to grasp opportunity for broader experience when it appears. Without preparation, you cannot do it."

In a perfect world, talent and having something to say would guarantee success. In the real world, knowing the publishing and speaking industries and having the ability to market oneself to the people in it can be even more pivotal to success.

The Internet can help you navigate the road to your goals, but you still need to know the marketing basics. *Sally Stuart's Guide to Getting Published* (Harold Shaw Publishers, 1999) and Dottie Walter's *Speak and Grow Rich* (Prentice Hall Press, 1997) are both excellent resources and can be found in many libraries and most bookstores—online or brick and mortar. No matter which book you pick up, though, you'll find the same basic tips:

Read and listen. One of the best things you can do for yourself as a writer is to read, and as a speaker, it's to listen to the presentations of others. Knowing your competition and learning from them, no matter what your occupation, helps you to be better in your field.

Join. Chapter 6 lists writer and speaker associations both online and off. Subscribing to and reading newsletters and becoming a regular in chat sessions and real-life meetings allow you to talk to and learn from others.

Work at your craft. Chapter 5 is filled with ideas for online learning opportunities, and real-life community colleges, workshops, and seminars also offer ways to become better at what you do.

Attend a writers' or speakers' conference or convention. Besides meeting people who can help you break into the industry, meetings are great places to learn about industry trends.

Know the publishing industry. Starting with your local markets and moving on to your particular genre, read book reviews and book publishing columns. *Publishers Weekly* has a daily subscription e-mail newsletter that's invaluable for those wanting to keep up-to-date. The Publisher's Marketing Association is the largest nonprofit trade association representing independent publishers of books, audio, video, and CDs. Their Web site has a wealth of industry news, including an online newsletter with a search engine to retrieve an excellent archive of articles.

Everyone agrees that the Internet is a great way to do research and to network with other writers and speakers. It also provides excellent online learning opportunities and up-to-date industry news. Beyond those valuable reasons for getting on the information superhighway, I'd like to suggest three more:

One, the Internet provides a way for writers and speakers to target their work to the editors and meeting planners who will be most interested in it.

Two, the Internet can help streamline the communication process between writers and editors, speakers and meeting planners. E-mail is definitely more dignified than yelling out the car window!

Three, the Internet provides a place for writers and speakers to showcase their work. You can't force someone to listen to your great idea, but you *can* invite an editor or meeting planner to view your work on Web sites designed especially for that purpose.

➤ Publisher's Marketing Association at *http://www.pma-online.org*

➤ *Publishers Weekly* at *http://www.publishersweekly.com*

TARGETING MARKETS FOR YOUR WORK

Sending an article on hydroponic gardening to a travel magazine is a waste of time and money. So is sending the proposal for your romance novel to a publisher whose line is almost entirely self-help books. The resources available to you on the Internet can help you not make those kinds of mistakes.

Book and magazine publishers often post their publishing guidelines online. Reading the online version of a magazine or newspaper is also a great way to get a feel for the publication. Writer Genetta Adair advises, however, "I try to follow up my online research with a hard copy of the guidelines.

Unfortunately, some Web sites are not kept current. Some magazines will send samples when you request them via e-mail," she continues. "Also, I like to research particular magazines online instead of sending for samples. This saves not only time, but money."

Some writers use publishers' guidelines to decide what they want to write. My advice is to instead look for a publisher who wants what you want to write—who, as Barbara Kingsolver says, can truly appreciate your subject matter and your approach to it.

There was once a young man, the story goes, who in his youth professed a desire to become a great writer. When asked to define "great," he said, "I want to write stuff that the whole world will read, stuff that people will react to on a truly emotional level, stuff that will make them scream, cry, wail, and howl in pain, desperation, and anger!"

He now works for Microsoft—writing error messages.

Since I received that story via e-mail from at least ten people, it may or may not be an urban legend. In any case, it's just too perfect to ignore!

You, too, can get paid to write what you really want to write—even if it's "stuff that will make them scream, cry, wail, and howl in pain, desperation, and anger!" The following list of publishers' guidelines and media sites can help you toward that goal. The list includes sites relevant to speakers as well.

> AJR Newslink *(http://ajr.newslink.org/mag.html)* includes newspapers, magazines, radio, and television resources.

> Association of American University Publishers (AAUP) *(http://aaup. pupress.princeton.edu)* is a cooperative, nonprofit organization of university presses. Links to AAUP member pages are here.

> The BookWire Index Web site *(http://www.bookwire.com/index/ publishers.html)* has links to a wide variety of publishers' home pages. Good listings, even without a search engine.

> Editor and Publisher *(http://www.mediainfo.com/ephome/index/ unihtml/siteindex.htm)* is an Adweek Magazines publication covering the newspaper industry in North America. Their site index has links to magazines, newspapers, and radio and television stations.

> Helpful Addresses *(http://www.acclaimed.com/helpful/new-add.htm)* has

links to over 1,500 U.S. newspapers and 9,000 libraries, organized by
state.

➤ Inscriptions Paying Markets *(http://www.inscriptionsmagazine.
com/Markets.html)* is a part of the *Inscriptions* newsletter. These are
new markets seeking submissions.

➤ Inspirational Romance Publishers *(http://members.aol.com/inspirlvg/pubs.
htm)* offers links to publishers of this genre.

➤ The iUniverse Data Base *(http://www.iuniverse.com/resources/iu_contact)*
has a great search engine for agencies, publishers, and magazines. The
engine searches by fiction or nonfiction, by state, and in categories from
action to travel and lots in-between.

➤ The Market List *(http://www.marketlist.com)* is a resource for science
fiction and fantasy writers. The site has guidelines and Web-site links to
publishers in this genre.

➤ News Directory.com *(http://www.newsdirectory.com)* has a searchable
database of newspapers, magazines, and other media.

➤ Newsletter Access Directory *(http://www.newsletteraccess.com/directory.
html)* has a searchable database of over 5,000 newsletters.

➤ Newspapers.com *(http://www.newspapers.com)* provides an easy-to-use
tool for referencing the world's newspapers.

➤ Publishers' Catalogue Home Page *(http://www.lights.com/publisher)* is a
free service of Northern Lights. Publishers each have a small bit of information listed. The site is broken down by category of publisher.

➤ Publisher's Marketing Association (PMA) *(http://www.pma-online.
org/pmalinks.html)* is a trade association of independent publishers. Links
to member Web sites are included.

➤ Sally Stuart's Christian Writers' Market Guide *(http://www.stuartmarket.
com/pubmain.htm)* is the companion Web site to her annual market
guide. Guidelines for both book and periodical publishers are listed.

➤ The Write Markets Report Web site *(http://www.writersmarkets.
com/index-guidelines.htm)* lists opportunities for writers to connect with
paying markets. The site also offers a weekly subscription e-mail
newsletter, featuring paying freelance jobs.

➤ WriteLinks: Commercial Book Publishers *(http://www.writelinks. com/resources/pub/pubsbk.htm)* is an alphabetical list of publishers with brief descriptions and contact information.

➤ Writer's Digest *(http://www.writersdigest.com)* is the world's largest magazine for writers. Their Web site has an ever-growing section devoted to guidelines posted by publishers of every genre.

➤ Writer's Guidelines Database *(http://mav.net/guidelines)* is a compilation of magazine guidelines broken into categories. Listings include a brief narrative, contact information, and pay rate.

➤ The Writer's Place Web site *(http://www.awoc.com/Guidelines.cfm)* features 650 publishers' guidelines. The search engine searches by pay scale, nonfiction, fiction, or market name.

➤ Writers Information Network *(http://www.bluejaypub.com/win/ publishers.htm)* has links to Christian publishers' Web pages.

➤ Writers Write *(http://www.writerswrite.com/books/bookpubs)* has an alphabetical book publisher index, as well as lists for computer, religious, and university presses.

STREAMLINING YOUR BUSINESS CORRESPONDENCE

"The last five pieces I had published were all queried and supplied over the Internet," says Australian-based freelance writer Ken Rolph. "In some cases the editors wrote to me, usually to fill a hole or respond to an ongoing issue."

According to Rolph, getting an assignment isn't the only benefit to using e-mail. "In the past, when I supplied printed articles to small publications, I found that their typists, often volunteers, would introduce lots of errors. Now I can be reasonably sure that what I wrote is what will make it to print."

Author Gail Welborn says e-mail correspondence has been vital in her writing career as well. "If it weren't for the Internet, I wouldn't be published to the extent I am," she claims. "Everything I write is sent over the Internet. Editors contact me at their leisure, and I reply within twenty-four hours of receiving the request. Audio reviews that I write for *AudioFile* magazine are sent e-mail, as are my monthly article assignments for *Northwest Christian Journal.*

My contact with *Guideposts Magazine* came through another writer on a mailing list, then I worked with the editor via e-mail. For me, Internet access has expanded my possibility of publication more than one hundredfold."

Canadian writer Nancy Lindquist, who sometimes also wears an editor's hat, loves the Internet. "As an editor, I worked with several writers entirely online, including Joel Comiskey who lives in Quito, Ecuador. We did one interview entirely by e-mail.... I got his pictures and everything by e-mail. The only thing I had to do by snail mail was send him copies of the magazine and his check."

Instant gratification—or almost instant gratification—is one of the greatest benefits to writers who submit their work through the Internet. "I've been writing more than eighteen years, and I began with a typewriter and carbon paper," declares Nanette Snipes. "E-mail has been a blessing to me as a writer because of the quick turnaround in responses. One that was particularly quick was the notification that I'd made the final stage with one of my stories for the *Chicken Soup for the Soul* book. The response time in that instance was less than a week, which included a snail mail 'Permission of Release' form." For writers who are all-too-familiar with stalking the mailman, this is great news.

Solicited E-Mail

At a booksellers' convention in the summer of 1999, I approached a publisher with little more than a sketchy verbal outline for *WriterSpeaker.com,* my business card, and enthusiasm. It must have been enough, because even with nothing on paper, he went back to work and told the editorial director about my idea. The director e-mailed me, requesting a copy of the nonexistent proposal.

Because the editor liked the idea for the book, she wanted my proposal as soon as possible so she could present it to a committee and discuss including it in the house's 2000 list. After frantically pulling together the best proposal I could, I prepared it for mailing, making sure it was presented and packaged to make the best impression possible.

I printed the cover letter on classic linen letterhead and placed the proposal in a forest green folder, complete with my business card in the slot. I tucked in four-color promotional cards from my first two books and a brochure about myself. Wanting both to make a good impression and to get the proposal there in timely fashion, I drove to the post office, stood in an outrageously long line, purchased postage for $3.20, and placed my baby in the priority-mail envelope. I knew my proposal was good—and in a couple of days, the publisher would too.

Think of my excitement when, on Friday, only two days after the scheduled Wednesday delivery, I discovered an e-mail in my mailbox from the editor. "Wow, she's fast," I thought.

My excitement quickly turned to confusion as I read her message asking if I'd sent the proposal, and if not, when I could get it in the mail. I was floored. By all calculations, they should already have received it.

A flurry of e-mails followed that day, but the proposal didn't arrive. Finally I asked her what word-processing program she used and told her I would send it out as an attachment in the next few minutes. "So much for my presentation," I thought as I converted my document into a format compatible to her PC and pushed the send button.

Within an hour of sending my electronic proposal, I got another e-mail from the editor. "She's a quick study," I thought. "She's read it already?"

But no, she hadn't read it yet. She'd e-mailed to inform me she'd unearthed my snail-mailed proposal from under one of the stacks of unsolicited manuscripts piled in the offices on chairs, desks, and the floor. Even though it was in a priority mailer with the words "Requested Material Enclosed" in full-capped, oversized letters, it had still ended up in the slush pile.

True, e-mailed proposals can't be presented as impressively as paper-and-ink proposals, but the method has distinct advantages—it saves postage, time, and paper, and e-mail rarely gets lost.

Using e-mail was advantageous in other ways during the process of getting this book published. The response to comments and requests on both our parts was immediate, usually within hours and sometimes within minutes. For instance, when my editor met with the committee to discuss the book, questions arose. She quickly popped off an e-mail, which I was able to answer that same day. When she wanted some revision to the proposal after we decided to approach the market a bit differently, I made the changes and within days sent her a revised version.

Via e-mail, my attorney and I discussed the book contract; eventually we included my editor in the discussion. The negotiations went smoothly and more quickly because everyone was involved at the same time.

My publisher is not alone in its use of electronic communications. In the 2000 *Writer's Market Guide* published by Writer's Digest Books, more than 6,500 e-mail and Web site addresses appear. Many publishers even accept complete solicited manuscripts by e-mail. This practice enables an editor to transfer the material directly into the house computer system. Be sure to include your submission and any supplementary materials in one document so they don't become separated. For shorter pieces, rather than depend on an attachment, you may want to cut and paste a submission into the body of an e-mail. If you have a longer manuscript or decide you prefer sending a shorter one as an attachment, ask the editor what type of word-processing software the house uses, and make sure your attachment can be opened and read error free.

Sally Stuart knows the Christian publishing industry better than most; the year 2000 will be her fifteenth year of producing the *Christian Writers' Market Guide.* "Although I've been reporting on which publishers are open to e-mail queries and submissions for about the last five years," she related in an e-mail conversation, "the changes in the last two years have been the most dramatic. At first there was a handful of editors and publishers who were really gung-ho about the new technology and embraced it wholeheartedly. The rest were reticent at best and willing to only reluctantly give it a try."

Just as writers are slowly beginning to understand the benefits of electronic queries and submissions, so, according to Stuart, are editors. "That reluctance began to lift for some of them in 1999, but as I worked on the 2000 edition, I saw the mood for most change from reluctance to enthusiasm, as many now indicate that e-mail is their first choice for correspondence with authors— whether for queries, answering questions, or submitting their manuscripts."

According to Stuart, last year the number of publishers who listed e-mail and Web site addresses almost doubled. "In the 2000 edition of the *Christian Writers' Market Guide,* of the 330 book publishers listed, 204 list e-mail addresses (20 percent more than last year), and 223 have Web sites (35 percent more than last year). Nearly 500 magazines have e-mail, and 325 are open to e-mail queries (more than 65 percent—up from 50 percent last year). Last year, 317 had Web sites—this year, 388 do."

Of course, the fact that editors have e-mail addresses doesn't mean they are anxious to hear from you via e-mail—especially if they have no idea who you are. As Andrew Scheer, managing editor of *Moody Magazine,* quips: "No e-mail on the first date."

Unsolicited E-Mail

While it's true that using e-mail to query editors is increasing in popularity and acceptance, by no means is the practice universal. Not every editor is willing to consider e-mail queries from unknown writers. Before sending an electronic query, make sure the editor you've targeted is willing to be contacted by e-mail.

Many editors still prefer the more traditional paper route for queries until they know a writer or have assigned a piece. Answering e-mail can be a drain for someone whose workload is already heavy. It's always a good idea to send a brief note by e-mail to an editor first, asking whether or not they accept e-mail queries. If he or she doesn't respond, take that as a no and send your query via snail mail.

There's a temptation to become overly chatty and informal when using e-mail. An electronic query should be just as well thought-out and formal as a paper one. When sending an electronic query, make sure that your name, not a nickname, is in the e-mail address. Nicknames are fine for family and friends, but that old cliché about "not getting a second chance to make a first impression" is just as true in cyberspace as it is in real life.

Your subject heading should be professional and to the point. Make sure the format of your well-written query is readable as well as understandable, and double-check the spelling even when using a spell checker. Don't use commands that create bold or italics in the e-mail. Not everyone uses the same e-mail client, and what you see as being the perfect query might look like gibberish to them. Emoticons and otherwise generally accepted e-mail abbreviations should not be used in your query. Double spacing between your paragraphs makes for easier reading. Like paper queries, electronic ones should be brief.

"My first [electronic] query is always just as professional as if sent in the mail," says writer T. Suzanne Eller. "But what I have found is that [the publishers'] responses are much less formal. I take their lead and respond, and soon an easy communication is built."

Do not, under any circumstances, send an attachment of your work unless asked. You can mention that clips are available upon request, or better yet, you can tell your correspondent where he or she can go on the Internet to view your clips or even your full proposal.

SHOWCASING YOUR WORK

Eller received one writing assignment because an editor for print magazine *Dunamis Life* saw an article she'd written in Focus on the Family's magazine *Teachers in Focus*. But, says Eller, the editor also checked her Web site, online résumé, and online writing, "which gave them a very solid idea of my writing before they ever approached me."

A Web page of your clips can be an excellent tool for marketing your writing. For ideas, check out some of the writers' Web sites listed in chapter 7. Speakers, too, thanks to the new Webcasting technology called "streaming media," can showcase their skills for potential clients.

Showcase Services for Writers

Despite the ease of contacting editors through the Internet, many publishers still do not accept unsolicited manuscripts. One service that is trying to make it easier for authors and publishers to connect is The Writer's Edge.

The Writer's Edge is a fee-based service that allows authors to submit information about their manuscript to over forty-five publishers. For a modest fee, authors can submit a completed copy of a "book information form." If your book is fiction, you may submit three sample book chapters and a one-page synopsis. Nonfiction books get a contents page and short descriptions of each chapter.

"I much prefer reading about a manuscript in The Writer's Edge than receiving it in the mail," says Joan Guest, editorial director at Shaw Publishers.

"The Writer's Edge people know how to best present the brief blurbs for publishing people to be interested, and Writer's Edge always includes marketing information, which is often more important than the blurb itself. Some writers leave marketing info out of their proposals.

"I usually request about a half-dozen manuscripts each month from Writer's Edge," says Guest. "One of our biggest books last year came from Writer's Edge."

While some authors might not see the need to pay a fee to have their work considered, for others the service is a godsend. For a writer outside the United States who has little access to publishers, submitting a proposal through Writer's Edge might pay for itself in postage savings alone.

Another similar program, First Edition, is offered by the Evangelical Christian Publishers Association (ECPA). First Edition acts as a clearinghouse for ECPA publishers looking for quality manuscripts without having to go through piles of unsolicited material.

GoodStory is another fee-based service for writers to market their work directly to agents, managers, and executives throughout the publishing and entertainment industries.

➤   First Edition at *http://www.ecpa.org/FE/index.html*
➤   GoodStory at *http://www.goodstory.com*
➤   The Writer's Edge at *http://members.xoom.com/WRITERSEDGE*

Showcase Opportunities for Speakers

The written word of a writer translates perfectly into e-mail. Speakers, however, need to be heard, and more and more they are embracing the Internet to showcase their skills. Dr. Susan Mitchell is a nutrition expert and nationally recognized author and speaker. Besides going on book tours to promote her two coauthored books, *I'd Kill for a Cookie* (Plume, 1998) and *Smart Cookies Don't Get Stale* (Kensington, 1999), she broadcasts her nutrition and health messages through television, radio, and now the Internet. Dr. Mitchell is host of the live online talk show *Focus on Nutrition* on the Web site *Your health.com.*

"The Internet is a fast way for the public to obtain health information," Dr. Mitchell says. "There is a vast array of health channels on the Net, many credible, many not. I enjoy the opportunity to serve as a nutrition expert to certain Internet sites and provide user-friendly, credible, scientifically based information that will help the public lead a healthier lifestyle."

Those who want a visual and audio presence on the Internet would do well to look at Webcasting—the delivery of audio and video content via the Internet using a technology known as "streaming media."

A quick search on Yahoo! under "Webcasting" shows a number of companies worldwide specializing in creating live, taped, and video-on-demand content, including C-SPAN2's weekend nonfiction book program, Book TV.

Online seminars and workshops, "interactive" book signings, and other multimedia activities are now possible through Webcasting. This means writers and speakers can use the Internet for presentations, training, video clips, and more, no matter where they live. Besides being a vehicle for those who pay to experience your presentations, Webcasting is a great way to show your skills to meeting planners and others. With the newness of the technology, standard pricing structures for filming have yet to emerge. But Internet filming technology is considerably less expensive than traditional television video quality and therefore should be a blessing for speakers and authors on a budget.

But what if you don't choose to invest in the tools to make Internet broadcast a personal reality? In some cases, Internet networks may encode existing content for broadcast at no cost to speakers in exchange for the exclusive Internet rights to the content. If the networks also have a studio, they may film speakers at no cost in exchange for the Internet broadcast rights.

The logistics of using the Internet for presentations, classes, and workshops are being worked out, but those who want an edge in this new century should look to the Internet and streaming media.

➤ Book TV at *http://www.booktv.org*

Ellen Edwards Kennedy, author of *Irregardless of Murder* (St. Kitts Press, 2000), sums up what writers worldwide are saying about the Internet. "I wouldn't be a published writer if I weren't on the Internet. It has provided me with writing courses, Web sites, links, updates, online magazines, sources of research, a critique group, several support groups, and the means of communicating quickly and concisely with publishers, other writers, and agents. I found my publisher online. The Internet is a blessing from God for this writer."

For those who are willing to invest the time needed to explore the multitude of Web sites designed to point you in the right direction, connecting with editors, publishers, meeting planners, and others who can help your career has never been easier. Just remember to be professional. Yelling out the window probably won't help your case!

Safer Than a Cell Phone

Networking with Other Writers and Speakers

In interpersonal communication, there must be an ongoing and perceived consistency between what you say and how you say it.—JANET G. ELSEA

In 1996, shortly after I began to learn the ins and outs of the Internet, we moved. Not down the block or around the corner—no, we *moved*. My need to spend more time taking care of my husband meant I couldn't work enough hours to afford staying in Hawaii. We had no medical insurance, and I knew that trying to find adequate medical care for him there would be futile. And there was no way I could meet my sons' needs if we continued to live in paradise. After researching various parts of the country, for many reasons we ended up five thousand miles away in Orlando, Florida—except for each other, alone.

We had no family or friends in Florida, and I was without a church, a job, or any support system. I quickly discovered that when your life is a train wreck—and having a husband with an incurable disease is exactly that—people don't seek you out.

It didn't take me long to realize that my computer gave me immediate access to one of the best support systems and networking resources available. I signed on to the Huntington's Disease support-group mailing list and shortly after decided to write a book. Since I knew little about the publishing industry, it seemed wise to connect with other writers. If there was a group for something as obscure as this disease, I decided there must be an abundance of groups for writers.

Finding groups of writers online changed my life. It not only gave me the information and resources I needed to write and publish my first book, it also helped me feel less isolated. Beyond the invaluable writing and publishing information I received, I met writers who have become close friends. An editor I met online who was living in Guam at the time even offered to edit my first book for free. She did it via e-mail.

Most of all, I learned more than ever to value others' input and support. As in real life, we socialize on the Internet for many reasons. While I was learning to read and utilize various information superhighway road maps, I was also experiencing the camaraderie and the free exchange of information that happens when one starts to spend a lot of time online. How we interact with our cyber-buddies is, in essence, no different from the way we interact with our closest neighbors and colleagues.

Online groups for writers and speakers come in different sizes and formats. Some groups exist simply as a means of discussing writing or speaking in general, while others are geared toward a specific genre or topic. Still others are in place for critique purposes and typically have more structure.

In chapter 2, we discussed the basics of online chats, mailing lists, forums, and newsgroups and the netiquette users should adhere to when doing research or pursuing hobbies online. In this chapter, we'll discuss using the same Internet options to connect on a regular basis with other writers and speakers. It's the perfect medium for support and networking. Better than a cell phone—one flat rate for unlimited hours!

MAILING LISTS: ONLINE CONFERENCING

Sandy Brooks is the executive director of Christian Writers Fellowship International (CWFI) and has seen firsthand the benefits of a mailing list for writers. "When our founder, Joan Unger, and her three friends started CWFI way back in 1976, the primary mission was to provide peer fellowship for lonely, isolated writers. One of the ways they would accomplish this mission was by linking everyone together through *Cross and Quill,* our organizational newsletter. The other way was to encourage and equip writers from all over the country to organize and operate writers' fellowships where they live or to use the mail to connect with one another by organizing round robins."

The Internet has revolutionized the way CWFI accomplishes its mission. Although still a membership-based group, CWFI members can also join an e-mail conference in addition to their traditional benefits.

Brooks explains how the Internet has virtually linked those who were particularly isolated in the past. "Some of our members are missionaries far from their homelands. Others are in the deep forests and plains of North America—places so isolated they would never be able to participate in a writers' group or attend a writers' conference. Through an e-mail conference we could provide personal contact, peer fellowship, and encouragement for writers in the remotest parts of the world."

"I can tell you I look forward to 'communicating' with the real world every day," says Eileen Zygarlicke, who lives in a remote region of the country. "The link the Internet has provided has been invaluable. I have found publishers [and] communicated with editors easily and more quickly via e-mail, but more importantly, I've found peers I respect and value as friends and collaborators in this frenzied writing world. A simple plea for help never goes unanswered, and wisdom I rarely possess, others do, and are willing to share."

List owner Lisa Weiner started the Christian Writers Group (CWG) for more personal reasons but has managed to accomplish many of the same things as Brooks. "About four years ago, my love of writing was reawakened.... I searched for an online Christian writers' group, only to find none. I began to pray about starting one myself."

Her initial reasons for starting a list were to receive online support from Christian writers and to help other writers with moral and prayer support and encouragement. She also wanted to help writers make contacts with editors and publishers and provide a pool of Christian writers for editors and publishers who might be interested.

Both Brooks and Weiner agree that their groups have succeeded beyond their expectations. However, conferences like theirs and others are not without drawbacks. Probably the number-one problem is getting list members to stick to writing topics when the temptation is to discuss burning social issues or personal problems and needs. The list owner or moderator is responsible for maintaining balance in this area.

Inevitably, some people leave lists. "Some have left the list because someone said something to offend them," says Brooks. "Others have left because they just couldn't handle the volume of e-mail the conference generated. Others have left because they weren't looking to develop relationships; they just wanted hard information. Although I'd like to please everyone, realistically that is impossible." Still, Brooks insists, "The advantages of peer fellowship and encouragement far outweigh the disadvantages."

To deal with the problem of bulging mailboxes, Weiner made the decision to place a limit of three e-mails per day sent to the group by any one individual. In an effort to cut down on the chitchat that is often prevalent, she also has the list controls set so that when the reply button is hit, the e-mail is sent only to the message originator. In this way, members stop to think about whether their reply has value to everyone in the group before they add the conference e-mail address to their message.

"I've learned a lot from others," Weiner says. "I've learned about writing techniques and tips, scheduling and creative ideas, submission advice, and so much more."

Brooks agrees that there is much to learn in a conference such as CWFI or CWG, describing her list as "a wonderful mix of information, experience, inspiration, humor, and prayer support. Many have formed friendships that have made it easier for them to venture into conference settings. Others have been encouraged to submit a manuscript that may have just lain in a drawer otherwise. Some have been confirmed in their writing gifts. Others have discovered that writing wasn't really their calling after all. The stories are as many and varied as the participants."

E-mail discussion lists are often geared to targeted markets, as is the case with Angela Adair-Hoy's self-publishers' discussion list. "We launched it as a forum enabling authors to share marketing tips, swap industry experiences, and help each other sell more books, online and off," says Hoy. Of course, her list is also a great place to promote her e-publishing company, Booklocker.com, home to three hundred electronic books.

The self-publishers' discussion list focuses on professional discussion of marketing strategies, results, studies, and tools for self-published authors. Those interested in electronic publishing especially appreciate sharing information with others who have already used the latest technology. Costly mistakes can be avoided through learning from others what to do and what to stay away from in this ever-changing industry.

Chapter 2 has a listing of Web sites to help you locate online mailing lists, including those for writers and speakers. To join the following groups, simply send a subscription request to the e-mail address listed.

➤ The Editors Forum *(Kat91@aol.com)* is an online group dedicated to discussion of publishing, editors, editorial issues, and writer-editor relations and communication. There's a monthly electronic newsletter and scheduled chats. You don't have to be an editor to join.

➤ Inklings *(Majordomo@home.samurai.com)* is an excellent newsletter filled with writing tips, articles, market news, and more.

➤ Self-Publishers Discussion List *(Publish-subscribe@onelist.com)* is for those engaged in self-publishing both print and electronic books and magazines.

➤ The Writers with Humor List (WWH) *(Majordomo@ns.kconline.com)* was created by a humorist for humorists. The list is moderated, and a newsletter is sent out once a day in digest form.

CHAT: ONLINE ENCOURAGEMENT

Mailing lists aren't the only form of online networking. Chats, both impromptu and scheduled, are easily accessible on the Internet.

Marita Littauer, founder and president of Christian Leaders, Authors and Speakers Services (CLASS), has found chatting to be an invaluable communication tool for both the writers and speakers her company represents. "The chat session has taken on a life of its own. There is a small core group of people who are there almost every week."

Unlike some, CLASS Chats welcomes newcomers whenever possible. "Those in the chat session encourage each other, offer input on various topics, and pray for one another during the week, checking in on the situations in each other's lives from week to week," says Littauer. "I think there is nothing else like

CLASS Chats out there for Christian speakers and writers. It is a place you can go every week and find fellowship and answers."

The drawback to the CLASS Chat is that you must be a member of AOL to participate. While some might argue that the weekly session isn't reason enough to stay with AOL, Eva Marie Everson disagrees. "My friend suggested that, because I am on AOL, I check out CLASS Chats. The first week I was fairly quiet though everyone was very friendly. Within a few weeks I felt like one of the group and was quickly learning valuable information about speaking and writing. Never have I seen a group of men and women so excited about the successes of others! Six months later I attended my first CLASS seminar, an experience that was life changing for me. The tools from the chat room and from the seminar have been invaluable! I am so thankful that God opened that door for me."

Her first book contract with Barbour Publishing, followed by a second one before the first book was even completed, came as a direct result of CLASS. Everson attended the CLASS Reunion, held for graduates of CLASS seminars each year in conjunction with the Christian Booksellers Association convention. She was able to meet many of those she chats with on a weekly basis. She has also been published in several compilation books authored by CLASS members she met in the chats.

Professional speaker Deb Haggerty says she owes her career to the Internet. "Without the Net, I don't think I'd still be a speaker. When I was first getting my feet wet as a professional speaker, I joined a chat group peopled by folks from the National Speakers Association (NSA). I 'met' them online so that when we met in person, we were already friends. They steered me to people I needed to meet and to opportunities I needed to be involved in. Without their advice and camaraderie, I'd be years behind where I am now!"

Haggerty, who is also a member of CLASS, says the CLASS Chats have been great from a networking standpoint, though they haven't really advanced her career. What has helped in that area have been the chats through the NSA. "I find the National Speakers Association site of great value. Most of the other 'speaker' sites are to promote speakers who have signed up with them. Those sites are of marginal use to the rest of us, except to see what fees are being quoted and what the 'hot' topics seem to be."

It's best to sample different chats and mailing lists to find what works well for you both professionally and socially. Like Haggerty, you might find that being a member of two or even more different groups would meet your needs.

iUniverse claims to be the world largest publishing portal with a variety of groups available for chatting. And the list keeps growing. Even if you're not interested in using their on-demand publishing services, the site offers many other opportunities for writers. With six years of online experience on America Online and Internet Relay Chat, freelance writer Kelly Millner Halls is the perfect choice as the paid iUniverse community host.

One of the arguments against joining online chat sessions and forums is that published writers rarely participate. But some do. Multipublished Millner Halls is one of them. Halls has an impressive writing résumé, with credits from *Writer's Digest, FamilyFun, Teen PEOPLE, Highlights for Children, Boys' Life, Guideposts for Kids,* and many others. She also has six books published, including *Dino-Trekking* (John Wiley), *Kids Go! Denver* (John Muir), *365 Afterschool Activities* (PIL), and *I Bought a Baby Chicken* (Boyds Mills Press).

Halls claims the Internet has rocketed her freelancing into the twenty-first century. No longer the realm only of the "cyber-geek," the Internet is "the most open and accessible information highway ever conceptualized. It's put a world of opportunity within my reach," she says.

iUniverse has regularly scheduled chat sessions on a variety of genres such as children's stories, romance, Christian writing, and science fiction. The site also has chats for and about editors, small publishers, agents, and many other targeted topics. Celebrity and well-known authors also have chats on iUniverse, providing a great opportunity to ask questions and learn more.

Communicating online, regardless of the method, is time-consuming. Many writers feel they would rather write what they can sell than write to other writers. It's a matter of personal opinion, but I find that connecting with other writers and speakers helps me grow professionally. An increasing number of writers and speakers feel the same way. If you're interested, check out the following Web sites for mailing lists, chat, and more. Those of you who are primarily speakers will want to take special note of the sites for Christian Leaders, Authors and Speakers Services, On Speakers, and Speakers Place.

➤ About.com's Writer's Exchange *(http://writerexchange.about. com/arts/writerexchange/mbody.htm)* offers forums and chats in many different areas.

➤ Authors Anonymous (AA) *(http://www.angelfire.com/wa/ AuthorsAnonymous/list.html)* is a collection of unmoderated message boards for writers. Boards include the Critique Exchange, Groups/ Partners, Writing Problems, For Fun/Chat, and an add-on storyboard.

➤ Blackwriters.org *(http://www.blackwriters.org/nsindex.html)* encourages African-American writers to communicate with each other through discussion lists, message boards, pen-pal listings, writing and critique groups, local events, chat rooms, and online workshops. This is a fee-based group.

➤ Christian Leaders, Authors and Speakers Services (CLASS) *(http://www.classervices.com)* has a weekly chat group for members of AOL and a weekly e-mail newsletter for all subscribers.

➤ Christian Writers' Fellowship International (CWFI) *(http://www. cwfi-online.org)* has a members-only e-mail forum.

➤ Christian Writers Group *(http://members.truepath.com/CWG)* has an e-mail discussion list for subscribers as well as a weekly chat session.

➤ Christian Writers Workshop *(http://www.billyates.com/cww)* brings together Christian writers of all genres and experience. The hourlong workshop is held twice weekly through iUniverse and America Online.

➤ Visit author Deb Haggerty's Web site *(http://www.PositiveConnect.com)*

➤ Eclectics Too *(http://www.delphi.com/eclecticstoo/start)* is a members-only forum with message boards and chats. Membership is free.

➤ eGroups *(http://www.egroups.com),* part of the Yahoo! family of communication tools, has a wide variety of mailing lists for writers and speakers. Simply enter keywords into their search engine to find targeted lists to join.

➤ Inspirational Romance Workshops *(http://members.aol.com/inspirlvg/ workshops. htm)* are available through the iUniverse chat room.

➤ iUniverse *(http://www.iuniverse.com/community/community_calendar.asp)* has a chat calendar posted with thirty regularly scheduled chats, conferences, and workshops.

➤ Local Writer's Workshop *(http://www.elanworks.com/lww.html)* is an online membership forum where writers can discuss the writing life and works in progress.

➤ Misc. Writing Mailing List *(http://www.scalar.com/mw/pages/mwmlist. shtml)* is a listing of mailing lists for different writing genres.

➤ My Writer Buddy *(http://www.writerbuddy.com)* is a free correspondence club for writers.

➤ Novel Advice *(http://www.noveladvice.com)* provides a message board for discussing the craft of writing as well as a chat room.

➤ On Speakers *(http://www.speaking.com/cafe.html)* has a speakers' chat room and various message boards.

➤ The Painted Rock Writers and Readers Colony *(http://www.paintedrock. com/index.html)* offers public message boards as well as topical mailing lists.

➤ Romance Central *(http://www.romance-central.com/index1.htm)* is a beautiful site devoted to romance writers. They feature both forums and chats. On my search, I found 78 writers' sites and over 300 sites for speakers. Many of the featured sites are actually archives of past chat sessions, including many from celebrities.

➤ Speakers Place *(http://www.speakersplace.com)* has message boards, an e-mail newsletter, and articles for speakers.

➤ Talk City *(http://www.talkcity.com)* has a search engine that allows you to find groups for writers and speakers.

➤ Tile.net *(http://www.tile.net)* lets you search for e-mail discussion, announcements, and information lists on the Internet.

➤ Visit the e-mail discussion page at Webcom.com *(http://www. webcom.com/impulse/list.html#Basic)* for information about mailing list commands.

➤ The Word Museum Web site *(http://www.wordmuseum.com)* has a twenty-four-hour chat room and a subscription newsletter for all writers.

➤ Writelink's Writeshop Chat Room *(http://www.writelinks.com/writeshop/ index.html)* brings many of the benefits of attending a writers' conference to the Internet, including workshops, Q&A sessions, and chats. There are logs of past chat sessions.

➤ The Writers BBS site *(http://www.writersbbs.com)* provides online discussion forums on over 50 different topics.

➤ WriterWorkshop.com *(http://www.writerworkshops.com/groups.html)* has an impressive listing of groups for writers of all genres.

The online networking opportunities listed in this chapter are only a few of those available. (Note that both AOL and CompuServe have many members-only forums and chat rooms available for writers and speakers.) As you find other relevant and helpful chats, lists, and forums, please e-mail me at *links@writerspeaker.com* so I can add them to the list on the *WriterSpeaker.com* Web site.

PART FOUR

Putting Yourself on the Road Map

From the Ground Up

Creating Your Web Site

Speech is power: speech is to persuade, to convert, to compel.—RALPH WALDO EMERSON

In June 1966, Rubin "Hurricane" Carter was a strong contender for the middle-weight boxing title. But his dreams were shattered when he was arrested and subsequently convicted and sentenced to three consecutive life terms—for a crime he did not commit.

In his highly acclaimed book, *The Sixteenth Round* (Viking Press, 1974), written while he was in prison, Carter pleaded: "I come to you in the only manner left open to me. I've tried the courts, exhausted my life's earnings, and tortured my two loved ones with little grains and tidbits of hope that may never materialize. Now the only chance I have is in appealing directly to you, the people, and showing you the wrongs that have yet to be righted…the injustice that has been done to me. For the first time in my entire existence I'm saying that I need some help."[1]

These words ultimately played a pivotal role, after twenty long years, in Carter's release from incarceration. The process began when a troubled Brook-lyn teenager named Lesra Martin bought a copy of *The Sixteenth Round* at a used-book sale. Martin wasn't illiterate, but he was reading far below his grade level and potential at the time. Carter's compelling story gave the young man an incentive to read and opened his eyes to the power of words. In fact, the story forever changed his life and the lives of his guardians, three Canadian activists who also came to believe in Carter's innocence as they fought to exonerate the former boxer.

The foursome's extraordinary efforts on Carter's behalf ultimately secured the prisoner's release, after which Carter was moved to remark: "Hate got me into this place, love got me out."

As I sat in the theater, mesmerized by Denzel Washington's portrayal of Carter in the movie *Hurricane,* based on *The Sixteenth Round* and Sam Chaiton and Terry Swinton's 1991 book, *Lazarus and the Hurricane: The Freeing of Rubin "Hurricane" Carter* (Griffin Trade Paperback), I was incredibly moved— not only by the injustice of Carter's incarceration and Martin's compassion and tenacity, but by the power of words.

Carol Burnett once said, "Words, once they're printed, have a life of their own." Each of you is a writer or speaker of words that have the power to change lives. But if those words never have an audience, their power can never be unleashed. A Web site is one way to reach an audience, to create compelling opportunities for those Internet users who find their way to your destination on the Internet superhighway to read and hear your words—words that may influence their lives in many ways.

WRITER AND SPEAKER WEB SITES: FAQS

Creating a Web page is becoming easier all the time as portals, search engines, and other sites offer free Web space as a way to encourage site traffic. Most ISPs also include free Web space as part of their basic service package; sites like Geocities, Truepath, and Yahoo! offer free space for noncommercial sites.

Do you really want a Web site of your own? Do you want to make yourself a "destination"?

To decide, your first step is to find the answers to some of the most frequently asked questions (FAQs) about the subject: Why should you have a Web site? If they're so great, why don't more writers and speakers have them? What needs to be included in a Web site? How do you go about creating one? What's a "domain"—and should you have one of your own? This chapter will give you the information you need to make up your mind.

➤ Truepath at *http://www.truepath.com*

➤ Yahoo! Geocities at *http://geocities.yahoo.com/home*

Why Should I Have a Web Site?

If it's designed correctly, a writer's or speaker's Web site will attract new audiences, educate cyber-visitors on whatever topic you're passionate about, promote your books or speaking engagements, and show off your writing or speaking skills. (Writers can post articles or sample chapters; speakers, audio clips.) You can also announce your conference, speaking, or book-signing schedule.

Author and speaker Linda Evans Shepherd embraced the marketing possibilities of hosting a Web site on the Internet and discovered her site could be a source of writing material as well. "My Web site has most certainly helped me gather material for both my writing and speaking. Not only can people check in to see what book I'm currently working on, they can contribute stories to that book. Many of those stories wind up in my books and talks."

Shepherd uses her site in other ways. "My Web site also lists a meeting planner's tip sheet. This has proved to be a popular feature. Meeting planners contact me based on my Web page to find out what dates are available and to ask other questions. This has been a great timesaver for all involved. As I always check my e-mail, I can get back to [my correspondents] usually before the end of the day. I also list my topics and endorsements so meeting planners can see if I am a good match for their event."

Realizing that one site may not be enough to address different ventures, Shepherd is currently working on a second one. "My new Web site," she says, "will support my new nonprofit, nationally syndicated radio show, *Right to the Heart.*"

According to Deb Haggerty, president of Positive Connections, "My Web site's been helpful when working with prospective clients to give them an idea of who I am and what I can do for them. Through the Internet, I was introduced to a client who has brought in major revenues."

The beauty of having your own Web site is in the variety of ways you can use it for your specific needs, using your unique talents. Do you want to sell your books? Provide meeting planners with audio clips of your talks? Promote your writing classes? Will a Web site help you sell more articles, connect with your readers, develop new clients?

Whatever your objectives, understanding them will help you create the perfect Web site. Only your imagination and your finances limit what you can do to create a site that stands out among others.

➤ Linda Evans Shepherd at *http://www.sheppro.com*

➤ Positive Connections at *http://www.PositiveConnect.com*

➤ Right to the Heart at *http://www.righttotheheart.com*

So Why Don't More Writers and Speakers Have Web Sites?

There's no question that having a Web site can open doors. When you have your own site, editors, customers, and other writers and speakers who previously didn't know about you or your projects have an efficient and economical way to find you through the Internet.

Okay, so if having a Web site is such a boon to writers and speakers, why aren't there more?

The reasons usually boil down to four things:

"I don't know how."

"I don't have time."

"I can't afford it."

"I don't have that much to say."

One difficulty in writing a book like *WriterSpeaker.com* is the massive amount of information available on the Internet, coupled with the miniscule amount of space available in which to present it. What and how much information is necessary to adequately cover the topic? There's enough material out there to write an entire book on the subject of each *chapter* included between these covers. This is particularly true in the areas of Web-site creation and promotion. My job in this chapter is twofold: to direct you to sites where you can find help in these areas and to address your excuses or fears—to eliminate your reasons—for not having your own Web site.

Let me start with a story. When I was a freshman in college, I developed a massive goiter due to an overactive thyroid. Emergency surgery also saw the removal of most of my parathyroid, which controls the body's calcium level. As a result, I got not only my very first tooth cavity, but eleven of them—in less than a year. Without any dental insurance, I couldn't remedy the situation for the rest of my college career.

After graduation, I joined the Peace Corps. Before I was scheduled to leave for Mali, West Africa, I was required to take care of all my medical and dental problems. Like most people, the prospect of dental work didn't thrill me, and I put off visiting the dentist until the Friday before my departure.

"Well, you've got quite a number of cavities to fill," the dentist announced, almost rubbing his hands in glee. "Let's schedule several appointments over the next few weeks."

"I'm leaving for a trip on Monday. They have to be filled in one sitting," I told him.

"No, that's not possible," he exclaimed. "Eleven fillings at once is too much. You've waited this long. We'll do it after your vacation. Two weeks won't make a difference."

"You don't understand. I'm leaving for Africa and won't be seeing a dentist for the next two years."

The next day I spent the better part of the morning with a numb tongue, listening to the whir of the drill. I hope never to repeat that day. I can truly say it was one of the most excruciating times of my life—except for the day I hand coded a massive Web site with hundreds of links…

I had my reasons for failing to get my cavities filled before the eleventh hour. I thought they were pretty good reasons too. But I would have made it a lot easier on myself had I dealt with the problem earlier—just as I would have made my life easier had I given myself more than a single day to create a monster Web site.

Whatever your reasons for not having your own Web site at this point in your writing or speaking career, we can deal with them. The experience of creating and promoting your site doesn't have to be excruciating. Trust me.

"I Don't Know How"

While writers and speakers may be excellent at writing and speaking, they usually know little about *HyperText Markup Language* (HTML), graphic design, and the other elements that go into designing a worthwhile site. But not having a Web site because you don't know how to create it is like saying you don't drive because you don't know *how* to drive. The fact is, we all start out not knowing how to drive. Yet somehow, thousands of new drivers are licensed each day.

There is no shortage of books and sites and software about Web-site development. Some of the sites are listed later in this chapter, and they're just a small sampling. But all those resources lead us to the next excuse—

"I Don't Have Time"

I hear you. This one is a toughie. After all, there are only twenty-four hours in a day.

All I can say is that we make time for what's important to us. If the goals you hope to reach as a writer or speaker by having your own Web site are important enough, you'll make the time.

Most of you reading this book probably don't write full time, and your hours are already packed with jobs, families, obligations, maybe even a little exercise. Whatever spare time you have is probably earmarked for writing the "great American novel" or creating those wonderful speeches that will someday command five-thousand-dollar honorariums. But what if a Web site can help get you there?

If you do write or speak full time, of course, you're doing just that—writing and speaking. Working. Making a living. But what if having a Web site can help you make that living?

Which leads nicely into reason number three for not having a site in place—

"I Can't Afford It"

While finding a place for your Web site on the Internet requires some thought, it doesn't necessarily need to cost money—at least not any more than you're currently spending for Internet service. As we discussed in chapter 1, part of selecting an ISP is making sure the amount of free space the server provides in its basic package is sufficient for a Web page. Remember, though, that the service you get from a free ISP often requires you to agree to terms stating that you won't have any commercial sites. If, after agreeing to the "no business clause," you do any sort of commerce through your site, the ISP has every right to shut you down.

Later we'll discuss other ways of getting affordable or free hosting, and you'll see that lack of money is the simplest of all problems to overcome.

"I Don't Have That Much to Say"

The idea of filling up an entire Web site seems overwhelming? True, creating an effective Web site is more than simply throwing together a few words and an outdated photo of yourself. The writers and speakers whose sites have pulled in actual sales, or at least generated ongoing interest in their work, have carefully planned the content of their sites.

But don't forget, a site can be as simple as a one-page announcement of your published books or speaking availability. Or it can be as complex as an interactive mega-portal, offering mailing lists, chats, and more. There are as many different reasons for having a Web site as there are writers and speakers; each of you is unique, and your Web site should reflect that. The content of your site depends entirely on your needs, desires, and goals.

What Should I Have on My Web Site?

My first Web page was actually one that announced my upcoming book. Mind you, I had not written a word of that book, nor did I know anything about writing or publishing. On the page, I established my expertise as that of a caregiver qualified to write a book about Huntington's Disease. I also used a portion of the page to ask for submissions and explain more about the disease. It was a small, clean page without bells and whistles, but it met the objective of establishing my expertise as the right person to write this particular book.

It's important to decide at the outset what your goals are for your Web site. Will a simple, one-page site meet your needs, or do you want a technologically intricate, monster marketing vehicle? Most of you will opt for something between the two extremes.

Whatever you decide, make sure your Web site is professional. The *American Heritage Dictionary* defines "professional" as "conforming to the standards of a profession." Professional writers and speakers need professional Web sites designed to advance their careers. Conforming to accepted standards is critical, even if you're not yet published or earning high fees for your speaking.

Every Web site should include the following:
- *an introductory page geared toward your subject and goal*
- *a table of contents*
- *copyright information on every page*
- *easily accessible contact information, including e-mail and mailing address, if appropriate*
- *an author or speaker bio*
- *an author's or speaker's résumé*

Depending on your site's purpose, consider adding the following:
- *writing samples (make sure you actually own the copyright before posting)*
- *links to related sites in your field*
- *frequently asked questions (FAQs)*
- *an online bookstore*
- *book covers and descriptions*
- *book excerpts*
- *ordering information*
- *writing tips*
- *speaking or book-signing schedule*
- *speaking topics*
- *speaking tips*
- *an audio or video file of a sample presentation*
- *autoresponders (sends automatic messages on requested topics)*
- *topical newsletters*
- *contests*
- *chat rooms*
- *message boards*
- *a search engine*

All Web sites are not created equal. With millions of sites being added to the Internet at mind-boggling speed, the search for good content is getting harder. However simple or complex you make your site, make sure your content is informative, accessible, and usable. Give people value during their stop at your personal Internet destination, and they'll be sure to find their way back—and maybe bring a friend along.

Of Special Interest to Speakers

After I wrote *Faces of Huntington's,* I began speaking to groups throughout the country. Even when I was speaking in a church or to another non-HD group, it was only natural for me to tell stories related to the disease. As I'm also a singer, I weave music into my presentations. Because so many people requested copies of my songs, I recorded the *Faces of Huntington's* CD. Today's technology allows me to have a sound clip from the CD on my Web site. It was easy to create and cost me nothing, and many people have ordered the CD, and even the book, based on hearing that one short demo.

Speakers can offer both audio and video presentations on their Web sites. Videos, for instance, can be encoded for viewing on Web sites and over Internet broadcast networks. One Huntington's Disease Society of America chapter has a library of over a dozen informative thirty-minute videos designed to educate and support families, doctors, and others interested in learning more about the disease. As a speaker and singer, I can add an introduction and my music to these videos and offer them to Internet broadcast networks. The presentations are the perfect vehicle to promote my book while helping to raise awareness of Huntington's Disease at a global level.

How Do I Go About Creating a Web Site?

After determining that you really want your own Web site, you have two additional decisions. Will you create your own site or hire someone to do it for you? And will you use a free service, a fee-based service, or your current ISP?

After you've answered these questions, you can begin to plan and design your site. The nice thing is that changing things around is easy. If you decide to do something differently after your initial decision, you'll have no problem making changes.

I can't possibly give you all the information you need to create a winning Web site. The good news is, an ample supply of free tutorial Web sites, Web tools, graphic sites, and lots more designed to get you started are available on the Internet. I've listed a number of Internet resources for Web design at the end of this chapter.

Teena Stewart is a writer as well as a Web designer, which means she understands the importance of content, especially for writers and speakers. "Rarely do writers plunge into a project without completing prerequisite work," says Stewart. "A good writer researches, then organizes his thoughts before actually sitting down to create the finished project. He or she moves logically from one point or chapter to another, fleshing out the outline as he goes. You should use the same approach for planning your Web site."

Stewart uses her own Web site as a platform for both her writing and her graphics abilities. Her company, SmartWorks, specializes in creating projects where the graphics and the writing are equally well done. Visit her Web site; it's an excellent example of using a site to feature samples of different styles of writing.

Stewart's comments and tips about Web design are located at the end of this book in appendix D. They will help you, whether you do all the work of designing your own Web site or hire someone else.

➤ SmartWorks at *http://www.smartwrks.com*

Designing Your Own Web Site

If you want to create your own site, there are several ways to learn what you need to know. For instance, many community colleges and private schools offer classes in basic Web-site development. Another resource may be your children; it's amazing what kids know when it comes to the Internet! My first site was actually a birthday gift from my son, who taught himself Web development with a book that included a CD tutorial. Part of my gift was having him sit down with me as we created the site together. I learned enough to make my own changes later on and, eventually, to create a more detailed site.

Web-site development how-to pages proliferate on the Internet. Anyone willing to take the time to review online tutorials can easily learn the basics of HTML. Several such sites are listed at the end of this chapter, as are helpful sites for site upkeep, expansion, and promotion.

Hiring a Web Designer or Webmaster

If you decide to hire someone to create your Web site instead of designing it yourself, do some research first. You'll get a good feel for different Web designers' creative abilities when you view their sites, which will also give you their clients' e-mail addresses. Use them to ask these questions:

- *Was the work done in a timely manner?*
- *Did the designer keep to the budget?*
- *What was included in the price? Graphics? Writing? Layout? Special add-ons?*
- *Was the designer patient? Did he/she explain what he/she was doing and why?*
- *Did the price include site maintenance?*
- *How many pages were included in the agreed-upon price?*
- *How much are additional pages and changes?*
- *Would you hire this person again?*

After checking references and choosing a Web designer, make sure you sign a written contract up-front, establishing what the price will cover and how long it will take to complete the work.

Prices vary as much as speaking fees and per-word compensation for writers do, so make sure you talk to a number of people about their services. "Inexpensive" doesn't always mean poor quality, just as "exorbitant" is no guarantee a professionally designed site will get results.

If you decide to hire someone to create your Web site, ask him or her how to make your own revisions. I maintain an online bookstore through Amazon.com, and I add books regularly that I think writers and speakers could use. If I had to wait for a Webmaster to make those changes and pay for him or her to do so, my site would soon become a nuisance and an expense I couldn't afford. A patient site designer can help you learn as much as you need to know to make your own revisions.

"Before engaging the services of a Web designer, both parties should read the extensive articles on my site under the link, 'Articles for Web Site Designers and Site Owners,'" says attorney Ivan Hoffman. "There are a wide variety of legal issues presented in this very complex relationship including but not limited to rights issues, warranties, deliverables, payment, failure of either party to perform, and so on."

- ➤ Ivan Hoffman at *http://www.ivanhoffman.com*
- ➤ My bookstore at *http://www.writerspeaker.com/bookstore.html*

USING A WYSIWYG EDITOR

When I first went online, there really were no other options for getting a Web page except learning how to create it myself from the ground up or hiring someone. These days there are two other alternatives that anyone can try.

The first is a *WYSIWYG* (pronounced WIZ-ee-wig), which is an acronym for "What You See Is What You Get." A WYSIWYG editor (program) allows you to create a Web page that lets you see what the end result will look like while the interface or document is being created. A WYSIWYG editor is a quick way to create a site without entering descriptive codes.

With an easy-to-use WYSIWYG editor, you can easily see the progress of your page as you work. A novice who follows a minimum of directions can create a Web page with very little hassle. Many professional Web designers and Webmasters use a blend of a WYSIWYG and HTML coding.

For the average writer or speaker needing a site, a WYSIWYG might be the perfect way to get started. Prices range from free to several hundred dollars. About.com has a great list of editors and links. Should you decide to go that route, Carl Davis's HTML Editor Reviews can help you decide which one is right for you. Also, Netscape and Microsoft's Internet Explorer both have a simple editor included.

➤ About.com Web Design at *http://webdesign.about.com/compute/ webdesign/ msubeditors.htm*

➤ HTML Editor Reviews at *http://www.webcommando.com/editrev/index.html*

Using Free Web Site Hosting

Another way to create your own Web page is to use one of the countless free community Web site hosting options available. Most of these free Web sites don't require you to be familiar with HTML.

"Free" is an attractive word, but there actually is a price to pay. Remember, the Internet is advertising driven, and advertising is the reason these Web sites are willing to give you free space. Viewers to your site will have to look at pop-up ads and/or banner advertising. Besides the fact that you have no control over the content of those banners and ads, visitors to your site could find them so irritating they might be tempted to move on to a competitor's site.

To receive free space, you have to register, which means at a minimum disclosing your name and e-mail address. Sometimes you're subjected to a complete survey. Information you give is often sold or given to advertisers. You think you're getting a lot of spam now?! Free Web hosting can also be unreliable and offer limited or nonexistent technical support and slow service.

The biggest concern with using free space for your Web site, however—whether from your provider or from one of the free community Web site hosting options—is protection of your copyright. In June 1999, copyright protection for Web sites made front-page news when Yahoo! bought Geo-Cities, a popular free Web-hosting service. After the sale, Yahoo! unveiled their new terms of service (TOS) agreement on their Web site. The following clause was buried deeply enough for most people to miss, even if they read the TOS before clicking to join or reregister their site:

> By submitting Content to any Yahoo property, you automatically grant, or warrant that the owner of such Content has expressly granted, Yahoo the royalty-free, perpetual, irrevocable, non-exclusive and fully sublicensable right and license to use, reproduce, modify, adapt, publish, translate, create derivative works from, distribute, perform and display such Content (in whole or part) worldwide and/or to incorporate it in other works in any form, media, or technology now known or later developed.[2]

What would that mean to writers, speakers, and anyone else with a Web site hosted by Yahoo/GeoCities? By signing an agreement that included this clause, developers of Web sites would have been acknowledging Yahoo!'s legal right to use the content of their sites for their own purposes, including selling it to any and all who expressed an interest in using the material, without compensation. Yahoo/GeoCities was also under no obligation to ask permission from or give notification or credit to the site developers.

A boycott of Yahoo! and the negative publicity caused the company to modify its TOS. The incident was a warning to those who create intellectual property for Internet publication of some of the pitfalls of free host sites.

Amy Gahran's e-zine for writers, editors, and others who create online content, *Contentious,* has a discussion about the Yahoo! copyright story you might be interested in reading. The linked article, "The Contentious Guide to 'Grabby' Web Hosts," is a great resource.

Free Web Hosting has links to hundreds of free Web-hosting services. For those who want a free Web site but are leery of banner and ad content on some free sites, you might want to chose a free Christian Web-hosting option. Truepath.com and IloveJesus.com are two excellent starting points.

For issues around Web-design contracts and law and other aspects of electronic publishing, visit attorney Ivan Hoffman's Web site.

> Contentious Guide to "Grabby" Web Hosts at *http://www.contentious. com/articles/V2/2-4/editorial2-4.html*

> Free Web Hosting at *http://www.free.com/index.asp?catid=67*

> IloveJesus.com at *http://www.ilovejesus.com*

> Ivan Hoffman at *http://www.ivanhoffman.com*

> Truepath.com at *http://www.truepath.com*

Should I Have My Own Domain?

What exactly—you might ask—is a *domain* or a *domain name?* Simply put, each server—the computer where your Web site is stored—has its own IP (Internet Proxie) address, which is a long string of numbers and dots. A long string of numbers and dots doesn't fit well on a business card, and it's hard to turn into a catchy jingle. So the domain name was created.

The domain name in my address is *writerspeaker.com* and is a replacement for those numbers I don't know and don't care about. As discussed in the first chapter, domains are listed by country code, but also by the following six categories:

- *.com = commercial businesses*
- *.net = network organizations*
- *.edu = educational institutions*
- *.org = nonprofit organizations*
- *.gov = government agencies*
- *.mil = military*

If I wanted to, I could register *writerspeaker* in other domains. Of course, that begins to get costly; there's a fee for each registered domain, and it has to be paid every two years. This is on top of any fee you pay to the server for hosting your site.

I recently heard commercials for a new category of domain called ".cc," which is the brainchild of Clear Channel Communications. Their contention is that all the "good dot-coms" are gone and everyone should rush out to secure a .cc domain. While brand names and obvious domains are gone, there are still lots of combinations left. Personally, I like having a ".com" or a ".net" instead of ".cc."

My first site was hosted by my ISP, which offered topnotch service and had twenty-four-hour customer support. So why did I drop my ISP service and switch to a different option? The dreaded tilde.

For those not familiar with the word, a tilde is the (~) symbol at either the far upper right or the far upper left of your keyboard. Giving out my Web-site address verbally was awkward because many people didn't know what "tilde" meant or didn't know where to find it on their keyboard. They invariably e-mailed, informing me that my URL didn't work. The problem? They were using the dash (-) instead of the tilde (~). My provider made the use of the tilde mandatory, and only by changing providers or getting my own domain was I able to eliminate the tilde.

Once I made the decision to move my site, I decided to register Writer-Speaker as a domain. The URL is certainly easier to remember. Not only is it the title of this book, it describes who I am. For me, having my own domain name gives me the security that I will never again have to change my Web-site address unless I want to.

Besides a more memorable address, there are a number of reasons to have a domain instead of using the space provided by your ISP or a free service:

1. *To show your credibility.* Having a Web site address with your name or business name or the name of a book you've written shows the world you're serious about your career and willing to spend the money it takes to have a marketable Internet presence.

2. *To enhance flexibility.* With Internet service providers cropping up everywhere and smaller companies swallowed up by the larger ones, it's possible that one day yours may cease to be. If your ISP does go out of business, having your own domain name allows you to go to another provider without changing your

Web-site address, which could be bad for your business as well as being troublesome.

3. *To create a "brand."* Having a domain name that is the same as the name of this book helps promote the book—and the book helps promote my Web site. With the name "writerspeaker.com," I've created my own "brand." The domain also brands me as a writer and a speaker, which ultimately adds to my credibility.

Your domain host can take care of registering your domain, or you can easily do it yourself. When obtaining a domain name, make certain that your host lists you or someone in your organization as the administrative contact or owner for the domain name. If you are not listed, the domain is actually owned by the provider, and should you decide to move to a different provider, there could be trouble in getting the domain transferred. Always ask who will be listed as the owner or contact, and only do business with firms that list you as the domain owner.

For a listing of Web-hosting options, visit CNET's Web site.

➤ CNET at *http://builder.com/Servers/webHosting*

ONLINE WEB SITE RESOURCES

An abundance of sites to help you create and promote your own Web site for personal and business purposes exists on the Internet. The following list will give you a few to get started.

To Help You Create Your Web Site

About.com, Suite101.com, Yahoo! and other portals have extensive lists of tutorials, guides, and checklists in their Internet listings. Other tutorials and guidelines follow. I've also included resources for Web tools and a couple of Web-designer sites that I'm familiar with. There are many more!

➤ About.com at *http://www.about.com*
➤ Suite101.com at *http://www.suite101.com*
➤ Yahoo! at *http://yahoo.com*

Tutorials and Style Guides

➤ The Bare Bones Guide to HTML *(http://www.werbach.com/barebones)* lists HTML tags and includes tutorials and links.

➤ A Basic HTML Style Guide can be found at *http://guinan.gsfc.nasa. gov:80/Style.html.*

➤ Making a WWW Flop *(http://www.ciolek.com/WWWVLPages/ QltyPages/FlopMaker.html)* is a tongue-in-cheek look at how not to create a Web site, by Dr. T. Matthew Ciolec.

➤ Net Tips for Writers and Designers *(http://www.dsiegel.com/tips)* can be found at the Web Wonk Web site.

➤ Richard Waller *(http://www.waller.co.uk/eval.htm)* has a valuable Web-site evaluation-rating checklist.

➤ So You Want To Make A Web Page *(http://junior.apk.net/~jbarta/ tutor/makapage/index.html)* is one of several helpful tutorials available.

➤ Unplugged Software *(http://www.unplug.com/great)* has tips for beginning, advanced, and expert designers. It also includes lots of links to free stuff.

➤ What Makes a Great Site? *(http://www.webreference.com/greatsite.html)* has an excellent article about Web design.

➤ Yale Style Guide *(http://info.med.yale.edu/caim/manual)* is a free, complete, online manual for Web-site design.

Web Tools

➤ Amazing Resources *(http://www.amazingresources.com)* offers free Web tools.

➤ Bravenet *(http://www .bravenet.com)* offers free Web space and a variety of Web tools even for those who have sites elsewhere.

➤ Cedge's HTML Cheat Sheet *(http://cedesign.net/help2j.htm)* is a must-have as an HTML quick reference.

➤ GIF Wizard *(http://usw est.gifwizard.com)* reduces the size of your site graphics. It features a free "test drive." Be prepared to pay for the service each month if you opt to register here.

➤ HomePage Tools *(http://homepagetools.com)* is filled with free tools for Web-site developers, including a guest book, bulletin board, Web-site counter, search engine, and lots more. All tools can be customized and branded for your site.

➤ MyComputer.com *(http://www.mycomputer.com)* has numerous free Web tools to help you with site creation and maintenance.

➤ Web Authoring Resources *(http://www.wwwscribe.com/resource.htm)* is maintained by Kenneth E. Johnson, a freelance writer who specializes in computer topics. Be prepared to spend quite a bit of time at this site filled with links to Web tools, articles, guides, etc.

➤ Website Garage *(http://websitegarage.netscape.com)* does automated site maintenance checks, optimizes graphics, and analyzes traffic.

Web Designers

➤ Nance Publishing at *http://www.nancepub.com*

➤ SmartWorks at *http://www.smartwrks.com*

➤ Web Imagine Design at *http://www.sandraryan.com*

➤ Workable Webs at *http://www.workablewebs.com*

To Help You Promote Your Web Site

The following is a quick checklist of self-explanatory tips for promoting your Web site and places to search for more information or resources.

- *Choose a good URL: short, "intuitive," and preferably with your own domain name.*
- *Place your Web address and e-mail address on all your print advertising (brochures, newspaper, magazines) and your letterhead and business cards.*
- *Submit your site to search engines or use a submission service.*

➤ Auto Submit at *http://autosubmit.com*

➤ Go Net-Wide at *http://www.gonetwide.com/gopublic.htm*

➤ The Internet Promotions MegaList at *http://www.2020tech.com/submit.html*

➤ Self Promotion.com at *http://selfpromotion.com*

➤ Submit It! at *http://www.submitit.com*

➤ WebMasterSuite.com at *http://www.webmastersuite.com*

- *Exchange links and banners with developers of relevant sites.*
➤ Hyper Banner Network at *http://bpath.com*
➤ Link Exchange at *http://www.linkexchange.com*
➤ Trafficx at *http://www.trafficx.com*

- *Frequent newsgroups, chat rooms, and mailing lists.*
➤ Chatseek.com at *http://www.chatseek.com*
➤ Copywriter.com at *http://www.copywriter.com*
➤ Deja.com at *http://www.deja.com*
➤ eGroups at *http://www.egroups.com*
➤ Tilenct.com at *http://www.tile.net*

- *Take advantage of word-of-mouth advertising.*
➤ Foxcontent.com at *http://www.foxcontent.com*
➤ Recommend-It at *http://www.recomendit.com*

- *Join a Web ring.*
➤ Ringworld at *http://www.ringworld.org*
➤ Web Ring at *http://www.webring.org*

- *Regularly check and fix any broken links and other site problems.*
➤ LinkAlarm at *http://www.linkalarm.com*

- *Offer freebies.*
➤ 123Greetings *(http://associates.123greetings.com)* offers free greeting cards.
➤ Bravenet *(http://www.bravenet.com/samples/e-mailforms.php)* offers free fill-in forms and search engines.
➤ Homepage Tools *(http://homepagetools.com/guestbook)* provides free guest books.
➤ Uproar *(http://www.uproar.com/webdevelopers)* provides free games.
➤ Vatagenet *(http://apps3.vantagenet.com/site/poll.asp)* provides free polls.
➤ Zap Zone *(http://www.zzn.com)* offers free Web-based e-mail.

EXAMPLES OF EFFECTIVE WEB SITES

A picture's worth a thousand words, the saying goes. So are well-constructed Web sites. The ones you'll find here demonstrate how writers and speakers are effectively promoting themselves and their work. Use them as examples as you design your own site.

Writer Sites

➤ April Clay, a chartered psychologist with an independent practice, is using her beautifully designed Web site *(http://www.telusplanet.net/ public/aclay)* to position herself as an expert in her field. Her Web site features information on her books and articles, her professional background, services, related links, and subscription details for her two e-zines.

➤ Holly Lisle, author of *Diplomacy of Wolves* and *Vengeance of Dragons* (Time-Warner/Aspect, 1998 and 1999 respectively) and seventeen novels published by Baen Books, has been supporting herself and her family solely by her fiction writing since 1992. Her page *(http://www. hollylisle.com)* is designed to meet her goals for the future. Lisle says, "I've recently started a free newsletter and some self-promotion at my writers' Web page, preparatory to bringing out a series of e-books detailing my methods for making a living by writing fiction." Lisle's site includes an excellent site index that points to a wealth of information targeted at people who would be interested in her books. By showcasing her own novels, she shows her prospective audience that she knows what she's talking about in the fiction-writing-for-publication area.

➤ Probably the premier Web site for writers is Inkspot *(http://www.inkspot. com)*. Debbie Ridpath Ohi's site is filled with great resources for both beginning and advanced writers. It's constantly updated and lives up to the site name: Writer's Resource, Writer's Community. Ohi's site is a great example of a site that educates and informs writers.

➤ Even best-selling author Lee Roddy, who has fifty published novels and fifteen nonfiction books with sales in the millions of copies, sees the value of having a Web site *(http://www.leeroddybooks.com)*. Roddy's credits include *Grizzly Adams,* which became a prime-time television series, and *The Lincoln Conspiracy,* which made the *New York Times* bestseller list. "I saw three great benefits in having a Web site," explains Roddy. "I can now sell my books online worldwide. My first two orders were from Australia and Canada. Furthermore, after 25 of my 51 novels went out of print, I bought remainders and got the plates back to possibly reprint my own. On my Web site," he continues, "I offer my autographed, hard-to-find but best-selling juvenile series Ladd Family Adventures (published by Focus on the Family); Between Two Flags and An American Adventure series (both Bethany House); two adult historical suspense trilogies: Giants on the Hill (Word) and The Lady Pinkerton Chronicles (Chariot Victor). When I speak or teach, I hand out fliers about my Web site and make some of these autographed books available to the audience. I'll soon offer unique online curriculum projects to my faithful readers in the Christian school and home-school markets."

➤ Author and speaker Terry Whalin has done an incredible job of creating a user-friendly Web site *(http://www.terrywhalin.com)* that accomplishes his goal of self-promotion without being pushy. "One of the keys with a Web site is figuring out your focus," he says. Whalin chose two. First, he wanted to include background material about himself—a résumé, a list of his books, articles about himself, a portfolio of his work—so editors could drop by and see what he'd done both in the distant and the recent past. That way, he says, they could "make an informed decision about my qualifications for their particular project." Second, Whalin decided his site needed to be a place where new writers could gain some insight about the marketplace from his perspective. "I've been helped by so many people over the years and profited from their teaching and insight," he says. The autoresponder messages and the Writer's Help section of his site are ways to pay back those who've helped him.

Speaker Sites

➤ Speaker and relationship coach Larry James has created a wonderful site *(http://www.celebratelove.com)* to promote his speaking and writing. One of the features of his site is the option to preview a rotation of his "LoveNotes" quotations by refreshing the Web page (make the page come up again with a new picture). A must-see on Larry's site is his link to "37 Ways to Make Your Next Book Signing an EVENT."

➤ Kathy and Larry Collard Miller have created a multipurpose Web site *(http://www.larryandkathy.com)*. "I think [the site] gives an image of quality and success to my ministry," says Kathy. The site has also been useful in getting submissions from site visitors for her compiled books. And at times she has been able to point people who were interested in finding a speaker to the Web site for information they might otherwise have had to wait several days for the mail carrier to bring.

➤ Nutrition expert Dr. Susan Mitchell, Ph.D., R.D., uses her site *(http://www.susanmitchell.org)* to establish her credibility, educate her customers, display her books, and preview her speaking. "I see the Internet as one more piece of the marketing pie," she says. "It's a terrific way for anyone, from a meeting planner or speakers' bureau to a company or media outlet such as a radio or television station, to find out more about you. By checking out my Web site, [site visitors] can hear audio and have access to printable documents, such as a bio, information on our books, or whatever they need to make their job easier. The great part is that this information is available 24/7 for their convenience."

➤ Parenting writer Brenda Nixon is hoping the Internet will extend her speaking engagements beyond the Midwest, where she is based. "Not only does my Web site *[http://www.parentpwr.com]* give me worldwide exposure, but I've been able to offer reciprocal Web links with others in my profession and [others who are] dedicated to the awesome responsibility of parenting."

➤ Susan Osborn is a writer and speaker who trains other writers and speakers to write salable books. "My critique service has gleaned a great deal of business from [my Web site *(http://www.christiancommunicator. com)*] and from the search engines I am listed on. [Connections with] several of my critique customers have led to actual speaking engagements in churches and writers' groups."

➤ Professional speaker and human resource trainer Beth Ratzlaff says her Web site *(http://www.lifelinespeaking.com)* "has heightened my credibility and given [me] an extra edge when new clients are considering me as a speaker or trainer. There aren't a lot of speakers out there with their own site! When [potential clients] phone to ask for my corporate portfolio, I tell them that it will go in the mail that day. In the meantime, I suggest that they check out my Web site. I have had [people] call me right back and tell me how impressed they are with the site, asking, 'Can you just look at your calendar and tell me if these dates are free?'" Ratzlaff claims the Internet has helped her speaking career by building relationships with other speakers all over North America. "Some of my toughest moments in the past stemmed from loneliness in this business. I longed for mentors, and...someone who understood. The Internet has opened that world for me, and I have a lot of support through national speaking associations and organizations."

You'll find many other examples of effective Web sites as you follow links from site to site—and probably even more not-so-effective ones. My advice is to learn from both.

"It has been said," quips professor Robert Silensky of California University, "that a million monkeys banging on a million typewriters would eventually reproduce the entire works of Shakespeare. Now, thanks to the Internet—we know this is not true."

Creating an effective Web site takes more than just "banging on a type-writer." If you want to be more than a traveler on the information superhighway—if you want to be a destination for other travelers—make sure your site is one that people will be pleased they came to see and that they'll want to revisit over and over again.

ELEVEN

Billboards and Bumper Stickers

Marketing Yourself on the Internet

North Americans communicate through buttons, T-shirts, and bumper stickers the way some cultures use drums.—TIM MCCARTHY

As I edged my way through the sea of traffic on the interstate the other day, I berated myself for being in this exact place at this exact time. I was fuming. I'm not one of the increasing droves of humanity in urban areas forced to face the daily commute, and I hadn't realized that traffic backups were starting earlier and lasting longer. The route I was taking is our one-and-only convenient north-south corridor from the suburbs to the congested downtown area.

Finally I saw an opening, flipped on my blinker, and carefully advanced my van toward the exit across three lanes of glassy-eyed commuters. There, at the bottom of the off-ramp, stood a disheveled, dirty man of indeterminate age. He wore what appeared to be a suit of above-average quality, albeit filthy. As I inched down the ramp, my mind played out different scenarios about what might have transpired to bring about his homelessness.

As I drew closer to him, I saw that he held a hand-lettered cardboard sign: "Hungry. Will work for food." My heart contracted with compassion, and I reached for my purse, quickly determining that although I didn't have much, I could give a little. Just as I reached for the handle to roll down the window, though, he flipped over the sign, where I read: "Or visit my Web site at www.hobo.com"!

Okay, so that didn't *really* happen. The traffic was real, but there was no homeless man holding a sign asking commuters to give via his Web site.

But trust me, it *could* happen. Actually, if you go to *www.hobo.com* you will find a Web site devoted to the National Hobo Foundation, so I'm not that far off the mark!

Most of us aren't interested in standing on a street corner holding a sign to let people know where to find us on the Internet. So how do we let them know? After all, if no one can find your Web site, what difference does it make how well you did your work creating it?

Too many people have an "if we build it, they will come" mentality about their Web sites. But with millions upon millions of sites out there along the information superhighway, why should anyone—and how *could* anyone—stumble across yours?

The checklist and accompanying Internet resources for promoting your Web site featured in the last chapter are a beginning, but there are many other things you can do, using the Internet, to promote your Web site and to promote yourself and your work in other ways.

Most writers and speakers prefer to focus on the part of their job they're good at—writing and speaking—and leave the marketing to someone else. But be warned that unless *someone* markets your work, your powerful words will go unnoticed. And since "someone else" usually means having to spend money you have yet to earn, you're better off learning how to harness the power of the Internet to help simplify the marketing process yourself. Not everyone can or even wants to be the next John Grisham or Zig Ziglar, but we can all sell more of our work by setting goals and following a plan.

Very few dollars, some common sense, and a lot of time can get you and your Web site in front of those same millions of people who see the "big boys." However, according to marketing guru Shel Horowitz, author of *Marketing Without Megabucks* (Accurate Writing & More/AWM Books, 1993) and *Grassroots Marketing: Getting Noticed in a Noisy World* (Chelsea Green, 2000), since "the big guys" have finally started "chewing up cyberspace," the task is a bit more of challenging than it was a few short years ago.

That doesn't mean individuals and small companies should write off the Internet as part of their marketing efforts. Internet marketing is "absolutely vital," says Horowitz. "Active participation in appropriate discussion groups can brand someone better than just about anything else, especially if [messages are] accompanied by a well-crafted signature. If you have a topic you speak or write about, find a community where people who hire people with your knowledge meet." Participating in discussion groups will also drive traffic to your Web site, says Horowitz, as will search engines, cross-links, etc. "You never know who's going to be strolling by that Web site," he adds. "I have a standing offer from a BBC producer to do a segment if I ever make it to London (or she to New York); she found me on a search engine."

PROMOTING YOURSELF

If ever a playing field was leveled for writers and speakers, marketing is it. Opportunities for marketing yourself on the Internet are limitless.

Getting your name out there is the first step toward promoting yourself and your work online. A number of opportunities exist to help make your name, if not a household word, at least recognizable to a much larger audience than you otherwise would have. Options to help make your name a "brand" include subscribing to mailing lists and newsgroups; participating in chats; and writing articles to post on portals, search engines, and Web sites—your own and others'. The more often people see your name linked to a particular topic, the more likely your "brand" will pop into their heads when they need information or service around that topic.

Subscribe to Mailing Lists and Newsgroups

According to chief executive officer Mary Westheimer, BookZone, the largest provider of Web services to the publishing industry, recently conducted a survey of nine thousand publishing Web sites to see what was working online. Not surprisingly, the survey revealed that those publishers who are using mailing lists and newsgroups are happiest with their traffic. Those resources are free to anyone willing to invest time and creativity in the marketing process. (Review chapter 2 for information about finding and using lists and newsgroups.) The same rules and advice about using e-mail, chats, newsgroups, and forums that you used for research and support apply to marketing yourself.

While joining lists and newsgroups helps connect you with writers and others in the publishing industry, you would also be wise to look for lists about subjects you've addressed in your writing. This works particularly well with nonfiction books, such as *The OCD Workbook—Your Guide to Breaking Free from Obsessive-Compulsive Disorder,* by Bruce M. Hyman, Ph.D., and Cherry Pedrick, R.N.

Pedrick uses mailing lists as a marketing tool for her book. "I have been a member of OCD-L, a huge OCD e-mail list for about four years," Pedrick says. "I was established on it before I started the book. It has helped me with marketing because it's like I am one of them. Well, I *am* one of them."

If there isn't a list devoted to your topic, then start one. "I also saw a need for a special prayer list for people with OCD and started my own mini e-mail list," explains Pedrick. Hers was the first of many specialized lists that were spawned from the main list, including a Christian OCD list called Serenity Bay, to which she also belongs.

Fiction writers can benefit from mailing lists about the subject matter their novel covers. Joining Civil War discussion lists, for example, is an excellent way to find potential readers for your fiction work set in that era.

Being part of the *momwriters@egroups.com* mailing list has been a benefit for author Mary Emma Allen. Her participation in the list, plus having a Web site to which to refer people for her credentials, has created some exciting professional opportunities. "I've been asked to participate in a Web site for teaching and encouraging youngsters to write," she says. "I will have a regular column on it with writing activities [for children]. I'm really excited about this.… It's an area I've wanted to expand upon, and now I will be able to reach and teach young people worldwide! All because of the Internet."

Participating in mailing lists and newsgroups even without having a Web site is a good idea, but having a site really makes a difference. Allen has published over two hundred poems and stories in addition to her books; the poems are featured on her Web site, which her nephew designed for her. "I think a Web site is really a necessity for an author nowadays. Having links to other sites has been helpful too. I've received inquiries about my books, classes, newsletter, etc. from the Web site."

Speakers usually develop expertise on specific subjects and often do well in targeted mailing lists relating to those topics. Attorney Ivan Hoffman has a niche in writing and publishing law. By subscribing to and being helpful on appropriate lists, Hoffman is able to promote his expertise by answering questions and offering advice with no strings attached. "The Internet is about giving away value," insists Hoffman. "My articles are just that. They also make for excellent marketing tools. Everyone wins."

Hoffman uses his signature file to market himself, including his name and a great tag line, "Lawyering with Integrity (sm)." He also lists his areas of expertise, including writing and publishing law, Web-design contracts and law, copyrights, trademarks, Internet law, Web-site audits, recording and music law, along with his URL.

Gail Showalter, a consultant and educator for the visually impaired, claims that participating in a professional list has led to speaking engagements in the coming year in Chicago, Maryland/D.C., and Denver on the topic of using art with blind students. Since she lives in southeast Texas, she would probably not have found those opportunities in any other way. Through her participation in the list, plus a Web site to give potential clients immediate access to her credentials, Showalter now has national and even international exposure.

One warning: Regardless of your genre, don't advertise your book to any list in which you're participating. The most effective way to use a mailing list is to become an active member and offer helpful advice in response to questions. Your research has probably given you some insight and experience that will make you a welcome, respected participant. Using a signature at the end of every e-mail that includes your book title, URL, and e-mail address gives others an opportunity to become familiar with your name and learn more about your writing.

What you never, under any circumstance, want to do is use spam as a marketing method. Sending unsolicited e-mail or posting inappropriate messages to newsgroups, even when your message is good, gives you and your company a negative image. Many online services and hosting companies have a no-spam clause in their service agreement; if you make a practice of sending spam and are found out, your e-mail account could be terminated by your provider. You could even lose your Web site. That's quite a risk to take for a practice that is usually unsuccessful and gives other writers and speakers a bad name.

- ➢ BookZone at *http://www.bookzone.com*
- ➢ Gail Showalter at *http://www.texasbiz.com/seeing*
- ➢ Ivan Hoffman, J.D. at *http://www.ivanhoffman.com*
- ➢ Mary Emma Allen at *http://homepage.fcgnetworks.net/jetent/mea*

Participate in Chat Rooms

In addition to joining chat sessions related to the topic of your book, look at those that discuss writing in general. What do you know about writing you could share with other list members? I successfully self-published my first two books and now enjoy giving workshops on self-publishing whenever possible. As a result of one self-publishing workshop for the online Christian Writers Workshop, I was invited to teach the subject at both the Colorado and Philadelphia Christian Writers' Conferences. While my intent was simply to offer my expertise, I'm thrilled with the invitations.

Bradley Kirkland, former CEO of the Writers Club and now executive producer of the iUniverse Writers Club, has worked with online chats, conferences, and events for over seven years, beginning on AOL and moving elsewhere on the Internet in 1998. "Honestly, the true value of chat depends on what each individual uses it for. Personally, one can meet new friends, renew acquaintances, and take a break from the normal grind of life. Professionally, the value of chat is limitless. You can join a regular work group or critique group, participate in Q&A as part of our writing courses, take part in a special event with a successful writer, or simply network. I've met everyone from Tom Clancy to agents to editors at major publishing houses."

The Internet is no different than real life, in many ways. Readers who enjoy the same types of books invariably interact with each other both online and off. There are online communities where people congregate and discuss particular topics and related books. The resource section in this and other chapters lists many chat opportunities and tips on locating chat venues for marketing your writing and speaking.

Provide Content for Web Sites, Portals, and Search Engines

Even if you don't have your own Web site, writing articles that focus on your area of expertise is an excellent way to promote both yourself and your books or speaking topics. Informational articles about the publishing or speaking industry, for instance, help to develop name recognition and establish credibility.

Web-site owners are always looking for content to bring repeat visitors to their site. For example, I'm always willing to consider solid, well-written articles on a full range of writing, publishing, and speaking topics for my site. Teena Stewart's article on Web-site design in appendix D is a wonderful example of how one article can reach potentially thousands of readers.

Many professionals feel they've already paid their dues and won't allow their work to appear without payment. While that is understandable, if an article published on a portal, search engine, or Web site provides links back to your site or an e-mail address for questions and feedback, you may find that the investment pays more than a one-time fee through traditional channels.

When you post new articles on your own Web site often, you give readers a reason to visit repeatedly—and to refer others to your site too. Professional speaker and human resource trainer Beth Ratzlaff features different articles monthly on her site. Each article is filled with helpful information that reflects Ratzlaff's extensive background as a workshop and seminar trainer, broadcast personality, and magazine and newspaper columnist. Because of the monthly change, there is always something fresh on her site to lure readers back for another look.

Whether your writing appears on your own or someone else's site, there are some potential downsides. More and more publishers are recognizing the validity of online publication. Even if you are not paid for your work, online writing is more often than not considered previously published work. When you submit a piece elsewhere, make sure to submit it as a reprint, or at least explain that the piece has appeared online.

Another problem is the possibility of your work appearing on Web sites and electronic newsletters other than your own. Having your work spread throughout cyberspace without your permission, without credit, and without compensation is not only frustrating but an infringement of copyright law.

I write short inspirational pieces that have proven quite popular on the Internet. Each month I use a meta search engine to do a search by my name as well as the names of some of my better-liked writings. I routinely find my work out in cyberspace and have to deal with each situation. After evaluating each site, I decide if this is a place where I'd like others to see my work. If I am willing to have my work on the Web site, I write a pleasant note pointing out the copyright laws and asking them to please include credit and contact information at the end of each piece.

On several occasions, when I have found the site or the use of my work to be contrary to my beliefs, I've given the site owner a specific amount of time to remove my work before I call my attorney. I've never had to follow through on the threat, but I still try to find out if anyone is posting my work without my permission. Another way to find out if your work is being used without permission is to use a search engine called EgoSurf. This unique engine allows you to type in your name and see where it appears on the Internet.

Amy Gahran is the author of an informative two-part article on this topic, "Content Creators: Have You Been Robbed?" in "Content Spotlight" in the *Content Exchange Newsletter* (see the following list to access). To find out how to file a complaint after finding unauthorized use of your content online, you might also want to visit the U.S. Federal Trade Commission Web site or the National Fraud Information Center and Internet Fraud Watch page at the site for the National Fraud Consumer's League.

Opportunities for paid writing assignments also exist on the Internet. Many portals and search sites are looking for content as a way to attract visitors. Increased visitors equals increased advertising revenue, which is what the Internet is all about these days.

Content is simply information in various formats written for a Web site's target market. There are a lot of experts out there who can't write. Thank goodness there are many who can. Besides being a paying "gig," writing content is sometimes another way for a writer or speaker to promote his or her own writing or speaking projects.

Site content material can include traditional articles on a set topic, book reviews, Web sites and music reviews, opinion, and Q&A columns, etc. If you're interested in this method of earning money while promoting your writing and speaking, search the Web. There's a good chance that sites you bookmarked months ago have gone through major overhauls, and the site owners are now seeking new and improved content. Just as your daily newspaper needs new content every day, so do these Web sites.

Those who write content need to be fast and dependable. Quick changes are the norm on the Internet, and content providers who can provide quick, professional writing will get repeat offers. Content providers need to write clearly and concisely and be comfortable doing extensive editing. They also need to be self-starters with little need for direction.

Just as you do for any work you publish, be sure what rights you're selling when you agree to provide content. What you don't want to do is sell all rights, which lets the site owners reuse your work in any and all other media, online and off, because the content no longer belongs to you. Whether they allow you to sell or even use that piece on any other Web site, including your own, should be negotiated up-front.

Another way to use your writing to promote yourself is to become an editor. The two best-known guide sites are About.com and Suite 101.com, but there are also niche sites on topics such as health and families. Many of these sites offer paid positions for individuals to edit topics in which they excel. If you're interested in becoming an editor guide, check out the listings at Argus Clearinghouse for a site that might need your specific knowledge.

For Cherry Pedrick, the token amount paid for her service was not the reason she applied as an editor for the Obsessive Compulsive Disorder section. "Last year I became a contributing editor for OCD at Suite 101.com. I did it well before publication so I could establish myself before the book came out. I am free to post news about the book and my coauthor's television appearances there." While surfing the Web for articles and Web sites of interest to her readers at Suite 101.com, Pedrick is able to promote her book and Web site in a nonthreatening way to targeted readers who want to know more.

Amy Gahran and Steve Outing are coeditors of *Content Spotlight: The Content Exchange Newsletter.* This is a must subscribe for anyone wanting to know more about this emerging market.

➤ Argus Clearinghouse at *http://www.clearinghouse.net*
➤ Beth Ratzlaff at *http://www.lifelinespeaking.com*

➤ "Content Creators: Have You Been Robbed?" Part 1 at *http://www. content-exchange.com/cx/html/newsletter/1-7/ttl-7.htm*

➤ "Content Creators: Have You Been Robbed?" Part 2 at *http://www. content-exchange.com/cx/html/newsletter/1-8/tt1-8.htm*

➤ Content Spotlight at *http://www.content-exchange.com/cx/html/newsletter*

➤ EgoSurf at *http://www.egosurf.com*

➤ National Fraud Consumer's League at *http://www.fraud.org/welcome.htm*

➤ U.S. Federal Trade Commission at *http://www.ftc.gov*

PROMOTING YOUR WORK

In his best-selling book *1001 Ways to Market Your Books* (Open Horizons, 1999), John Kremer gives us his own philosophy about publishing: "I am dedicated to selling my books—not just for the money, or the prestige, or whatever—but because I don't believe in wasting my time. If I'm going to publish a book, then I'm going to do my best to make sure that anyone and everyone who might benefit from the book gets a chance to read it." Writers and speakers who have published books to promote, and have the same philosophy, would be wise to turn to the Internet to promote and sell their books.

Romance writer Lori Soard believes the Internet offers a new and inexpensive opportunity for a "new generation of authors to become household names." Authors can take advantage of lists targeted to specific readers, purchase inexpensive advertising in online newsletters and through banner ads, post Web pages, and participate in online chats "where they can speak to large groups of people at one time without ever leaving their home," she says.

Soard's site showcases her books and short stories, features polls and contests to get visitors involved, and includes information for writers. Soard also designs Web sites for authors.

While she is quick to credit her Web site as a helpful tool for increasing her book sales, Soard also "works the Web" through her newsletter and other online promotional efforts. Along with using your own Web site, here are a few other ways to promote and sell your work through the Internet.

➤ John Kremer at *http://www.bookmarket.com*

➤ Lori Soard at *http://www.lorisoard.com*

Get Your Book Reviewed

It makes a lot of sense to get your book reviewed in online newsletters and e-zines—particularly those related to your book's topic—and even on individual Web sites, as well as in the more obvious print review sources. But book reviews can be difficult if not downright impossible to obtain.

Sometimes, however, all you have to do is to ask. When *Faces of Huntington's* was released, I e-mailed individuals, universities, medical centers, caregiver sites, and others with an interest in this disease and asked them to review the book and to include a link. Some had a no-review policy, but almost every site added a link to my book from their site and, in many cases, the cover art too.

January Magazine bills itself as the site "where the Web looks for books." In addition to author interviews and profiles, January Magazine reviews fiction, nonfiction, crime fiction, science fiction, cookbooks, and more. Contact them about reviewing your book.

Guide and niche sites such as About.com and Suite 101.com are great places to shop for reviews. After you've targeted your market and looked at the different categories, contact the site guide and ask for a review of your book. Web-site owners need content to fill their sites as well as to furnish helpful resources to their readers.

➤ January Magazine at *http://www.JanuaryMagazine.com*

Link to Other Author/Speaker Sites

In addition to her own personal Web page, Lori Soard has an author site called Word Museum. Her site does have a free option, but she also has fee packages available in three different plans. Soard believes that her site offers great value for the money. It also tenders extensive promotion, including search-engine listings for Word Museum and every individual-author page, and a newsletter that goes out to over fifteen hundred readers. Another service her site provides for other writers and authors is a set of links to several high-traffic sites that utilize mailing lists and message boards to announce the authors.

Author Rick Kamen recently launched an author site, AutographedBy-Author, with an unusual twist. According to Kamen, his novel concept is simple:

"Readers are referred to authors for autographed books at no extra cost. Authors can list their books and contribute a small percentage of their sales to support this site. Because there's no risk for authors to list, we expect the number of participating authors to grow dramatically in the coming months."

Kamen strongly believes in the marketing potential of the Internet. "I'm putting 99 percent of my publicity efforts into drawing interested buyers to my Web site," he says. "Increasing the traffic to AutographedByAuthor is the best thing I can do for sales of my own Heirloom Stories books."

Depending on your book's topic, TTC Publishing offers an easy-link option for authors. On his Para Publishing Web site, Dan Poynter allows authors to list their books complete with an e-mail address, Web site URL, and additional information. To list your book, go to his home page and click on "Success Stories."

Don't overlook regional listings either. For example, Footprint Press, based in Rochester, New York, offers free listings for books by Rochester authors.

➤ Autographed By Author at *http://AutographedByAuthor.com*
➤ Footprint Press at *http://www.footprintpress.com*
➤ Para Publishing–Dan Poynter at *http://www.parapub.com*
➤ TTC Publishing at *http://www.toupin.com*
➤ Word Museum at *http://www.wordmuseum.com*

Join a Web Ring

Author Web rings are another way to get readers to your page, as are Web rings related to the topic of your book. A Web ring is a group of Web pages that are linked to one another by virtue of sharing a similar topic or interest. These Web sites voluntarily trade visitors and drive new traffic to each other's sites. A Web ring makes it easier for visitors who have already expressed an interest in your site's topic to find your site.

Author Nancy Lindquist is a member of the Writers' Realm Writing Ring for the purpose of promoting her three teen novels. It's too early to tell if being a member of the ring is actually responsible for sales, but as there was no cost or effort involved, she feels it was well worth joining.

Webring.org can help you find author, genre-specific, and any other type of Web ring to join or surf. Like newsgroups, Web rings are too numerous to count, with more popping up each day. The theme-oriented nature of Web rings makes them a smart addition to more traditional Web search tools—if you're willing to invest the time to find one or more rings to complement your writing and speaking projects.

➤ Webring.org at *http://www.ringworld.org*

➤ Writers' Realm Writing Ring at *http://members.home.net/thats-life*

Utilize Online Bookstores

Maybe it's the Amazon.com success story or something else entirely, but books appear to be the perfect product to sell over the Internet. I figure that if online auction sites can sell cars, selling books should be easy.

So what's the best way to sell books and services online?

The right audience for your book is shopping more and more at online bookstores. Amazon.com is the biggest, and many say the best, of all the thousands of Internet bookstores and also an easy-to-use resource for authors. There are more and more mega, regional, and themed bookstores on the Internet where authors can promote and sell their books. While listing with any bookstore should not replace having your own site, online bookstores do offer their author-customers additional promotion and the ease of online sales without the hassle of handling credit cards. Having your books available on these sites also gives international customers an uncomplicated way to order your book.

About.com has listings of online bookstores that offer promotional opportunities. Many online bookstores feature author interviews and review sections where you can include information about your book. There is a price to pay for these added features, however. Bookstores take a percentage of the retail price to feature your book. Adding cover art, reviews, author interviews, and other items that help sell the book often increase the percentage you pay to the store. Make sure to check the various programs so that you understand all costs—and get the most out of this marketing opportunity.

Once your book is listed with a store that features reviews, ask friends, relatives, and customers to provide reviews for the sites. A good review can go a long way toward more sales.

Other sources of online "bookstores" are those found on individual Web sites. For example, my Web site includes a list of books I recommend in the area of writing and publishing. I receive a 5 to 15 percent commission on my own and any other books I sell from my site. As you search the Web for appropriate sites for link exchange, be on the lookout for site bookstores, and ask the site owners to include your book.

➤ About.com at *http://publishing.about.com/business/publishing/ msubonlinebookstores.htm*

➤ WriterSpeaker.com Bookstore through Amazon.com at *http://www. writerspeaker.com/bookstore.html* or *http://www.amazon.com*

Sponsor Contests and Giveaways

The Internet is a great place to try innovative and grassroots-style marketing. Giving your book away through your Web site or through a forum where potential readers congregate often results in increased sales. If well-written and placed in the correct hands, your book itself is the best advertising you'll ever get.

Fern Reiss, publisher of *The Infertility Diet: Get Pregnant and Prevent Miscarriage* (Peanut Butter and Jelly Press, 1999), developed a novel way for independent-bookstore owners to capture customer information for future mailings. Reiss has a contest for visitors to the Peanut Butter and Jelly Press Infertility Diet Web site. The contest, named "Why I Love My Independent Bookstore," is designed to get readers off the Web and into bookstores. This creative contest encourages booksellers to hang a poster in their store and accept entries for the monthly event. Winners are announced monthly from the finalists submitted through participating bookstores. Reiss sends out a press release to all the national media announcing each month's winner and mentioning the independent bookstore involved. Of course, in the Web site information about the contest, they include a postscript on how to order their book.

Whether the contest generates big sales for the book or not, it certainly has helped Reiss gain recognition. "I'm not sure yet how successful [the contest] will be in terms of sales, but the total cost will be about $1,000 (including photocopying, mailings to one thousand bookstores, and the monthly prize). So far it's been written up in *Publishers Weekly, Foreword This Week, Independent*

Publisher, Holt Uncensored, ABA This Week, and many of the regional bookstore association newsletters."

BookZone is an "old-timer" in Internet promotion, having just celebrated its fifth year online. The BookZone Web site is a must-visit for those wanting to make sure they still have time to write while they're promoting what they've already written.

"The Internet is a powerful tool for speakers and writers," says Terri Firebaugh of Firebaugh Communications. Speakers can create audio clips for their Web sites so that potential clients can visit their Web site and get a good idea of what they sound and look like without having to wait for a videotape via snail mail or FedEx. Clients have never had this kind of access to speakers before, she claims.

Writers, too, can market themselves through their Web sites by including samples of their work, feedback from clients, etc.—creating something "almost like an online brochure," says Firebaugh, "but without length and cost constraints."

She is quick to point out a common trap many writers and speakers fall into though: limiting the content of their Web sites to simple brochures. A Web site "should be interactive and keep the reader coming back." For example, she suggests a speaker might include tips on how to select a speaker for an event or a writer might include a quiz on writing savvy.

- ➤ BookZone at *http://www.bookzone.com*
- ➤ Firebaugh Communications at *http://www.firepub.com*
- ➤ The Infertility Diet (PB&J Press) at *http://www.InfertilityDiet.com*

Hire a Publicist

While the Internet is a great tool, it's not the only venue for self-promotion. "A publicist not only frees up [writers' and speakers'] time so they can focus on [the work at which] they excel, publicists deal with the media all day long, every day," Terri Firebaugh says. "They have information on what editors need what information, how to appeal to a particular audience, how to create press materials with the strongest hooks, how the editor likes to receive their information, and many little quirks that could otherwise get the professional's PR materials thrown in the 'circular file.'"

Which brings up another great use for the Internet: finding the right team of marketing professionals. Most organizations now have Web sites that give referrals as well as information about a specific topic. Visiting the Public Relations Society of America site might help you find a publicist in your area. The Small Publishers, Artists and Writers Network (SPAWN) Web site has a member search engine that allows both members and nonmembers access to find publicists or other professionals.

Getting referrals is important, but so is knowing what to look for in a publicist. Publisher's Marketing Association (PMA) is an excellent way to learn more about book publicity and publicists. "Hiring a Freelance vs. an In-House Publicist" is an informative article by Katherine Brandenburg in the June 1998 newsletter.

One of the best online resources is a Web site by the Littfin Pratt Agency, a book publicity firm. Its free publicity workshop includes topics such as general publicity principles, workflow, publicity planning and organizing, mailing schedule, author questionnaires, press releases, and interview how-tos.

- ➤ Hiring a Freelance vs. an In-House Publicist at *http://www.pma-online.org/newsletr/may5-98.html*
- ➤ Littfin Pratt Agency at *http://www.littfinpratt.com*
- ➤ Publisher's Marketing Association (PMA) at *http://www.pma-online.org*
- ➤ Small Publishers, Artists and Writers Network at *http://www.spawn.org*

Whether you do your own promotion, hire a professional, or use a combination approach, the Internet is a powerful marketing tool.

INTERNET RESOURCES: MARKETING AND PROMOTION

- ➤ All About Lists from A to Z *(http://www.listhost.net/fromatoz.htm)* is a comprehensive document about list publishing for beginners and professionals.
- ➤ Book Marketing Update *(http://www.bookmarket.com)* has some terrific marketing and promotional links for both writers and speakers.

➤ Gebbie Press *(http://www.gebbieinc.com)* is the home of the All-in-One Media Directory. The site includes U.S. radio and television stations, daily and weekly newspapers, and lots of other resources, including an autoresponder library of PR tips and tricks.

➤ Internet Monitor *(http://www.internet-monitor.com/arti_plan.html)* has a basic marketing plan outline. The site also includes the iTips newsletter.

➤ Internet Publicity Resources *(http://marketing.tenagra.com/pubnet)* is packed with articles, links, and resources about Internet marketing by Steve O'Keefe.

➤ Para Publishing is Dan Poynter's Web site *(http://www.ParaPub.com)* and is filled with a huge array of free marketing information. Of course it also has information on all his books and fee reports. This site is a must.

➤ Promotion World *(http://www.promotionworld.com)* has tutorials, articles, interviews, and resources on promoting your Web site.

Author Web-Site Hosts

➤ African American Authors on Tour at *http://www.authorsontour.com*

➤ Autographed By Author at *http://AutographedByAuthor.com*

➤ BookBrowser's Authors Online at *http://www.bookbrowser.com/Authors/index.html*

➤ BookZone's Author's Indexes at *http://www.bookwire.com/index/Author-indexes.html*

➤ The Healing Place, CWGBookstore at *http://users.1st.net/imsaved/BRMAIN.html*

➤ Homeschoolzone's Meet the Author at *http://www.homeschoolzone.com/amazon/meettheauthor.htm*

➤ Light Communications, Inc. at *http://www.light-communications.com*

➤ Mystery Writers of America at *http://www.mysterynet.com/mwa*

➤ NightSky Publishing at *http://www.nightskypublishing.com*

➤ Para Publishing–Dan Poynter at *http://www.parapub.com*

➤ Romance Writers of America at *http://www.rwanational.com*

➤ Science Fiction Writers of America at *http://www.sfwa.org/site_index.htp*

➤ TTC Publishing at http://www.toupin.com

Chat Opportunities
➤ CNN Interactive Interviews at *http://www.cnn.com/chat*
➤ Reader's Choice Book Chat at *http://www.thegrid.net/dakaiser/books/chat.htm*
➤ TalkCity at *http://www.talkcity.com/calendar/category/books.htmpl*
➤ WordsWorth at *http://www.wordsworth.com/www/present/interviews*
➤ The Writer's BBS at *http://www.writers-bbs.com/chat.html*
➤ Writer'sClub.com at *http://www.writersclub.com/chatschedules*
➤ Writers Write Chat at *http://www.writerswrite.com*

Fee-Based Press Release Services
➤ Internet to Media Fax Service at *http://www.imediafax.com*
➤ Press Flash at *http://www.pressflash.com*
➤ The U.S. Congressional Fax Service at *http://www.uscongress-fax.com*

Marketing and Book-Promotion Professionals
➤ Andrea Reynolds at *http://www.ExpertsWhoSpeak.org*
➤ Book Marketing Update at *http://bookmarket.com*
➤ BookZone at *http://www.bookzone.com*
➤ Firebaugh Communications at *http://www.firepub.com*
➤ The Littfin Pratt Agency at *http://www.littfinpratt.com*
➤ Marketability at *http://www.marketability.com*
➤ Sensible Solutions at *http://www.happilypublished.com*

Miscellaneous Marketing Tools
➤ The All Media Jumpstation at *http://www.owt.com/dircon/mediajum.htm*
➤ Ed's Internet Book Review at *http://www.clark.net/~bell/eibr/book_review.html*
➤ NetRead Event Calendar at *http://www.NetRead.com/calendar*
➤ RoseDog.com at *http://www.rosedog.com*
➤ Show Ideas.com at *http://showideas.com*
➤ The U.S. All Media E-Mail Directory at *http://www.owt.com/dircon*

Online Bookstores (Many of Which Feature Chat and Forum Opportunities)
- ➤ Bookstreet.com at *http://www.1bookstreet.com*
- ➤ Amazon.com at *http://www.amazon.com*
- ➤ Barnes and Noble at *http://www.barnesandnoble.com*
- ➤ Books-A-Million at *http://www.booksamillion.com*
- ➤ Borders at *http://www.borders.com*
- ➤ Chapters at *http://www.chapters.ca*
- ➤ Christian Superstore at *http://www.christianbooks.com*
- ➤ Indigo at *http://www.indigo.ca*
- ➤ WordsWorth at *http://www.wordsworth.com*

The next chapter deals with alternative forms of publishing, including e-zines and online newsletters. These, too, can be excellent promotional vehicles for writers and speakers. For other invaluable tips, see marketing consultant and strategist Andrea Reynolds's excellent article "Sixteen Ways for Speakers to Harness the Power of the Internet," reprinted as appendix E at the end of this book.

However you choose to market yourself—and I recommend using a variety of approaches—remember that the magnificent site you've built along the information superhighway will stand empty unless you make every effort to let people know about it and help them get there.

TWELVE

The Future Is Here, and We Are It!

Down deep in every soul is a hidden longing, impulse, and ambition to do something fine and enduring.—GRENVILLE KLEISER

Shortly after my oldest son returned from his year as a foreign exchange student in the Czech Republic, we discussed his future. It's not every day a seventeen-year-old American comes home speaking fluent Czech. Our conversation went from which college he might attend to what career he might pursue.

"I don't know, Mom," he said. "But whatever I do with my languages, I want to make a decent living. In fact, I want to make a lot of money. I'm tired of being poor."

"We're not poor," I assured him. "We just don't have any money. One day you'll understand the difference."

"Mom, I hate to be the bearer of bad news, but we're poor. You know how poor, according to a Czech proverb?"

"No, Nicholas, I don't. But since you know so much, I'm sure you'll tell me."

Self-righteously complacent, Nicholas said, "*Mam hlad jako spisovatel.* That means 'I'm as hungry as a writer,' and the reason he's hungry is because he's poor, Mom."

That wasn't even the end of it. "*On je chudy jako spisovatel,*" he added. "That means, 'He's as poor as a writer.' I'll never be a writer, Mom. I want to have money!"

What could I say? Proverbs come from somewhere! So do terms like "struggling writer" and "starving artist."

I still don't think I'm poor, but then again, money has never been the goal of my writing. It may be a reason some people write (or speak), but even then, it's only one reason. Most beginning writers and speakers know better than to quit their day jobs. Many, like myself, simply have a subject about which they are passionate and feel they have no choice but to communicate that passion beyond their own circles of influence. Even those who think of themselves primarily as speakers often find writing to be a means of enhancing their oral presentations and supplementing their speaking fees.

Whatever the reason you write, publication always begins with a dream. Unfortunately, sometimes even when you put feet to your dreams and produce a manuscript, dreaming of your name on the spine of a book or as a byline on a magazine article often remains just that—a dream.

We've discussed ways in this book that you might use the information highway to research, network, learn, and hone your craft and market yourself and your work.

Guess what? There's more.

You can use the Internet to make your dream of publication come true too.

TRADITIONAL VS. NONTRADITIONAL FORMS OF PUBLICATION

Traditionally, when a book is published, the publisher pays all costs to produce the book, as well as marketing costs. But with recent trends toward consolidation in the publishing industry and publishing houses making million-dollar deals with mega-authors, how does a new writer become a published author? Even when the subject is an interesting one and the text is well written, a writer's attempts at getting published through mainstream channels can be the proverbial exercise in futility.

The publishing industry has changed, according to multipublished author Dorothy Jane Mills. "Today's publishers aren't looking for the so-called midlist authors," she says. "Mergers and consolidations have changed the industry into a small set of mega-publishers who look only for the few manuscripts they believe will make the most money for the company."

Despite the fact that she's a published author with fifteen books to her credit, Mills couldn't, after two years, find a publisher interested in her newest book. "This is by far my best work," she says of *The Sceptre,* a historical novel about the 1930s Austrian Nazis. *The Sceptre* was based on extensive research as well as personal background and family history. As a longtime editor and a writer, Mills knew the book was good. But publishers weren't interested.

Fortunately for Mills and others like her, a traditional publishing house isn't the only route to publication. Independent publishing, long ridiculed as the "poor stepchild" of the publishing industry, is—like Cinderella—finally coming into its own. Writers have more and more opportunities for self-publication, both in print and electronic media. Print options include contracting with a book packager or printing company to produce one's book or using the services of a print-on-demand publisher. Electronic options include publishing on the Internet or producing e-books meant to be read on electronic book readers.

Frustrated with traditional approaches to publishing and knowing her book deserved to be published, Mills went the e-publishing route with *The Sceptre.* "I got a letter from an e-publisher, 1stBooks Library," she says, "asking me in my capacity as editor if I knew of any writers who might be interested in their services. I did, and the list included me."

Mills ended up publishing her novel through another electronic publisher, Xlibris, when she discovered the company published both electronically and in print. While she remains the publisher of record, Xlibris produced her book in both hard copy and electronic forms and handles marketing and distribution through its Web site. The "virtual book" route, says Mills, has exposed her work to the public, but hard-copy sales have been stronger. She's pleased to have her book available in both formats.

> ➤ 1stBooks Library at *http://www.1stbooks.com*
> ➤ Xlibris at *http://www.xlibris.com*

Why Go Alternative?

Mills chose to publish through nontraditional channels because she couldn't find a publisher interested in her book. The reasons other authors choose an alternative route to publication are as varied as the authors themselves. There are, however, some consistent reasons why writers choose self-publishing, either print or electronic, over traditional forms of publishing. Jacqueline Marcell tells a typical story: "After nine months of struggling to get control over my elderly, combative father and save my invalid mother, I decided to write a book about all I had been through," says Marcell. Her book, *Elder Rage (Or, Take My Father—Please!): How to Survive Caring for Aging Parents,* is a book she hopes will help others deal with similar situations.

"I bought *Writer's Market Guide* to locate all the names and phone numbers of the editors and called 130 publishers who had done books on elder care or aging," she says. Sixty editors responded to the pitch she left on their voice mails, asking her to send the manuscript, even without an agent. She was on her way!

Her enthusiasm faded, however, as she received one wonderful, glowing rejection notice after the other. Then she received an offer and, not long after, two more.

She was elated, Marcell says, until she understood exactly what the publishers had in mind for her as a first-time author: "A couple hundred dollars up-front and a very minimal royalty. Then they all wanted the rights to my next book. I said I had no idea if I was ever going to write another one, but if I did, I didn't want to be bound to them legally."

They also wanted her to sign away the movie rights to the book. "Since I come from the television business and [didn't] need any help getting it looked at there, I said no and tried to negotiate out of it," she says. "They wouldn't budge. They figured I'd cave in and settle." In addition, two of the publishers couldn't get to the book for a year, and the other was so small it only did one book a year. Marcell also had qualms regarding control, money, and the publishers' credibility. Finally, after negative feedback about the companies from two authors she'd contacted, she decided to look into self-publishing.

Marcell's concerns are all frequently voiced arguments for going the independent route. Other reasons abound. Writers who have been frustrated by not having an agent or knowing the "right" people can now publish their own books for a relatively small cost. Others who write to a niche market smaller than that which most publishers regard as potentially profitable have an option for getting their message to readers.

Even established authors—like Dorothy Jane Mills—are choosing the route of independent publishing. Published writers who can't find a publisher interested in their current project, or whose last book didn't do well, or who want a bigger piece of the financial pie than traditional publishers offer might want to look more closely at self-publishing. And of course, for authors more interested in sharing their knowledge or leaving a legacy than making a profit, self-publication is a sensible option.

Can writers make a living by self-publishing? According to Angela Adair-Hoy, owner of Booklocker.com and author of a how-to book on e-publishing as well as four other e-books, "If authors are willing to spend the time it takes to market their books, yes, they can make a living at it. I still earn more than four thousand dollars every month from sales of my five e-books."

Established independent publishers, too, are taking a look at how they might benefit from the changes taking place in the publishing industry as a result of new technologies. Says David Visser of Essence Publishing, "We've always billed ourselves as short-run book publishing specialists, and the new trend toward smaller print runs is a natural extension of our services. On-demand printing capabilities will benefit our authors. Smaller print runs allow authors to test the waters and make sure they have a product that will sell and that they actually want to be in the publishing business."

Regardless of your reasons for considering a nontraditional publishing approach, it makes sense to know as much as possible about the forms independent publishing can take before you make a decision.

➤ Booklocker.com at *http://www.booklocker.com*

> ➤ Essence Publishing at *http://www.essencegroup.com*
> ➤ Jacqueline Marcell's *Elder Rage* at *http://www.ElderRage.com*

FORMS OF ALTERNATIVE PUBLISHING

We've made an analogy in these pages between the Internet and a superhighway. We've talked about getting on the road, exploring the neighborhood, learning to read the road maps, and setting out on an information journey. We've discussed stops we might make: to take classes, to make business calls, and to simply explore the sights along the way. We've learned how to carry on conversations in transit with editors and meeting planners and other writers and speakers.

Finally, we've learned how to put ourselves on the map—to create an interesting destination of our own, get it in the guidebooks, and establish a marketing campaign to attract tourists and convince them to stay awhile and come back often.

To continue the analogy, we might think of our projects—our books, our articles, our poems and stories—as offerings at the movie house in the center of town. Or better yet, anachronistic as they might be, offerings at drive-in theaters along the highway at the edge of town.

Some of our work is in the form of short takes and some in the form of full-length feature presentations. Documentaries and dramas, cartoons and comedies, action films and art films—whatever our passion has created is showing at the local theater.

Sometimes they're big-budget films produced by one of the big studios. But more and more, our films are independently produced and distributed. This chapter is designed to help you do just that—to independently produce and distribute your own "short takes" and "feature presentations" when working with the big guys, for whatever reason, doesn't suit your needs.

Short Takes: E-mail Newsletters and E-Zines

An e-mail newsletter is just that: a newsletter that is sent directly to someone's e-mail address. An e-mag or an e-zine is an electronic publication delivered by e-mail or published online to paying or nonpaying subscribers.

The best way to learn which type of publication is right for you is to visit current e-zines and subscribe to a variety of newsletters. Zine Scene and ePublishing are two monthly columns from *Writer's Digest* magazine. Reviewing the sites featured in these columns and surfing the Web to see different examples of newsletters and e-zines will help you become familiar with what works and what doesn't.

Deciding the topic and audience of your publication should help you determine whether a newsletter or an e-zine is better for your needs. Other considerations should include how much time you have to devote to the project, publishing frequency, whether the publication will be fee-based or free, and how you will promote it.

Many terrific online resources exist to help you learn about creating, promoting, and making money from your online newsletter or e-zine. The same promotional efforts described throughout this book should be used to promote and market your e-zine or newsletter. Search engine directories, reciprocal links, e-zine database listings, judicious use of your signature file, and seeking reviews are just some of the ways to increase your circulation and awareness. I've listed resources at the end of this chapter that should answer any questions you may have.

It's impossible to say just how many newsletters and e-zines there are today or how many more there might be tomorrow. If it's a good idea, someone has probably done it. As wise Solomon said, there truly is nothing new under the sun. But if you can come up with a fresh angle or a hook to reel subscribers in, your publication can shine as a "must-subscribe."

E-mail Newsletters

People launch e-mail newsletters for many reasons: to share information, to market a book or speaking platform, to begin a business venture, or all of the above. Some newsletters are designed to point readers to the owner's Web site, where they can buy products, hear speaking clips, or see what's new on the site.

Lee Simonson, founder of Heartwarmers4u, started his newsletter out of frustration. "I was drowning in a sea of negativity," he says. "I already knew that negativity feeds on itself and can actually be contagious, so I was looking for ways to escape the onslaught and to keep myself in an optimistic frame of mind."

According to Simonson, the result of his frustration was to find a way "to spread a little optimism" in cyberspace by creating a scrapbook of stories that provided "an alternative to the depressing day-to-day news."

Simonson already worked out of his home and spent a lot of time on the Internet, so a newsletter seemed the perfect vehicle to spread cheer throughout cyberspace. "I thought, why not have a free e-mail service that people could subscribe to that sent out short stories and poems every day? Stories that would help people overcome their day-to-day stresses and help them to look at the bright side."

On May 27, 1998, Simonson sent out his first Heartwarmer to a few friends whom he took the liberty of putting on his mailing list. Within a few months, there were tens of thousands of subscribers in over a hundred countries throughout the world, most of whom had found out about his newsletter when friends or relatives had forwarded a copy to them via e-mail.

The beauty of Heartwarmers is that the original daily stories are submitted by the members themselves. It turned out that there were dozens of excellent writers who had little or no opportunities for exposure and who jumped at the chance to have their stories published online. Simonson says, "I couldn't pay them, but I could give them a big plug. Beyond that, I could give them something the mainstream publishing industry could never give them—instant gratification."

Heartwarmers4u has grown to over seventy thousand subscribers worldwide. Subscribers can now get free Web pages and can participate in the Heartwarmers message board and twenty-four-hour chat room. The community recently had its first real-life conference in Niagara Falls, and community member Azriela Jaffe has collected the best of the real-life tales from the newsletter for readers everywhere to enjoy. (*Heartwarmers: Award-Winning Stories of Love, Courage, and Inspiration* is available through my WriterSpeaker.com bookstore.)

Some people start their e-mail newsletters for fun and end up turning them into a money-making venture. One such person is Doug Helsel, whose humor newsletter is called Aiken Drum's ~ *a laugh a day*.

"I started out by making a Web page for fun," says Helsel, who featured his family, himself, and a few of his interests in the first issues. Then he heard about a Web page competition and entered it. "Drumming up votes was hard," he continues. "I found myself writing to my friends, pestering them. It dawned on me that if I had a good reason for writing them daily, then the begging for votes would not be so rude. Hence the jokes."

Helsel competed in the Site Fights contest for several months and built up a large list of friends-subscribers. "I started naming the daily mailing 'Aiken Drum's ~ *a laugh a day*' and sent jokes of all sorts." Eventually he changed his focus slightly and published only clean jokes and inspiring stories.

Helsel now has eight lists with over thirty-one thousand subscribers. "I've recently started making almost half the amount of income [from the newsletters] that I receive from my regular job. The money comes from the ads that I run for others, of course. It has been a slow process, but I have hopes of being able to use this as my sole source of income."

Helsel says his efforts are as much about the people as about the money. He's had threats from some subscribers, flowers from others; a beautiful, illustrated book of some of the inspirational pieces he's published, put together by a subscriber; and he's even visited a boy in Canada who had become a friend of his daughter's through the Internet.

One of my favorite newsletters of all times is the informative advertising-driven Tourbus, from Bob Rankin and Patrick Douglas Crispen. Tourbus is a free e-mail newsletter published twice a week and read by over ninety thousand people in 130 countries around the globe. In their newsletter, Rankin and Crispen explain Internet technology in plain English with a dash of humor. "Since 1995, Tourbus riders have been getting the scoop on search engines, spam, viruses, cookies, urban legends, and other topics," they explain. "We also give you in-depth reviews of the most useful, fun, and interesting sites on the Net." Also available to Tourbus subscribers is an additional fee-based newsletter called "Tourbus Plus!" for people who want an additional post every weekend.

I highly recommend Angela Adair-Hoy's e-book *How to Publish a Profitable E-mag!* (published by her own online company, Deep South Publishing Company) for anyone who is considering starting an e-mail newsletter or an e-mail–based electronic magazine. (Adair-Hoy draws a distinction between e-mags, which are e-mail based, and e-zines, which are usually site based.) Her book covers all the basics and much more.

Be aware that e-mail–based publications do have some drawbacks in comparison to site-based e-zines. Because they're created by cutting and pasting text files into the body of an e-mail, they can't be enhanced with graphics or sound. They also must be kept short in order for those subscribers with slow modems to be able to download them without frustration.

On the other hand, newsletters are easier to publish than e-zines and more accessible to more subscribers. Not everyone connected to the Internet has state-of-the-art equipment. Slow modems, an inability to view frames or use Java, and other technological limitations on the receiving end can frustrate your intended audience and send them back into cyberspace to find something more suited to their needs—an e-mag or e-mail newsletter, perhaps.

- ➤ Aiken Drum's at *http://www.AikensLaughs.com*
- ➤ Deep South Publishing Company at *http://www.writersmarkets.com*
- ➤ Heartwarmers4u at *http://www.heartwarmers4u.com*
- ➤ Tourbus at *http://www.tourbus.com*
- ➤ WriterSpeaker.com at *http://www.writerspeaker.com/Bookstore.html*

E-Zines

Site-based electronic magazines, rather than being mailed directly to subscribers, are at a site that readers must access through the Web. An e-zine can be a part of a larger site—your current Web site, for instance—or the sole reason for a site's existence. They differ from regular Web sites in that they are updated with greater frequency, usually on a schedule of some sort. Readers are encouraged to browse and read new content and, often, retrieve and read past issues from a site archive. Some e-zines include a search engine as the archives become larger.

E-zines range from simple sites to those with articles, advertising, sidebars, graphics, and sound and video clips. They usually include links to other pages within the site as well as to other related sites. Again, realize that as fun as it might be to create a showy e-zine filled with the latest and greatest toys, the technological complexity will limit your audience to those whose computer equipment can support the format.

David Bruce is the creator of the two-year-old e-zine HollywoodJesus.com and a companion e-mail newsletter. "HollywoodJesus.com is all about pop culture from a spiritual point of view," says Bruce.

For Bruce and his wife, Mary Nella, who both have backgrounds in media, the e-zine is a ministry. "There's no money in it. I did it as a way of communicating Jesus within the context of modern culture. It's been the best experience of my life. I'm in touch with people all over the world! [There are] lots of hurting people out there—I can't keep up with all the e-mail coming in." Bruce contends that assisting people spiritually is a "high privilege." "I live for this," he says. "The Internet is a writer's dream, unless money is the motivation—by that standard I am a failure."

However, if numbers are the standard, he's anything but a failure. HollywoodJesus.com has consistently new content, sometimes daily, and receives over 750,000 hits per month. Their little-advertised newsletter has over six thousand subscribers. Thanks in large part to his e-zine, Bruce is also a much-sought-after speaker.

➤ HollywoodJesus.com at *http://www.hollywoodjesus.com*

Feature Presentations: Self-Publishing, Print on Demand, and E-Publishing

Several options are available for authors who want to consider alternative forms of publishing: self-publishing (either in print, electronically, or both), print on demand, and e-publishing. Understanding the benefits and drawbacks of each can help you make an intelligent decision about which of these options might be a good fit for you—or whether independent publishing is a route you want to take at all.

Self-Publishing

In the past, one alternative to royalty publishing was vanity publishing. The author paid all production costs—often thousands of dollars—to a company that paid little attention to editing and spent minimal money on marketing because it had already made its profit from the author. The author, on the other hand, usually had little to show for his or her investment except the majority of the stock.

An alternative to royalty and vanity publishing, then and now, is self-publishing. Self-publishing is simply contracting with a book packager or a printing company to actually produce the book. The author retains all rights and profits to the book and is liable for any financial losses. Marketing and distribution of the finished product is also the responsibility of the author.

In the past, both vanity presses and self-publishing companies were notorious for producing inferior, unprofessional, badly written and edited books, and authors who used them were also branded as inferior and unprofessional. Consequently, many wonderful writers—and their products—were overlooked.

Fortunately, these perceptions are changing as more and more success stories emerge. In fact, the premier magazine for writing professionals, *Writer's Digest*, sponsors an annual self-publishing contest and devotes an entire issue a year to the topic.

A self-published book can also catch the attention of royalty publishers. Author Richard Paul Evans made publishing history with the unheard-of advance of $4.2 million from Simon and Schuster for his self-published book, *The Christmas Box*. His little story about a struggling young family and a wealthy widow who lost an infant daughter has since been made into a movie. Today, Evans continues to write and command large advances. I have other similar success stories posted on my WriterSpeaker.com Web site.

John Vonhof, author of *Fixing Your Feet: Prevention and Treatments for Athletes*, self-published the first edition of his book because "I knew my audience, where they were, and how to reach them," he says. "The benefits far outweighed the costs. I am now self-publishing the second edition, a much larger and improved book, for the same reasons. I have a winner. The people who are involved in sports that stress the feet call my book the 'bible' of footcare. World-class athletes have endorsed the book. Its success has helped promote me as an authority on feet, has given me credence as an author, and has helped me gain acceptance [from] national magazines as an article writer."

Vonhof, who still has his "day job," markets the book primarily through his Web site, sporting events, sport-specific magazine ads, and by writing articles for magazines and Web sites.

Self-published author Faithe Finley began her publishing company with her own devotional book, *Stay in the Breeze*, in 1998. She started The Master Design for two main reasons. "First, I wanted the control over design and layout.

Second, I knew that the traditional route [to publication] would have taken much, much longer. So time was a factor."

Finley has since expanded her concept into a publishing ministry to serve a specific niche. "Originally, I started my publishing company in order to legally sell my book in my state. However, in the process, I found others in ministry who also desired self-publishing. The end result was the founding of Master Design Ministries, a nonprofit corporation that provides affordable publishing services for religious and educational organizations. Authors who are not from a religious or educational organization can [also] be published through The Master Design. So, in essence, I have two publishing companies. The pricing structure is different, but otherwise they are the same in vision."

Finley stresses that Master Design is unique even for most self-publishing companies. "We want to produce books which make a difference, even if that difference is only in one life. We are very 'hands-on.' We make an effort to really get to know the heart of the author and to educate the author in the process of publishing. For us, the project is not just a project that needs to get done. It is an investment in the life of the author as well as all those the book will reach."

With technology becoming more affordable, increasing numbers of self-publishing companies have emerged, and local printers and book binderies also offer services for writers interested in self-publishing. *U-Publish.com* by self-publishing guru Dan Poynter and coauthor Danny O. Snow is "a revolutionary new book," say the authors, "that shows today's writers how to publish high-quality books with worldwide distribution at a small fraction of the cost of conventional methods."

According to Poynter and Snow, "*U-Publish.com* is intended to keep today's writers informed about the latest technologies for publishing books independently, and about new—and proven—methods to promote them. The combination of leading-edge technologies and proven principles for marketing and promotion offers writers the chance to compete effectively with major publishing houses," the authors contend. "For the first time in history, it is possible for writers to bring their work more directly to readers around the world."

U-Publish.com is available in print through the company's Web site and also as an electronic book at the 1stBooks Library Web site.

Before signing a contract with any self-publishing company, learn as much as possible about the company and about the industry to make sure you are working with someone reputable. Tips for choosing a company through which to self-publish, either in print or electronically, are featured at the end of this chapter along with other alternative publishing resources.

➤ 1stBooks Library at *http://www.1stbooks.com*

➤ Fixing Your Feet (Vonhof) at *http://www.footworkpub.com*

➤ The Master Design at *http://www.masterdesign.org*

➤ U-Publish.com at *http://www.u-publish.com*

➤ WriterSpeaker.com at *http://www.writerspeaker.com/success.html*

Print on Demand

A second alternative to traditional publishers for book-length manuscripts is a print-on-demand publisher. As the name suggests, on-demand printing allows books to be stored electronically and printed, one at a time, after an order has been placed by wholesalers, booksellers, librarians, and the general public.

Although using this type of service means you never have the expense of printing and warehousing thousands of books at once, print on demand is typically a more expensive publishing option per book than other forms of self-publishing. On the other hand, authors can test the waters with only a minor up-front investment.

Print on demand is also a great option for keeping a book in print, even when sales are few and far between. Instead of reprinting hundreds or thousands of books, print on demand allows an author or publisher to print books only as needed. In fact, on-demand printing could conceivably mean that a book never goes out of print. This is a good news/bad news scenario, depending on who holds the rights to the book. If you as the author own the rights, you can keep earning money on a book in perpetuity. If a publisher owns the rights to your book, however, and has stopped printing and marketing it, because the possibility to print and sell just one more copy always exists, the book is never officially "out of print." In the future, as print on demand becomes more common, contracts with publishers may have to specify how and when the rights to a book will revert to the author.

Using the latest technology and their considerable marketing muscle,

Writer's Digest, iUniverse, and the Writer's Club have joined forces to offer publishing options for authors wanting to see their words in print.

Author T. Suzanne Eller has a print-on-demand novel, *Blood of the Fathers*, currently available through iUniverse. *Blood of the Fathers* is a print-on-demand book available at BarnesandNoble.com and Amazon.com as well as through Barnes and Noble stores.

Eller says her decision to go through iUniverse was "borne out of prayer." "I believe in this book," she says, "and I know that God is in it. I kept getting rejection slips that read, 'This is definitely worth publishing; however, our fiction line is full until 2001.' "

Eller had trouble selling this particular book for other reasons. "I met a wall because those who did ask for the manuscript told me they loved the writing and the story, but that some of my scenes were too 'real' for the Christian fiction world. [My protagonist] Jacob is lost and he finds solace in a world of drugs and darkness. [My novel] portrays sin and the hold of sin. I couldn't change that because the heart of the story is the 'lostness' of sin and the mercy of a Savior who follows you even into the darkness."

For an author like Eller, who believes passionately in her work, the iUniverse publishing alternatives make a dream come true. There are different options with iUniverse, including Writers Club Press, Writer's Showcase by *Writer's Digest*, People's Press, Back in Print, and toExcel Press. The iUniverse Web site has a quick comparison chart to help authors decide which is the best for them.

"I went through an iUniverse program called Writer's Showcase, by *Writer's Digest*," explains Eller. "One writer asked me why I paid more when I could have the same services at iUniverse for less by going through one of their other programs. *Writer's Digest* is a name I respect, and they were the only [iUniverse option] that had a manuscript committee that qualified manuscripts. I didn't want it out there unless it passed the test of this committee and the scrutiny of a company that has mentored writers for longer than I've been alive."

Print on demand is also a perfect fit for those involved in electronic publishing. One argument against e-publishing is that many customers don't want to read a book on their computer monitors or to print out a manuscript on their own printer. In addition to offering books in an electronic format, with a print-on-demand option, e-publishers can print out individual copies of electronically archived manuscripts. Customers get what most of them want—a "real" book—while publishers are able to maintain the low costs of electronic publishing. Since the book does not have to be physically printed until it is ordered, the publisher has no inventory investment or warehousing costs. The expense of printing isn't incurred until the book is actually sold.

Lightning Source, a subsidiary of Ingram Book Group, is one of the largest and best-funded print-on-demand publishers. However, a quick look at the results of a search-engine query for "print on demand" will give other worldwide options. Before signing a contract with any print-on-demand publisher, do your research. Check out the quality of different companies' work, the strength of their distribution system, and, of course, the cost for their services.

Print-on-demand books are now produced not only by print-on-demand publishers but by a few traditional publishers as well. In fact, print on demand enables traditional publishers to release or rerelease titles at virtually no cost. Customers can order these books through bookstores and other outlets, including online bookstores, the Web sites of various print-on-demand companies, and individual Web sites—even your own.

➤ iUniverse at *http://www.iuniverse.com/publish/pubProgramCompareChart. html*

➤ Lightning Source at *http://www.lightningsource.com*

➤ T. Suzanne Eller at *http://www.intellex.com/~eller/tseller.html*

E-Publishing

In an interview with *Time* magazine (March 20, 2000), Stephen King had this to say about electronic publishing: "There's this space on the Internet—this infinite space—for people to publish, for the midlist to be re-created, for people who have been disenfranchised by the shrinking lists of publishers to actually do their stuff."

The reception of King's e-book *Riding the Bullet* (it sold 500,000 copies in forty-eight hours) has given sudden respectability to e-publishing. People who had never heard of or accepted the value of electronic publishing now think it's a great idea.

What exactly is an e-book? Generally defined, it's any book in any genre produced in a format that can be read on a computer or other electronic device. It might come on a disk for Mac or PC, on a CD-ROM, or exist as an electronic file to be downloaded to an e-book reader. E-books can also be sent and received via e-mail or downloaded by the reader from a Web site.

There are several ways to publish an electronic book. The easiest, but least attractive, is to distribute a book by cutting and pasting the text into an e-mail message and sending it on request. Publishers can also set up a system whereby all requests are answered automatically through an autoresponder. (An e-mail autoresponder automatically reads the e-mail address of the person who sent the message and then automatically e-mails him or her your text message.) While e-mail is an easy way to send a book, the method has some obvious disadvantages. One, downloading large e-mail messages can take time and may irritate some people, and two, a book sent by e-mail loses its original formatting.

Another way to publish a book electronically is through a series of Web pages produced in HTML or with the use of a good WYSIWYG editor. Books may also be published online as plain text files, although plain text is less attractive and doesn't allow the use of graphics, hyperlinks, etc. Like books sent via e-mail, books produced as Web pages require the reader to view the screen and/or print a hard copy.

A third option, also requiring the reader to view the screen or print the pages, is to produce the book using PDF (Portable Document Format). PDF is a special file format created by Adobe Systems, Inc. Documents in this format can be distributed electronically across the Web and on a variety of platforms, all the while retaining their original look. Whether readers are using a PC or a Mac, as long as they have a copy of Adobe Acrobat Reader installed on their computer, they can see the text, layout, and graphics just as you created them. The process involves uploading PDF files to a Web site and sending readers a link to the site, where they have access to download your book.

A fourth e-publishing option is to produce a book for use with an electronic book reader. These readers are about the size of a traditional print book and weigh a couple of pounds. They are powered by batteries and have a life of several hours. Readers display a digital version of your book on a flat screen or pair of screens and users can "turn" pages electronically, bookmark passages, and even make notes as they read. Publishers or publisher-authors submit their books, usually as PDF files, to an e-book distribution company such as Every-Book, Inc., NuvoMedia, Inc., or SoftBook Press, Inc. The company adds each new file to their database of titles, all of which are available for download by their customers.

The readers are portable and hold multiple books. One nice feature is that they are usually backlighted to allow reading even in the dark. However, they are heavier than a single book, and they have still not come down to an afford-able price for most consumers. Another drawback to working with an e-book distribution company is that more people are involved in making decisions about your book—and in sharing the profits. Authors lose some control over their product and usually earn lower royalties than they might with other forms of electronic publishing.

E-publishing as a whole offers some distinct advantages to authors, includ-ing shorter response times from publishers, more control over the content and cover design, faster publication, and higher royalties than traditional publishers pay. E-books also tend to stay in print longer than traditional books and don't require warehousing.

But e-publishing isn't for everyone. Security issues deter some authors from considering it as an option; it's relatively simple to make and distribute pirated copies of an e-book. Another disadvantage to publishing electronically is that most e-book publishers do not pay an advance to authors and may even charge an up-front fee. Royalty arrangements differ from publisher to pub-lisher too. Angela Adair-Hoy, e-publisher and owner of Booklocker.com, offers no advances but also charges no fees and gives authors a generous 70 percent royalty. Do your research, and regardless of whom you choose to e-publish your book, make sure to confirm the royalty arrangement before signing any contract.

Although Dorothy Jane Mills is pleased with her e-publishing experience and would definitely publish electronically again, she acknowledges it isn't easy. Perhaps the most frustrating aspect of her experience so far is trying to get reviews for her novel. "I've got great pre-publication endorsements and great reader comments [for *The Sceptre*]," she says, "but few reviews, despite hard promotional work."

James A. Cox, editor-in-chief for Midwest Book Review and an online book review magazine called Internet Bookwatch, is, however, encouraging about the future of reviews for e-books. Although it's true that very few publications are currently willing to review e-books, he says, that's bound to change soon. In December 1999 Internet Bookwatch ran its first column dedicated to reviews of e-books. "I had one reviewer," he says, "and she covered three e-books on the equivalent of one page. Three months later, an issue featured nine e-book reviews, and I have a roster of five volunteer reviewers for e-books."

Another problem Mills has encountered trying to promote her book is that many bookstores are prohibited contractually from carrying any books other than those of the big publishers. "Some bookstore managers who want to give me a book signing can't do it for that reason," Mills says.

A big problem the e-publishing industry is facing is a lack of quality control. The fact that anyone who decides to be an e-publisher *can* be one is not necessarily a good thing. Without controls, e-publishers may end up with the same reputation that vanity publishers have: that they will print anything for a profit, whether or not it's really publishable.

Some e-publishers are already addressing this problem. Adair-Hoy's Booklocker.com carries more than four hundred e-books as of this writing. "Contrary to most e-publishing sites," she says, "Booklocker.com has a strict screening policy in place to ensure that we carry only quality works of literature." The company publishes all genres, but their best-selling books at this time are nonfiction how-to books.

Adair-Hoy says that though there might be an online market for every book written, Booklocker isn't it. "We were offered *Satan's Bible* and turned that one down without a second thought," she says. "We also choose not to publish adult material; we refer authors elsewhere."

Like books produced by traditional methods, e-books require a marketing effort. Since e-book readers are likely to be Internet savvy and spend time surfing the Web and frequenting chat and forum sites, the online marketing suggestions discussed throughout this book work especially well for e-books. Some e-publishers also provide their authors with marketing tips.

All new Booklocker.com authors, for instance, receive a free copy of Adair-Hoy's Online Book Promotion E-kit. "In addition," she says, "we distribute a weekly e-magazine via e-mail, highlighting new additions [to our line], best-sellers, and free e-book excerpts. We also provide a book page for each book [we have] for sale on Booklocker."

Mayapriya Long of Bookwrights, a book-jacket design and production company, reminds publishers and publisher-authors that even books produced electronically need appealing covers. "As the Internet segment of bookselling grows," she says, "and with the widespread use of the PDF format, competition will require the same attention to detail by e-book publishers as is required in traditional publishing. I am already being called upon by savvy e-book authors and publishers to design e-book covers and attractive page-top graphics. I look for this segment of my business to grow drastically in the next few years." Long concludes, "A poorly designed book cover is like a plaid sports jacket at a black-tie dinner—it speaks volumes about you in a significant instant."

Finding the right person to design a book cover or jacket is important to the overall success of the publishing project. In addition to checking the yellow pages and search engines for designers, try asking other authors from mailing lists and chat rooms for referrals. One question to a small publisher's mailing list netted me several suggestions from various list members, as well as an e-mail from Dan Poynter with his recommended book writing and publishing suppliers (see the following list).

By far the biggest disadvantage of publishing electronically is the small volume of sales compared to what you might get through traditional publishing. Some of that is due to poor marketing, but distribution is also a factor. Many online bookstores sell e-books, but traditional bookstores have not yet fully embraced the idea.

High e-book prices may be one reason consumers have not gone out of their way to find and purchase e-books. Even those books comparable to mass-market hard-copy books seem high to some, given the need to print it on their own paper or purchase an electronic reader to make it portable.

Probably the main reason consumers haven't embraced e-books is that they don't yet know much about them. But as established houses, as well as new-comers, turn to e-publishing to complement traditional methods of publication, more and more readers are becoming aware of the option. It can't be long before e-books are a simple addition to the variety of formats—hardback, trade paper, mass market, audio—in which books already come.

For anyone thinking of e-publishing, both About.com and Suite 101.com have several helpful articles on the subject, as well as links to relevant Web sites. If the idea appeals to you, pursue it! The fact of the matter is, the future is here —and we are it.

- ➤ Adobe Acrobat Reader at *http://www.adobe.com/products/acrobat/readstep.html*
- ➤ Aeonix Publishing Group at *http://www.aeonix.com*
- ➤ The Art Core at *http://www.theartcore.com*
- ➤ Booklocker.com at *http://www.booklocker.com*
- ➤ Bookwrights at *http://www.bookwrights.com*
- ➤ Cover Art by P3 at *http://hometown.aol.com/PubPromos/Art.html*
- ➤ Desktop Miracles, Inc. at *http://www.desktopmiracles.com*
- ➤ EveryBook, Inc. at *http://www.everybook.net*
- ➤ Internet Bookwatch at *http://www.execpc.com/~mbr/bookwatch/ibw*
- ➤ Knockout Books at *http://www.knockoutbooks.com*
- ➤ Midwest Book Review at *http://www.execpc.com/~mbr/bookwatch/mbr*
- ➤ NuvoMedia, Inc. at *http://www.rocket-eBook.com*
- ➤ Para Publishing Dan Poynter at *http://parapublishing.com/supplier.cfm*
- ➤ SoftBook Press, Inc. at *http://www.softbook.com*
- ➤ TLC Graphics at *http://www.tlcgraphics.com*

INDEPENDENT PUBLISHING: HERE TO STAY

Angela Adair-Hoy and M. J. Rose are convinced that e-books are here to stay. One of their own e-books, *The Secrets of Our Success—How to Publish and Promote Online,* has caught the eye of more than just the Internet community.

"In an auction, St. Martin's Press bested HarperCollins and bought the rights," says Rose. "It is the first book about e-publishing to be purchased by a major New York house. They see making it the 'bible of e-publishing,' updating it, and keeping it in print and marketing it. It will be available in print and e-format."

Fabjob.com is a new online publisher with a specific niche—electronic career guides. They publish a new guide every month with the goal of eventually having two hundred guides for perceived fabulous jobs such as actor, baseball player, cartoonist, event planner, massage therapist, speaker, and more.

Fabjob.com is currently looking for writers with hands-on experience to become Fabjob authors, complete with a signing bonus and up to 50 percent royalties. Authors Jeannie Harmon and Sheila Seifert coauthored *Become a Children's Book Author*. "I have really enjoyed working with the staff at Fabjob," says Harmon. "As a full-time editor by profession, I usually spend my days working on things that others have written. When Sheila contacted me about doing a book for Fabjob, it sounded like a challenge I was ready to take."

"Following their concise guidelines made our job easier," she explains. "We wrote from our areas of expertise and then combined the copy. To give our book continuity, we sat down and read every line out loud and made corrections as needed. It was a fulfilling and rewarding experience to complete our book, and since e-books are growing in popularity, it was fun being a part of the new technology. We hope that *Become a Children's Book Author* will help all of those onliners who are aspiring to write good books for kids."

Editor and reviewer James Cox believes electronic books will eventually take over the paper market. "It will take another generation of readers to make it so," he says, adding that the children who are coming of age in an environment of rapidly evolving technology will be "as comfortable with [e-books] as you and I are with the telephones, televisions, and computer stations of today."

John Kremer, author of *1001 Ways to Market Your Books* and editor of the popular *Book Marketing Update* newsletter, is also convinced that e-publishing is here to stay. "Most self-publishing," he asserts, "will be done via e-books and on-demand publishing. You will see few self-publishers printing books before they've established a market via e-books and on-demand. These technologies allow anyone to test the market for their books, poems, music, whatever—and do it in a cost-effective way that reaches an international audience."

Kremer intends to self-publish a number of books via "e/o" publishing (his shorthand term for e-books and on-demand publishing). "These are books that I would not have attempted to print," he says, "because I don't know how good the market will be. But I can easily set them up via e/o publishing and let the market tell me how many people are interested.

"I believe we'll see some incredibly adventurous novels and nonfiction formats arise out of this new technology," Kremer adds. "It's an exciting time. And a wide-open opportunity for authors." He believes there will be a price to pay, however: the publication of "a lot of junk…things that no one will read or want to read. But, in short time, we'll develop some way to sift out the good stuff from the bad stuff, a way that doesn't rely on the opinions of a few editors in New York, but instead relies on the money votes of people around the world."

More than simply putting out a book, independent publishing—either self-, on-demand, or electronic—means a writer is actually starting and operating his or her own business. It can be an incredibly rewarding experience personally, professionally, and financially. It can also be time-consuming and financially risky. Like any owner of a start-up company, author-publishers should develop a business plan and seek appropriate state, local, and federal tax and legal advice.

Author-publishers also need to be focused, have a passion about their subject, be good organizers—and remember that the real work begins after the finished book is off the press. Whatever you decide, make sure that you understand the 80/20 rule: Writing takes only 20 percent of your effort, marketing and promotion the other 80 percent.

Is Independent Publishing for Me?

Addressing the following list of questions can help you decide if independent publishing, whether in print or electronically, is a route you want to take to make your manuscript available to readers:
- *What is my motivation and purpose for publishing my book?*
- *Is my book written for a specific market niche or group of people?*
- *Do I have a way to sell books direct?*
- *Who will buy this book?*
- *Is it my intention to make money on this book or to simply get my work published?*
- *Have I:*
  …thought through marketing from the very beginning?
  …studied the competition?

> *...written something other people want to read?*
> *...written where there is a void in the market?*
> *...procured professional editing?*
> *...created a memorable title?*
> *...created a fabulous cover?*
> *...given attention to the inside pages? (Are they clean and easy to read?)*
> *...included the ISBN, LCCN, EAN Bookland scanning symbol, etc.?*

- *Am I willing to publicize and promote my book?*

Resources for Independent Publishing

The following Web sites and print resources will help you get started on your independent publishing venture. The more you know before you go in, the more you will enjoy the experience—and the more you enjoy the experience, the better chance you'll have of making it successful.

Books on Demand
- Book Marketing Update (list) at *http://www.bookmarket.com/ondemand.html*
- iUniverse at *http://www.iuniverse.com*
- Lightning Printing at *http://www.lightningprinting.com*
- Omni PublishXpress at *http://www.publishxpress.com/index.html*
- Unlimited Publishing Services at *http://www.unlimitedpublishing.com*

Books for the Independent Publisher*
- *1001 Ways to Market Your Books* at *http://www.bookmarket.com/1001index.html*
- *The Complete Guide to Self-Publishing* at *http://www.About-Books.com*
- *Grassroots Marketing: Getting Noticed in a Noisy World* at *http://www.frugalfun.com*
- *Marketing Without Megabucks* at *http://www.frugalfun.com*
- *The Prepublishing Handbook* at *http://hometown.aol.com/catspawpre/ToolShed.html*

* All books may be ordered through http://www.writerspeaker.com/Bookstore.html

➤ *The Self-Publishing Manual* at *http://www.parapublishing.com*

➤ *Smart Self-Publishing* at *http://www.tabbyhouse.com/ssp.htm*

Cover and Jacket Design

➤ Adobe Acrobat Reader at *http://www.adobe.com/products/acrobat/readstep.html*

➤ Aeonix Publishing Group at *http://www.aeonix.com*

➤ The Art Core at *http://www.theartcore.com*

➤ Booklocker.com at *http://www.booklocker.com*

➤ Bookwrights at *http://www.bookwrights.com*

➤ Cover Art by P3 at *http://hometown.aol.com/PubPromos/Art.html*

➤ Desktop Miracles, Inc. at *http://www.desktopmiracles.com*

➤ EveryBook, Inc. at *http://www.everybook.net*

➤ Internet Bookwatch at *http://www.execpc.com/~mbr/bookwatch/ibw*

➤ Knockout Books at *http://www.knockoutbooks.com*

➤ Midwest Book Review at *http://www.execpc.com/~mbr/bookwatch/mbr*

➤ NuvoMedia, Inc. at *http://www.rocket-eBook.com*

➤ Para Publishing–Dan Poynter at *http://parapublishing.com/supplier.cfm*

➤ SoftBook Press, Inc. at *http://www.softbook.com*

➤ TLC Graphics at *http://www.tlcgraphics.com*

E-book Publishers

➤ 1stBooks.com at *http://www.1stbooks.com*

➤ Awe Struck Books at *http://www.awe-struck.net*

➤ Bibliomania-free e-books (classics) at *http://www.bibliomania.com/Fiction*

➤ Booklocker.com at *http://www.booklocker.com*

➤ BookZone at *http://www.bookzone.com*

➤ Boson Books at *http://www.cmonline.com*

➤ Domhan Books at *http://www.domhanbooks.com*

➤ Dreams Unlimited at *http://www.dreams-unlimited.com*

➤ E-books connections at *http://www.ebookconnections.com*

➤ Fatbrain.com at *http://www.fatbrain.com*

➤ The Fiction Works at *http://www.fictionworks.com*

➤ Hard Shell Word Factory at *http://www.hardshell.com*

➤ Hyperbooks at *http://www.hardshell.com*

➤ New Concepts at *http://www.newconceptspublishing.com*

➤ Peanut Press at *http://www.peanutpress.com*

➤ Project Gutenberg e-Texts at *http://promo.net/pg/list.html*

➤ Sugarbakers at *http://www.juliasugarbaker.com*

➤ Xlibris Publishing at *http://www.Xlibris.com*

E-book Readers

➤ EveryBook, Inc. at *http://www.everybook.net*

➤ Librius at *http://www.librius.com*

➤ NuvoMedia, Inc at *http://www.rocket-eBook.com*

➤ SoftBook Press, Inc. at *http://www.softbook.com*

E-book Review Sites

➤ eBookAd at *http://www.eBookAd.com*

➤ eBook Connections at *http://www.ebookconnections.com*

➤ January Magazine at *http://www.JanuaryMagazine.com*

➤ Midwest Book Review at *http://www.execpc.com/~mbr/bookwatch*

E-zine and Newsletter Information and Tips

➤ Association of Electronic Publishers at *http://www.welcome.to/AEP*

➤ The Book of Zines at *http://www.zinebook.com/roll.html*

➤ Contentious E-Zine Article at *http://www.contentious.com/articles/ 1-10/editorial1-10.html*

➤ Electronically Published Internet Connection (EPCIC) at *http://www.eclectics.com/epic*

➤ Inkspot at *http://www.inkspot.com/craft/newsletterinfo.html*

➤ Newsletter Access Directory at *http://www.newsletteraccess.com*

➤ VirtualPROMOTE at *http://www.virtualpromote.com*

E-zine Databases

➤ E-zine Master Index at *http://www.site-city.com/members/ e-zine-master*

➤ E-zine Search (over 3,000 e-zines) at *http://www.homeincome.com/search-it/ezine/index.html*

➤ New E-zine Directory at *http://foxcities.com/ims/ezine.htm*

E-zine Links

➤ The E-text Archives at *http://dmoz.org/Arts/Literature/Electronic_Text_Archives*

➤ John Labovitz's E-zine List at *http://www.etext.org/zines*

Magazines for the Independent Publisher

➤ Contentious at *http://www.contentious.com*

➤ ForeWord Magazine at *http://www.forewordmagazine.com*

➤ Self-Publishing Magazine at *http://www.self-publishing.com/index.html*

Miscellaneous Resources

➤ Copyright Information and Forms at *http://lcweb.loc.gov/copyright*

➤ ISBN numbers and ABI forms at *http://www.bowker.com*

➤ Printing Industry Exchange at *http://www.printindustry.com*

Newsletter and Mailing List Hosting Services

➤ E-Groups at *http://www.egroups.com*

➤ ListBot at *http://www.listbot.com*

➤ OakNet Publishing at *http://Oaknetpub.com*

➤ ONEList at *http:// www.egroups.com*

PDF Converters and Readers

➤ Adobe Acrobat at *http://www.adobe.com*

➤ PrintToPDF (Shareware, Mac) at *http://www.jwwalker.com*

Self-Publishing Companies

➤ ACW at *http://www.acwpress.com*

➤ Essence Publishing at *http://www.essencegroup.com*

➤ Morris at *http://www.morrispublishing.com*

➤ Wine Press at *http://www.winepresspub.com*

Wholesalers, Distributors, and Fulfillment Houses

- ➤ Baker & Taylor at *http://www.baker-taylor.com*
- ➤ Book Clearing House at *http://www.bookch.com*
- ➤ Book World at *http://www.bookworld.com*
- ➤ Bookpeople at *http://www.bponline.com*
- ➤ Ingram Book Company at *http://www.ingrambook.com*
- ➤ National Book Network at *http://www.nbnbooks.com*
- ➤ Partners Book Distributing at *http://bookexpo.reedexpo.com*
- ➤ Quality Books at *http://www.quality-books.com*
- ➤ Small Press Distribution at *http://www.spdbooks.org*

A FINAL WORD

Book publishing is clearly changing. Thanks in large part to the Internet, writers and speakers who have something to say can break into print faster, more easily, and less expensively than ever before. New techniques and technology are making everyone from royalty publishers to individual authors think differently about writing, producing, selling, and promoting books.

Back at the beginning of *this* book, I suggested you might want to buckle your seat belt to get ready for an amazing ride.

Well, keep it buckled.

The ride is getting more amazing all the time.

Living Links

The resources listed here are also part of the *WriterSpeaker.com* Web site. The ISBN number of this book acts as your password to enter the site, and anyone who registers will receive quarterly updates. All links are checked regularly, dead Web sites are eliminated, and each new Web site comes with a brief description.

➤ WriterSpeaker.com Living Links at *http://www.writerspeaker.com/ LL.html*

Agents

➤ Agent Research and Evaluation at *http://www.agentresearch.com*

➤ The Association of Authors' Representatives, Inc. (AAR) at *http://www. publishersweekly.com/AAR/Topics.html*

➤ Authorlink! (database) at *http://www.authorlink*

➤ Inkspot at *http://www.inkspot.com/market/agents.html*

➤ LiteraryAgent.com at *http://www.literaryagent.com/index.htm*

➤ Preditors & Editors at *http://www.sfwa.org/prededitors/peala.htm*

➤ Writers.net at *http://www.writers.net/agents.html*

➤ Writing.org at *http://www.writing.org/html/a_agents.htm*

Author Web-Site Hosts

➤ African American Authors on Tour at *http://authorsontour.com*

➤ Autographed By Author at *http://AutographedByAuthor.com*

➤ BookBrowser's Authors Online at *http://www.bookbrowser.com/Authors/ index.html*

➤ BookZone's Author Indexes at *http://www.bookzone.com*

➤ First Edition at *http://www.ecpa.org/FE/index.html*

➤ GoodStory at *http://www.goodstory.com*

➤ The Healing Place, CWGBookstore at *http://users.1st.net/imsaved/BRMAIN.html*

➤ Homeschoolzone's Meet the Author at *http://www.homeschoolzone.com/amazon/meettheauthor.htm*

➤ Light Communications, Inc. at *http://www.light-communications.com*

➤ Mystery Writers of America at *http://www.mysterynet.com/mwa*

➤ NightSky Publishing at *http://www.nightskypublishing.com*

➤ Para Publishing–Dan Poynter at *http://www.parapub.com*

➤ Romance Writers of America at *http://www.rwanational.com*

➤ Science Fiction Writers of America at *http://www.sfwa.org/site_index.htp*

➤ TTC Publishing at *http://www.toupin.com*

➤ The Writer's Edge at *http://members.xoom.com/WRITERSEDGE*

Books on Demand

➤ Book Marketing Update (list) at *http://www.bookmarket.com/ondemand.html*

➤ iUniverse at *http://www.iuniverse.com*

➤ Lightning Source at *http://www.lightningsource.com*

➤ Omni PublishXpress at *http://www.publishxpress.com/index.html*

➤ Unlimited Publishing Services at *http://www.unlimitedpublishing.com*

Bookstores Online

➤ 1Bookstreet.com at *http://www.lbookstreet.com*

➤ Amazon.com at *http://www.amazon.com*

➤ Barnes and Noble at *http://www.barnesandnoble.com*

➤ Books-A-Million at *http://www.booksamillion.com*

➤ Borders at *http://www.borders.com*

➤ Chapters at *http://www.chapters.ca*

➤ Christian Superstore at *http://www.christianbooks.com*

➤ Indigo at *http://www.indigo.ca*

➤ WordsWorth at *http://www.wordsworth.com*

Chat Resources

- AOL Instant Messenger at *http://www.aol.com/aim*
- Beseen's The Chat Zone at *http://www.beseen.com/chat/topics.html*
- Excite at *http://www.excite.com/communities/pal/home*
- ICQ ("I seek you") at *http://www.icq.com*
- Ircle at *http://www.ircle.com*
- LookSmart at *http://looksmart.yack.com/categories/Books*
- mIRC at *http://www.mirc.com*
- Pueblo at *http://www.chaco.com/pueblo*
- Savitar at *http://www.heynow.com/Savitar*
- Yahoo! at *http://chat.yahoo.com*

Cliche and Quote Sites

- Cliché Finder at *http://www.westegg.com/cliche*
- Link Bank's Quotation Links at *http://www.linkbank.net/get_links/ default/quotes/8*
- The Quotations Archive at *http://www.aphids.com/quotes/index.shtml*
- The Quotations Page at *http://www.starlingtech.com/quotes*
- Quoteland at *http://www.quoteland.com*
- Quotez at *http://business.virgin.net/mark.fryer/intro.html*

Conferences

- American Christian Writers (ACW) at *http://www.ecpa.org/acw/ schedule.html*
- Authorlink! at *http://www.authorlink.com/confren.html*
- Inkspot at *http://www.inkspot.com/tk/network/conf.html*
- IRE at *http://www.ire.org/training*
- Sally Stuart's Christian Writers' Market Guide at *http://www. stuartmarket.com*
- Screenwriters Online Guide to Writers' Conference at *http://www. screenwriter.com/insider/WritersCalendar.html*

➤ Shaw Guides at *http://www.shawguides.com/writing*
➤ Writers' Conferences and Festivals at *http://www.gmu.edu/departments/awp/wcf/wcfmembers.html*
➤ Writers Information Network at *http://www.bluejaypub.com/win/conferences.htm*
➤ YWAM Woodcrest at *http://www.ywamwoodcrest.com*

Contracts

➤ The American Society of Journalists and Authors at *http://www.asja.org/resource.htm*
➤ The Freelance Editorial Association's Code of Fair Practice at *http://www.tiac.net/users/freelanc/Code.html*
➤ Ivan Hoffman, J.D. at *http://home.earthlink.net/~ivanlove/points.html*
➤ The National Writers Union at *http://www.nwu.org/grv/grvcont.htm*
➤ The Publishing Law Center at *http://www.publaw.com*
➤ Science Fiction Writers of America at *http://www.sfwa.org/contracts/index.htm*
➤ Tom Brosnahan at *http://www.infoexchange.com/Author%20Table%20Pages/Contracts.html*
➤ The Writers Union of Canada at *http://www.writersunion.ca*

Copyright

➤ Books A to Z Copyright Basics at *http://www.booksatoz.com/copyrigh/whatis.htm*
➤ Copyright Clearance Center at *http://www.copyright.com*
➤ The Copyright Law site at *http://www.duq.edu/Technology/copy/copylaw1.html*
➤ Intellectual Property Law at *http://www.intelproplaw.com*
➤ Ivan Hoffman, J.D. at *http://www.ivanhoffman.com*
➤ National Fraud Consumer's League's National Fraud Information Center & Internet Fraud Watch at *http://www.fraud.org/welcome.htm*

- So You Want to Write a Book at *http://www.oreilly.com/oreilly/author/permission*
- Stanford University Libraries Council on Library Resources and Find-Law Internet Legal Resources at *http://fairuse.stanford.edu*
- Ten Big Myths About Copyright Explained at *http://www.templetons.com/brad/copymyths.html*
- U.S. Copyright Office at *http://lcweb.loc.gov/copyright*
- U.S. Federal Trade Commission at *http://www.ftc.gov*
- Writers Write at *http://www.writerswrite.com/journal/dec97/cew3.htm*

Copyright Music

- The American Society of Composers, Authors and Publishers (ASCAP) at *http://www.ascap.com/ascap.html*
- Christian Copyright Licensing Information (CCLI) at *http://www.ccli.com*
- Harry Fox Agency (HFA) at *http://www.nmpa.org/hfa.html*
- Sesac, Inc. at *http://www.sesac.com*

Cover and Jacket Design

- Bookwrights at *http://www.bookwrights.com*

Critique Groups

- Amy Foundation at *http://www.amyfound.org/onlinecwg.html*
- Coffee House for Writers at *http://members.tripod.com/coffeehouse4writers/groups.html*
- Critters Workshop at *http://brain-of-pooh.tech-soft.com/users/critters*
- Fictech for Novelists' Inner Circle Writers Club at *http://www.geocities.com/SoHo/Lofts/1498/circlefaq.htm*
- Internet Writers Fantasy List at *http://www.fantasytoday.com*
- IRC #Undernet Writers Site at *http://www.getset.com/writers*
- Kingdom Writers at *http://www.angelfire.com/ks/kingwrit*
- Local Writers Workshop at *http://members.tripod.com/~lww_2*

- ➤ Misc.Writing Mailing Lists at *http://www.scalar.com/mw/pages/mwmlist. shtml*
- ➤ Preditors & Editors at *http://www.sfwa.org/prededitors/pubwork.htm*
- ➤ The Six Foot Ferret Writers' Group at *http://pages.cthome.net/6ft_ferrets/ index.html*
- ➤ Write Links at *http://www.writelinks.com/critgroup/critgroupa.htm*
- ➤ The Writers Write at *http://www.writerswrite.com/groups.htm*
- ➤ Young Writer's Clubhouse at *http://www.realkids.com/critique.htm*

Dictionaries

- ➤ Encyberpedia at *http://encyberpedia.com/glossary.htm*
- ➤ OneLook Dictionaries at *http://www.onelook.com*
- ➤ The Roget's Thesaurus at *http://humanities.uchicago.edu/forms_unrest/ ROGET.html*
- ➤ Web of Online Dictionaries at *http://www.facstaff.bucknell.edu/ rbeard/diction.html*
- ➤ WWWebster Dictionary at *http://www.m-w.com/netdict.htm*

Directories

- ➤ 555-1212.com at *http://www.555-1212.com*
- ➤ AT&T Internet Directory at *http://www.att.com/directory/internet.html*
- ➤ BigFoot at *http://www.bigfoot.com*
- ➤ Internet Address Finder at *http://www.iaf.net*
- ➤ Telephone Directories on the Web at *http://www.teldir.com/eng*
- ➤ World Email Directory at *http://www.worldemail.com*

Electronic Book Resources

E-book publishers

- ➤ 1stBooks.com at *http://www.1stbooks.com*
- ➤ Awe Struck Books at *http://www.awe-struck.net*
- ➤ Bibliomania-free e-books (classics) at *http://www.bibliomania.com/Fiction*

- Booklocker.com at *http://www.booklocker.com*
- BookZone at *http://www.bookzone.com*
- Boson Books at *http://www.cmonline.com*
- Domhan Books at *http://www.domhanbooks.com*
- Dreams Unlimited at *http://www.dreams-unlimited.com*
- E-books connections at *http://www.ebookconnections.com*
- Eclectics at *http://www.eclectics.com*
- Fatbrain.com at *http://www.fatbrain.com*
- The Fiction Works at *http://www.fictionworks.com*
- Hard Shell Word Factory at *http://www.hardshell.com*
- Hyperbooks at *http://www.hardshell.com*
- New Concepts at *http://www.newconceptspublishing.com*
- Peanut Press at *http://www.peanutpress.com*
- Project Gutenberg e-Texts at *http://promo.net/pg/list.html*
- Sugarbakers at *http://www.juliasugarbaker.com*
- Xlibris Publishing at *http://www.Xlibris.com*

E-book Readers

- EveryBook, Inc. at *http://www.everybook.net*
- Librius at *http://www.librius.com*
- NuvoMedia, Inc at *http://www.rocket-eBook.com*
- SoftBook Press, Inc. at *http://www.softbook.com*

E-book Review Sites

- eBookAd at *http://www.eBookAd.com*
- eBook Connections at *http://www.ebookconnections.com*
- January Magazine at *http://www.JanuaryMagazine.com*
- Midwest Book Review at *http://www.execpc.com/~mbr/bookwatch*

Electronic Magazines and Newsletter Resources

E-zine and Newsletter Information and Tips

- Association of Electronic Publishers at *http://www.welcome.to/AEP*
- The Book of Zines at *http://www.zinebook.com/roll.html*

➤ Content Spotlight: The Content Exchange Newsletter at *http://www.content-exchange.com/cx/html/newsletter*

➤ Contentious E-Zine Article at *http://www.contentious.com/articles/1-10/editorial1-10.html*

➤ Electronically Published Internet Connection (EPCIC) at *http://www.eclectics.com/epic*

➤ Inkspot at *http://www.inkspot.com/craft/newsletterinfo.html*

➤ Newsletter Access Directory at *http://www.newsletteraccess.com*

➤ VirtualPROMOTE at *http://www.virtualpromote.com*

E-zine Databases

➤ E-zine Master Index at *http://www.site-city.com/members/e-zine-master*

➤ E-zine Search at *http://www.homeincome.com/search-it/ezine/index.html*

➤ New E-zine Directory at *http://foxcities.com/ims/ezine.htm*

E-zine Links

➤ The E-text Archives at *http://dmoz.org/Arts/Literature/Electronic_Text_Archives*

➤ John Labovitz's E-zine List at *http://www.etext.org/zines*

E-mail Resources

E-mail Clients

➤ Eudora at *http://www.eudora.com*

➤ Netscape at *http://www.netscape.com*

➤ Outlook Express at *http://www.microsoft.com*

Free E-Mail

➤ Free Email Address Directory at *http://www.emailaddresses.com*

➤ ILoveJesus.com at *http://www.ilovejesus.com*

➤ Juno at *http://www.juno.com*

➤ Truepath at *http://www.truepath.com*

Web-Based E-Mail

➤ Hotmail at *http://www.hotmail.com*

➤ ThatWeb.com at *http://www.thatweb.com*

E-mail Tips

➤ Everything Email at *http://everythingemail.net*

➤ Netiquette at *http://www.albion.com/netiquette/book/index.
html*

Encyclopedias

➤ Britannica.com site at *http://www.britannica.com*

➤ Encyclopedia.com at *http://www.encyclopedia.com*

Expert Links

➤ Ask An Expert at *http://www.askanexpert.com*

➤ Associations on the Net at *http://www.ipl.org/ref/AON*

➤ The Dot.com Directory at *http://www.dotcomdirectory.com*

➤ Experts.com at *http://www.experts.com*

➤ Profnet at *http://www.profnet.com*

➤ YearbookNews.com at *http://www.YearbookNews.com*

Government Sites

➤ Canada Post at *http://www.canadapost.ca*

➤ The Internal Revenue Service (IRS) at *http://www.irs.treas.gov*

➤ Revenue Canada at *http://www.ccra-adrc.gc.ca/menu-e.html*

➤ TaxPlanet at *http://www.taxplanet.com*

➤ United States Postal Service at *http://www.usps.com*

➤ The Writer's Pocket Tax Guide at *http://foolscap-quill.com/
wptg2000.html*

Grammar Sites

- The Arrow at *http://www.wport.com/~cawilcox/mainpath/page1.htm*
- Common Errors in English at *http://www.wsu.edu:8080/~brians/errors/index.html*
- Copy Editor at *http://www.copyeditor.com*
- Elements of Style at *http://www.bartleby.com*
- The English Grammar Clinic at *http://www.lydbury.co.uk/grammar*
- The Grammar Hotline at *http://www.tc.cc.va.us/writcent/gh/hotlinol.htm*
- The Grammar Lady Online at *http://www.grammarlady.com*
- Guide to Grammar and Writing at *http://webster.commnet.edu/HP/pages/darling/original.htm*
- Jesse's Word of the Day at *http://www.randomhouse.com/jesse*
- The Phrase Finder at *http://www.shu.ac.uk/web-admin/phrases/go.html*
- The Slot at *http://www.theslot.com*
- The University of Wisconsin at *http://www.library.wisc.edu/libraries/Memorial/citing.htm*
- The Word Detective on the Web at *http://www.word-detective.com*
- The Writing Center at *http://www.rpi.edu/dept/llc/writecenter/web/handouts.html*

Guide Sites

- About.com at h*ttp://www.about.com*
- Suite 101.com at *http://www.suite101.com*

Internet Service Provider Resources

Commercial Online Services

- America Online at *http://www.aol.com*
- Compuserve at *http://www.compuserve.com*
- Prodigy at *http://www.prodigy.com*

Filtered ISPs

➤ CleanWeb at *http://home.cleanweb.net*

➤ ClearSail at *http://www.clearsail.net*

➤ DotSafe at *http://www.dotsafe.net/staticindex.html*

➤ Family.Net at *http://www.family.net*

➤ Integrity Online at *http://www.integrityonline.com*

➤ Mayberry at *http://www.mayberryusa.com*

Filtering Software

➤ CyberPatrol at *http://www.cyberpatrol.com*

➤ Cyber Sitter at *http://www.solidoak.com/cysitter.htm*

➤ Net Nanny at *http://www.netnanny.com/netnanny*

Free ISPs

➤ About.com at *http://www.about.com*

➤ Aid4 Free ISPs at *http://www.y4i.com/freeaccess2.html*

➤ AltaVista at *http://www.freealtavista.com*

➤ Freei.Net at *http://go.freei.net/www*

➤ FreePPP at *http://www.freeppp.com*

➤ WorldSpy.com at *http://www.worldspy.com/freeisp/ free-isp-nav.asp*

Internet Service Providers

➤ A+Net at *http://www.aplus.net*

➤ EarthLink at *http://www.earthlink.com*

➤ MindSpring at *http://www.mindspring.net*

ISP Locators

➤ ComputerCurrents at *http://www.currents.net/resources/ispsearch*

➤ ISPcheck at *http://webpedia.ispcheck.com*

➤ ISPs.com at *http://www.isps.com*

➤ The List at *http://thelist.internet.com/internet.com*

➤ The Ultimate Web ISP List at *http://webisplist.internetlist.com*

Learning Sites

Fee-Based Learning

- ➤ Coffee House for Writers at *http://www.coffeehouse4writers.com*
- ➤ Diversity University at *http://www.du.org/duSvcs/teachers.htm*
- ➤ Explorations Unlimited at *http://www.explorationsu.com*
- ➤ F2K at *http://fiction.4-writers.com/creative-writing-classes.shtml*
- ➤ Fiction Writer's Connection at *http://www.fictionwriters.com*
- ➤ Gotham Writers' Workshop at *http://www.write.org/gwwOnline/olCourses.html*
- ➤ The Institute for Children's Literature at *http://www.institutechildrenslit.com*
- ➤ Novel Craft at *http://www.noveladvice.com/craft/index.html*
- ➤ Online Course Centre at *http://www.accesstv.ab.ca/courses.html*
- ➤ Painted Rock Writers and Readers Colony at *http://www.paintedrock.com/conference/wrtclass.htm*
- ➤ Poynter Online at *http://www.poynter.org/class/q1-2000sked.htm*
- ➤ The Screenwriters & Playwrights page at *http://www.teleport.com/~cdeemer/Distance.html*
- ➤ Scribe and Quill Mailing List at *http://come.to/ScribeQuill*
- ➤ Simple Steps to Landing Profitable Assignments at *http://members.aol.com/bugsley/doug.htm*
- ➤ Sponsored by 4-Writers.Com at *http://4-writers.com*
- ➤ Word Museum at *http://www.wordmuseum.com/classes.htm*
- ➤ The Write Site at *http://www.thewritesite.com/corkboard.html*
- ➤ Writers Club University at *http://www.iuniverse.com*
- ➤ Writers.com at *http://www.writers.com*
- ➤ Writing Unlimited at *http://www.writing-unlimited.com*

Free Learning

- ➤ Inkspot at *http://www.inkspot.com/craft/courses.html*
- ➤ Purdue at *http://owl.english.purdue.edu/writers/#guides*
- ➤ Simple Steps to Landing Profitable Assignments at *http://members.aol.com/bugsley/doug.htm*
- ➤ Wordweave Creative Writing Lab at *http://www.welcome.to/wordweave*
- ➤ The Write Life at *http://welcome.to/thewritelife*

Mailing-List Resources

Mailing-List Search Sites
- CataList at *http://www.listserv.net/lists/listref.html*
- The Directory of Publicly Accessible Mailing Lists at *http://www.neosoft.com/internet/paml*
- Internet for Christians Newsletter at *http://www.gospelcom.net/ifc/mail/view/?ifc*
- IRE at *http://www.ire.org/membership/listserv.html*
- The Liszt at *http://www.liszt.com*
- Tile.net at *http://tile.net/lists*

Mailing-List Tips
- Email Discussion Groups/Lists and Resources at *http://www.webcom.com/impulse/list.html*
- Emily Post News at *http://www.templetons.com/brad/emily.html*

Newsletters and Mailing-List Hosting Services
- E-Groups at *http://www.egroups.com*
- ListBot at *http://www.listbot.com*
- OakNet Publishing at *http://Oaknetpub.com*
- ONEList at *http://onelist.com*

Marketing Resources

Fee-Based Press Release Services
- Internet to Media Fax Service at *http://www.imediafax.com*
- Press Flash at *http://www.pressflash.com*
- The U.S. Congressional Fax Service at *http://www.uscongress-fax.com*

Marketing and Promotional Resources
- All About Lists from A to Z at *http://www.listhost.net/fromatoz.htm*
- Gebbie Press at *http://www.gebbieinc.com*
- Internet Monitor at *http://www.internet-monitor.com/arti_plan.html*

➤ Internet Publicity Resources at *http://marketing.tenagra.com/pubnet*

➤ Para Publishing–Dan Poynter at *http://www.ParaPub.com*

Marketing/Book-Promotion Professionals

➤ Andrea Reynolds at *http://www.ExpertsWhoSpeak.org*

➤ Book Marketing Update at *http://bookmarket.com*

➤ BookZone at *http://www.bookzone.com*

➤ Firebaugh Communications at *http://www.firepub.com*

➤ The Littfin Pratt Agency at *http://www.littfinpratt.com*

➤ Marketability at *http://www.marketability.com*

➤ Sensible Solutions at *http://www.happilypublished.com*

Miscellaneous Marketing Tools

➤ The All Media Jumpstation at *http://www.owt.com/dircon/mediajum.htm*

➤ Ed's Internet Book Review at *http://www.clark.net/~bell/eibr/book_review.html*

➤ NetRead Event Calendar at *http://www.NetRead.com/calendar*

➤ RoseDog.com at *http://www.rosedog.com*

➤ Show Ideas.com at *http://showideas.com*

➤ The U.S. All Media E-Mail Directory at *http://www.owt.com/dircon*

Markets

➤ AJR Newslink at *http://ajr.newslink.org/mag.html*

➤ Association of American University Publishers (AAUP) at *http://aaup.pupress.princeton.edu*

➤ The BookWire Index at *http://www.bookwire.com/index/publishers.html*

➤ Editor and Publisher at *http://www.mediainfo.com/ephome/index/unihtm/siteindex.htm*

➤ Helpful Addresses at *http://www.acclaimed.com/helpful/new-add.htm*

➤ Inscriptions Paying Markets at *http://www.inscriptionsmagazine.com/Markets.html*

➤ Inspirational Romance Publishers at *http://members.aol.com/inspirlvg/pubs.htm*

➤ The iUniverse Data Base at *http://www.iuniverse.com/resources/iu_contact*

➤ The Market List at *http://www.marketlist.com*

➤ Newsletter Access Directory at *http://www.newsletteraccess.com/ directory.html*

➤ News Directory.com at *http://www.newsdirectory.com*

➤ Newspapers.com at *http://www.newspapers.com*

➤ Publishers' Catalogue Home Page at *http://www.lights.com/publisher*

➤ Publisher's Marketing Association (PMA) at *http://www.pma-online. org/pmalinks.html*

➤ Sally Stuart's Christian Writers' Market Guide at *http://www. stuartmarket.com/pubmain.htm*

➤ The Write Markets Report at *http://www.writersmarkets.com/index-guidelines.htm*

➤ WriteLinks: Commercial Book Publishers at *http://www.writelinks.com/ resources/pub/pubsbk.htm*

➤ Writer's Digest at *http://www.writersdigest.com*

➤ Writer's Guidelines Database at *http://mav.net/guidelines*

➤ Writers Information Network at *http://www.bluejaypub.com/ win/publishers.htm*

➤ The Writer's Place at *http://www.awoc.com/Guidelines.cfm*

➤ Writers Write at *http://www.writerswrite.com/books/bookpubs*

Message Boards

➤ Research Forum at *http://writers-bbs.com/inkspot/threads. cgi?forum=research*

➤ Speakers Place at *http://www.speakersplace.com/forum*

➤ Yahoo! at *http://messenger.yahoo.com*

Newsgroups

➤ Deja News at *http://www.deja.com*

➤ Deja Power Search at *http://www.exit109.com/~jeremy/news/deja.html*

➤ Misc.Writing at *http://www.scalar.com/mw*

➤ Newsgroup Terminology at *http://www.newbie-u.com/news/terms.html*
➤ Usenet Info Center at *http://metalab.unc.edu/usenet-i/usenet-help.html*

PDF Converters and Readers

➤ Adobe Acrobat at *http://www.adobe.com*
➤ PrintToPDF (Shareware,Mac) at *http://www.jwwalker.com*

Postage Online

➤ Estamp.com at *http://www.estamp.com*
➤ Stamps.com at *http://www.stamps.com*
➤ Stamps Online at *http://www.stampsonline.com*

Professional Associations Online

➤ American Advertising Federation (AAF) at *http://www.aaf.org*
➤ American Crimewriter's League at *http://members.aol.com/theACWL*
➤ American Marketing Association (AMA) at *http://www.ama.org*
➤ American Society of Journalists and Authors (ASJA) at *http://www.asja.org*
➤ The Association of American Publishers at (AAP) *http://www.publishers.org/home/index.htm*
➤ Associations on the Net (AON) at *http://www.ipl.org/ref/AON*
➤ Authors Guild Online at *http://www.authorsguild.org/welcome.html*
➤ Business Marketing Association (BMA) at *http://www.marketing.org*
➤ The Children's Book Council (CBC) at *http://www.cbcbooks.org*
➤ Christian Writers Fellowship International (CWFI) at *http://www.cwfi-online.org*
➤ Crime Writers of Canada at *http://www.crimewriterscanada.com*
➤ Direct Marketing Association (DMA) at *http://www.the-dma.org*
➤ The Editorial Freelancers Association at *http://www.the-efa.org/main.html*
➤ The Evangelical Christian Publishers Association at *http://www.ecpa.org*
➤ Evangelical Press Association at *http://www.gospelcom.net/epa/aboutepa.htm*

➤ The Freelance Editorial Association at *http://www.tiac.net/users/freelanc*
➤ InScribe Christian Writers' Fellowship in Canada (CWF) at *http://www.inscribe.org*
➤ Investigative Reporters and Editors, Inc. (IRE) at *http://www.ire.org*
➤ Mystery Writers of America, Inc. at *http://www.mysterywriters.net*
➤ National Speakers Association (NSA) at *http://www.nsaspeaker.org*
➤ National Writers Union (NWU) at *http://www.nwu.org/nwutoc.htm*
➤ The Public Relations Society of America (PRSA) at *http://www.prsa.org*
➤ Romance Writers of America at *http://www.rwanational.com*
➤ Sales and Marketing Executives International (SME) at *http://www. smei.org*
➤ Science Fiction and Fantasy Writers of America at *http://www.sfwa.org*
➤ The Society of Children's Book Writers and Illustrators (SCBWI) at *http://www.scbwi.org*
➤ The Society of Professional Journalists at *http://www.spj.org*
➤ Toastmasters International at *http://www.toastmasters.org*
➤ Writers Guild of America, West (WGAw) at *http://www.wga.org*
➤ Writers Information Network (WIN) at *http://www.bluejaypub.com/win*
➤ The Writers Union of Canada at *http://www.writersunion.ca*

Search Sites

Major Search Sites

➤ AltaVista at *http://www.altavista.com*
➤ Excite at *http://www.excite.com*
➤ Go Network at *http://www.go.com*
➤ HotBot at *http://www.hotbot.com*
➤ Infoseek at *http://www.infoseek.com*
➤ Lycos at *http://www.lycos.com*
➤ Northern Light at *http://www.northernlight.com*
➤ TheTrip.com at *http://www.TheTrip.com*
➤ WebCrawler at *http://www.webcrawler.com*
➤ Yahoo! at *http://www.yahoo.com*

Meta Sites

➤ Ask Jeeves at *http://www.askjeeves.com*

➤ Beaucoup at *http://www.beaucoup.com*

➤ CNET Search.com at *http://www.search.com*

➤ Dogpile at *http://www.dogpile.com*

➤ Google at *http://www.google.com*

➤ Inference Find at *http://www.InferenceFind.com*

➤ Librarian's Index to the Internet at *http://sunsite.berkeley. edu/InternetIndex*

➤ MetaCrawler at *http://www.metacrawler.com*

➤ Mamma at *http://www.mamma.com*

Portals

➤ About.com at *http://www.about.com*

➤ Canada.Com at *http://www.canada.com*

➤ Christianity.com at *http://www.christianity.com*

➤ CNN at *http://www.cnn.com*

➤ Crosswalk.com at *http://www.goshen.net*

➤ MSN at *http://www.msn.com*

➤ OnePlace at *http://www.oneplace.com*

➤ Snap.com at *http://www.snap.com*

➤ Suite101.com at *http://www.suite101.com*

Self-Publishing Resources

Miscellaneous Resources

➤ Copyright Information and Forms at *http://lcweb.loc.gov/copyright*

➤ ISBN numbers and ABI forms at *http://www.bowker.com*

➤ Printing Industry Exchange at *http://www.printindustry.com*

➤ Unlimited Publishing Services at *http://www.unlimitedpublishing. com*

Self-Publishing Companies

➤ ACW at *http://www.acwpress.com*

> Essence Publishing at *http://www.essencegroup.com*
> Morris at *http://www.morrispublishing.com*
> Wine Press at *http://www.winepresspub.com*

Speaker Resources

> Ambassador Agency at *http://www.ambassadoragency.com*
> Canadian Association of Professional Speakers (CAPS) at *http://www.canadianspeakers.org*
> Christian Leaders, Authors and Speakers Services (CLASS) at *http://www.classervices.com*
> Experts Who Speak at *http://www.ExpertsWhoSpeak.org*
> Great Speaking at *http://www.antion.com/ezinesubscribe.htm*
> Jim Watkins at *http://www2.fwi.com/~watkins/speak.htm*
> National Speakers Association (NSA) at *http://www.nsaspeaker.org*
> OnSpeakers.com at *http://www.speaking.com*
> Presenters Online at *http://www.presentersonline.com*
> SpeakerNet News at *http://www.SpeakerNetNews.com*
> Speakers.com at *http://speakers.com/database/speakersonline.asp*
> The Speakers Place at *http://www.speakersplace.com*
> Speeches.com at *http://speeches.com/gentips.htm*
> Sullivan Speaker Services at *http://www.sullivanspeaker.com*
> Toastmasters International at *http://www.toastmasters.org*

Search Engines for Speakers (Fee-Based)
> Christian Speakers International at *http://www.journeypubs.com/csi*
> Speakers.com at *http://speakers.com*
> Women's Ministry Network at *http://www.womensministry.net*

Speakers' Bureaus
> Christian Leaders, Authors and Speakers Services (CLASS) at *http://www.classervices.com*
> Leading Authorities, Inc. at *http://www.leadingauthorities.com*
> Professional Woman Speakers Bureau at *http://www.protrain.net*

➤ Speakers.com at *http://speakers.com/database/agentindex.asp*
➤ Speakers Spotlight at *http://www.speakers.ca*
➤ Walters Speakers Services at *http://www.walters-intl.com*

Specialty Engines and Search Sites

➤ The Argus Clearinghouse at *http://www.clearinghouse.net*
➤ B.J. Pinchbeck's Homework Helper at *http://www.bjpinchbeck.com*
➤ Ditto.com at *http://www.ditto.com*
➤ EgoSurf at *http://www.egosurf.com*
➤ Everything Search Engine at *http://www.searchenginewatch.com*
➤ FedWorld Information Network at *http://www.fedworld.gov*
➤ HomeworkCentral at *http://www.homeworkcentral.com*
➤ Inomics at *http://www.inomics.com*
➤ Internet Scout Project at *http://scout.cs.wisc.edu/index.html*
➤ The Megasite Project at *http://www.lib.umich.edu/megasite*
➤ Pilot-Search.com at *http://www.pilot-search.com*
➤ Refdesk.com at *http://www.refdesk.com*
➤ Search Power at *http://www.searchpower.com*
➤ TekMom: Resources for Students at *http://www.tekmom.com/students/index.html*

Urban Legends

➤ The AFU and Urban Legends Archive at *http://www.urbanlegends.com*
➤ Tourbus at *http://www.tourbus.com*

Web-Site Resources

Link Exchange and Banners
➤ Hyper Banner Network at *http://bpath.com*
➤ Link Exchange at *http://www.linkexchange.com*
➤ Recommend-It at *http://www.recomendit.com*
➤ Trafficx at *http://www.trafficx.com*

Search Engine and Submission Services

➤ Auto Submit at *http://autosubmit.com*

➤ Go Net-Wide at *http://www.gonetwide.com/gopublic.html*

➤ The Internet Promotions MegaList at *http://www.2020tech.com/submit.html*

➤ Self Promotion.com at *http://selfpromotion.com*

➤ Submit It! at *http://www.submitit.com*

➤ WebMasterSuite.com at *http://www.webmastersuite.com*

Site Maintenance

➤ LinkAlarm at *http://www.linkalarm.com*

Tutorials and Style Guides

➤ The Bare Bones Guide to HTML at *http://www.werbach.com/barebones*

➤ A Basic HTML Style Guide at *http://guinan.gsfc.nasa.gov:80/Style.html*

➤ Making a WWW Flop at *http://www.ciolek.com/WWWVLPages/QltyPages/FlopMaker.html*

➤ Net Tips for Writers and Designers at *http://www.dsiegel.com/tips*

➤ Promotion World at *http://www.promotionworld.com*

➤ Richard Wallace at *http://www.waller.co.uk/eval.htm*

➤ So You Want to Make a Web Page at *http://junior.apk.net/~jbarta/tutor/makapage/index.html*

➤ Unplugged Software at *http://www.unplug.com/great*

➤ What Makes a Great Site? at *http://www.webreference.com/greatsite.html*

➤ Yale Style Guide at *http://info.med.yale.edu/caim/manual*

Web Designers

➤ BookZone at *http://www.bookzone.com*

➤ Nance Publishing at *http://www.nancepub.com*

➤ SmartWorks at *http://www.smartwrks.com*

➤ Web Imagine Design at *http://www.sandraryan.com*

➤ Workable Webs at *http://www.workablewebs.com*

Web Hosting

- ➤ CNET Hosting List at *http://builder.com/Servers/WebHosting*
- ➤ Free Web Hosting at *http://www.free.com/index.asp?catid=67*
- ➤ IloveJesus.com at *http://www.ilovejesus.com*
- ➤ Truepath.com at *http://www.truepath.com*

Web Rings

- ➤ Web Ring at *http://www.webring.org*

Web Tools

- ➤ 123Greetings at *http://associates.123greetings.com*
- ➤ Bravenet at *http://www.bravenet.com*
- ➤ Cedge's HTML Cheat Sheet at *http://cedesign.net/help2j.htm*
- ➤ GIF Wizard at *http://uswest.gifwizard.com*
- ➤ Homepage Tools at *http://homepagetools.com/guestbook*
- ➤ MyComputer.com at *http://www.mycomputer.com*
- ➤ Uproar at *http://www.uproar.com/webdevelopers*
- ➤ Vatagenet at *http://apps3.vantagenet.com*
- ➤ Web Authoring Resources at *http://www.wwwscribe.com/resource.htm*
- ➤ WebSite Garage at *http://websitegarage.netscape.com*
- ➤ Zap Zone at *http://www.zzn.com*

Wholesalers, Distributors, and Fulfillment Houses

- ➤ Baker & Taylor at *http://www.baker-taylor.com*
- ➤ Book Clearing House at *http://www.bookch.com*
- ➤ Book World at *http://www.bookworld.com*
- ➤ Bookpeople at *http://www.bponline.com*
- ➤ Ingram Book Company at *http://www.ingrambook.com*
- ➤ National Book Network at *http://www.nbnbooks.com*
- ➤ Partners Book Distributing at *http://bookexpo.reedexpo.com*
- ➤ Quality Books at *http://www.quality-books.com*
- ➤ Small Press Distribution at *http://www.spdbooks.org*

Writers' and Speakers' Chats, Forums, and Mailing Lists

- ➤ About.com's Writer's Exchange at *http://writerexchange.about.com/ arts/writerexchange/mbody.htm*
- ➤ Authors Anonymous AA at *http://www.angelfire.com/wa/ AuthorsAnonymous/list.html*
- ➤ Blackwriters.org at *http://www.blackwriters.org/nsindex.html*
- ➤ Chatseek.com at *http://www.chatseek.com*
- ➤ Christian Writers' Fellowship International (CWFI) at *http://www. cwfi-online.org*
- ➤ Christian Writers Group at *http://members.truepath.com/CWG*
- ➤ Christian Writers Workshop at *http://www.billyates.com/cww/default.html*
- ➤ CNN Interactive Interviews at *http://www.cnn.com/chat*
- ➤ Copywriter.com at *http://www.copywriter.com*
- ➤ Eclectics Too at *http://www.delphi.com/eclecticstoo/start*
- ➤ Inspirational Romance Workshops at *http://members.aol.com/inspirlvg*
- ➤ iUniverse at *http://www.iuniverse.com/community/community_calendar.asp*
- ➤ Local Writer's Workshop at *http://www.elanworks.com/lww.html*
- ➤ My Writer Buddy at *http://www.writerbuddy.com*
- ➤ Novel Advice at *http://www.noveladvice.com*
- ➤ The Painted Rock Writers and Readers Colony at *http://www. paintedrock.com/index.html*
- ➤ Reader's Choice Book Chat at *http://www.thegrid.net/dakaiser/ books/chat.htm*
- ➤ Romance Central at *http://www.romance-central.com/index1.htm*
- ➤ Talk City at *http://www.talkcity.com*
- ➤ Tile.net at *http://www.tile.net*
- ➤ The Word Museum at *http://www.wordmuseum.com*
- ➤ WordsWorth at *http://www.wordsworth.com/www/present/interviews*
- ➤ Writelink's Writeshop Chat Room at *http://www.writelinks.com/ writeshop/index.html*
- ➤ The Writers BBS at *http://www.writersbbs.com/*
- ➤ Writers Write Chat at *http://www.writerswrite.com*
- ➤ Writer'sClub.com at *http://www.writersclub.com/chatschedules*

➤ WriterWorkshop.com at *http://www.writerworkshops.com/groups.html*

Writers' Mailing Lists

To subscribe, send an e-mail to the address listed or see instructions at the listed Web site.

➤ The Editors Forum at *Kat91@aol.com*
➤ Inklings at *Majordomo@home.samurai.com*
➤ Misc.Writing Mailing List at *http://www.scalar.com/mw/pages/mwmlist.shtml*
➤ Onelist at *http://www.onelist.com/directory/3/24*
➤ Self-Publishers Discussion List at *Publish-subscribe@onelist.com*
➤ The Writers With Humor List (WWH) at *Majordomo@ns.kconline.com*

Writing Sites

➤ Absolute Write at *http://www.absolutewrite.com*
➤ Black on White at *http://www.bfree.on.ca/bow*
➤ Business Writer's Free Library at *http://www.mapnp.org/library/commskls/cmm_writ.htm*
➤ The Eclectic Writer at *http://www.eclectics.com/writing/writing.html*
➤ ForWriters.com at *http://www.forwriters.com*
➤ Inkspot at *http://www.inkspot.com*
➤ iUniverse at *http://www.iuniverse.com*
➤ John Hewitt's Writer's Resource Center at *http://www.poewar.com*
➤ Mom Writers at *http://www.momwriters.com*
➤ The Official Misc.Writing Web Site at *http://www.scalar.com/mw*
➤ Pure Fiction at *http://www.purefiction.com*
➤ SharpWriter.com at *http://www.sharpwriter.com*
➤ Tips for Writers at *http://www.tipsforwriters.com*
➤ Write Links at *http://www.writelinks.com*
➤ The Write Page at *http://www.writepage.com*
➤ Writercise at *http://www.writercise.net*

➤ Writers.com at *http://www.writers.com*

➤ The Writer's BBS at *http://www.writers-bbs.com/home.shtml*

➤ Writer's Digest at *http://www.writersdigest.com*

➤ Writer's Links from Bricolage at *http://bricolage.bel-epa.com/ scripts/links.py?wo*

➤ WritersNet at *http://www.writers.net*

➤ Writer's Toolbox at *http://www.writerstoolbox.com*

➤ Writer's Tools at *http://www.writetools.com*

➤ Writing Corner at *http://www.writingcorner.com*

➤ Zuzu Petal's Literary Resources at *http://www.zuzu.com*

Children's Writing

➤ The BookWire Index Publishing for Young Readers at *http://www. insead.fr/Programmes/Case/ReadersInn/docs/bajado/bookstor/ bookwire/00328.htm*

➤ The Children's Book Council (CBC Online) at *http://www.cbcbooks.org*

➤ Children's Book Publishers at *http://www.scils.rutgers.edu/special/kay/ publish.html*

➤ The Children's Literature Web Guide at *http://www.acs.ucalgary. ca/~dkbrown/index.html*

➤ The Children's Writing SuperSite at *http://www.write4kids.com/ index.html*

➤ Cyberteens at *http://www.stonesoup.com*

➤ Inkspot for Young Writers at *http://www.inkspot.com/young*

➤ The Institute for Children's Literature at *http://www.institutechildrenslit. com*

➤ KidsWeb at *http://www.kidsvista.com/Arts/literature.html*

➤ Kidword at *http://www.bconnex.net/~kidworld*

➤ Patricia Polacco at *http://www.patriciapolacco.com/h.html*

➤ The Purple Crayon at *http://www.users.interport.net/~hdu/index. html*

➤ The Quill Society at *http://www.quill.net*

➤ The Society of Children's Book Writers and Illustrators (SCBWI) at *http://www.scbwi.org*

➤ Stone Soup Magazine at *http://www.stonesoup.com*

➤ Verla Kay's Web Site at *http://www.verlakay.com*

Christian Writing

➤ American Christian Writers at *http://www.ecpa.org/acw/index.html*

➤ The Amy Foundation at *http://www.amyfound.org*

➤ Christian Writers' Fellowship International (CWFI) at *http://www. cwfi-online.org*

➤ Christian Writers Group at *http://members.truepath.com/CWG*

➤ Christian Writers Workshop at *http://www.billyates.com/ cww/default.html*

➤ Kingdom Writers at *http://www.angelfire.com/ks/kingwrit*

➤ Marlene Bagnull's Write His Answers Ministries at *http://www. writehisanswer.com*

➤ W. Terry Whalin at *http://www.terrywhalin.com*

➤ Writers Information Network (WIN) at *http://www.bluejaypub.com/win*

Freelance Writing

➤ Ants.com at *http://www.ants.com/ants*

➤ Community Writers Association at *http://www.communitywriters.org/ index.html*

➤ Creative Freelancers at *http://www.freelancers.com*

➤ Freelance Editorial Association at *http://www.tiac.net/users/freelanc*

➤ Freelance Online at *http://www.FreelanceOnline.com/index2.html*

➤ Freelance Success at *http://www.freelancesuccess.com*

➤ Freelance Writing.com at *http://www.freelancewriting.com*

➤ NetRead at *http://www.netread.com/jobs/jobs*

➤ Sun Oasis Jobs at *http://www.sunoasis.com*

➤ T. Suzanne Eller at *http://www.intellex.com/~eller/tseller.html*

➤ WritersWeekly.com at *http://www.writersweekly.com*

➤ Writing Employment Center at *http://www.poewar.com/jobs.htm*

Journalism Sites

➤ American Journalism Review at *http://ajr.newslink.org/news.html*

- The Associated Press at *http://wire.ap.org*
- Business and Science News at *http://www.businesswire.com*
- Doug Millison at *http://www.online-journalist.com*
- Executive's Toolbox at *http://ceoexpress.com/*
- FACSNET at *http://www.facsnet.org*
- Guide to Electronic and Print Resources for Journalists at *http://www.cio.com/central/journalism.html*
- JournalismJobs.com at *http://www.journalismjobs.com*
- Monique's Newsjobs at *http://www.newsjobs.net*
- National Institute for Computer-Assisted Reporting (NICAR) at *http://www.nicar.org*
- National Press Club Reporter's Internet Resources at *http://npc.press.org/what/library/reporter.htm*
- NewsDirectory.com at *http://www.newsd.com*
- The Newsroom Home Page at AssignmentEditor.com at *http://assignmenteditor.com*
- Newstream.com at *http://www.newstream.com*
- Poynter Online at *http://www.poynter.org*
- PubList.com at *http://www.publist.com*
- Reporter.org at *http://www.reporter.org*
- Reporter's Internet Guide at *http://www.crl.com/~jshenry/home.html*
- Scoop Cybersleuth's Internet Guide at *http://www.courierpress.com/courier//scoop/journalism.html*
- Ultimate Collection of News Links at *http://www.pppp.net/links/news*

Mystery and Crime Writing

- Bibliomysteries at *http://www.bibliomysteries.com*
- ClueLass at *http://www.cluelass.com*
- Crime Writers of Canada at *http://www.crimewriterscanada.com/links/mystery.htm*
- Hollywood Crimewriting Network at *http://crimewriters.com/Crime/index.html*
- Mystery Pages at *http://www.mysterypages.com*

Playwriting and Screenwriting

➤ Act One Writing for Hollywood at *http://www.actoneprogram.com*

➤ The Dramatic Exchange at *http://www.dramex.org*

➤ Essays on the Craft of Dramatic Writing at *http://www.teleport. com/~bjscript/index.htm*

➤ Fade In Through Fade Out at *http://members.aol.com/anniraff/contents.htm*

➤ Hollywood Screenwriters Network at *http://hollywoodnet.com//scriptindex.html*

➤ Moviebytes.com at *http://www.moviebytes.com*

➤ The Online Communicator at *http://www.communicator.com/toppage.html*

➤ The Playwrights Union of Canada at *http://www.puc.ca*

➤ Richard Toscan, The Playwriting Seminars at *http://www.vcu.edu/artweb/playwriting/seminar.html*

➤ ScreenTalk at *http://www.screentalk.org*

➤ The Screenwriters Homepage at *http://home.earthlink.net/~scribbler*

➤ Screenwriters Online at *http://www.screenwriter.com/insider/main.html*

➤ Screenwriters Utopia at *http://www.screenwritersutopia.com*

➤ TV Writer.com at *http://www.tvwriter.com*

➤ The Visual Writer, Ltd. at *http://visualwriter.com/descript.htm*

➤ The Writers Guild of Canada at *http://www.writersguildofcanada.com*

Poetry Sites

➤ The Academy of American Poets at *http://www.poets.org*

➤ Aha! Poetry at *http://www.ahapoetry.com*

➤ AlienFlower at *http://www.sonic.net/web/albany/workshop*

➤ Christianity and the Arts at *http://www.christianarts.net/literature/literature.html*

➤ The Electronic Poetry Center (EPC) at *http://wings.buffalo.edu/epc*

➤ The Glossary of Poetic Terms at *http://shoga.wwa.com/~rgs/glossary.html*

➤ GreetingCardWriter at *http://www.greetingcardwriter.com*

➤ The Internet Poetry Archive at *http://metalab.unc.edu/ipa*

➤ Kurt McCullum, Editor: Adoration, A Journal of Christian Poetry at *http://www.mccullumsoftware.com/adoration/*

➤ Neile's Advice on How to Sell Poetry at *http://www.patriciapolacco. com/h.html*

➤ The Online Writery at *http://web.missouri.edu/~writery*

➤ Poets and Writers Online at *http://www.pw.org*

➤ Semantic Rhyming Dictionary at *http://www.link.cs.cmu.edu/dough/ rhyme-doc.html*

Romance Writing

➤ Harlequin Books at *http://www.romance.net*

➤ The Literary Times at *http://www.tlt.com/news/itiner.htm*

➤ Lori Soard at *http://www.wordmuseum.com*

➤ Romance and Women's Fiction Exchange (RomEx) at *http://www. romex.dm.net*

➤ Romance Writer and Reader Retreat at Simegen.com at *http://www. simegen.com/romance/index.html*

➤ Romance Writers of America (RWA) at *http://www.rwanational.com*

➤ Romancing the Web at *http://www.romanceweb.com/index5.cfm*

Science Fiction and Fantasy Sites

➤ Christopher Holliday, The Market List at *http://www.marketlist.com*

➤ Critters Workshop at *http://brain-of-pooh.tech-soft.com/users/critters*

➤ Internet Fantasy Writers Association at *http://www.fantasytoday.com*

➤ Moira Allen at *http://www.tipsforwriters.com/fantasy.shtml*

➤ Ralan's Webstravaganza at *http://www.ralan.com*

➤ Science Fiction and Fantasy Writers of America at *http://www.sfwa.org*

➤ Science Fiction Resource Guide at *http://www2.lysator.liu. se/sf_archive/sf-texts/SF_resource_guide*

➤ The SF Site at *http://www.sfsite.com*

➤ SFRT on the Web at *http://www.sfrt.com/sfrt2.htm*

➤ The Ultimate Science Fiction Web Guide at *http://www.magicdragon. com/UltimateSF*

Technical and Scientific Writing

➤ Gary Conroy at *http://techwriting.about.com/arts/techwriting*

- Inkspot's resources for science and technical writers at *http://www.inkspot.com/ss/genres/tech.html*
- John December Technical Communication Information Sources at *http://www.december.com/john/study/techcomm/info.html*
- John Hewitt's Technical Writing Center at *http://www.poewar.com/links/technical.htm*
- Society for Technical Communication (STC) at *http://stc.org*

Sample Sites

AUTHOR AND SPEAKER SITES

➤ Mary Allen at *http://homepage.fcgnetworks.net/jetent/mea*

➤ April Clay at *http://www.telusplanet.net/public/aclay*

➤ Gary Conroy at *http://techwriting.about.com/arts/techwriting*

➤ Kate Derie/ClueLass HomePage at *http://www.cluelass.com*

➤ T. Suzanne Eller at *http://www.intellex.com/~eller/tseller.html*

➤ Faithe Finley/The Master Design at *http://www.masterdesign.org*

➤ Deb Haggerty at http://www.PositiveConnect.com

➤ Doug Helsel at *http://www.AikensLaughs.com*

➤ Christopher Holliday, The Market List at *http://www.marketlist.com*

➤ Larry James at *http://www.celebratelove.com*

➤ Nancy Lindquist at *http://members.home.net/thats-life*

➤ Holly Lisle at *http://www.hollylisle.com*

➤ Jacqueline Marcell at *http://www.ElderRage.com*

➤ Kurt McCullum, editor, *Adoration, A Journal of Christian Poetry* at *http://www.mccullumsoftware.com/adoration*

➤ Kathy and Larry Collard Miller at *http://www.larryandkathy.com*

➤ Doug Millison at *http://www.online-journalist.com*

➤ Dr. Susan Mitchell, Ph.D., R.D. at *http://www.susanmitchell.org*

➤ Brenda Nixon at *http://www.parentpwr.com*

➤ Susan Osborn at *http://www.christiancommunicator.com*

➤ Patricia Polacco at *http://www.patriciapolacco.com/h.html*

➤ Beth Ratzlaff at *http://www.lifelinespeaking.com*

➤ Fern Reiss at *http://www.InfertilityDiet.com*

➤ Georgia Shaffer at *http://www.georgiashaffer.com*

➤ Linda Shepherd at *http://www.sheppro.com*

➤ Gail Showalter at *http://www.texasbiz.com/seeing*

➤ Lori Soard at *http://www.wordmuseum.com*

➤ Richard Toscan, The Playwriting Seminars at *http://www.vcu.edu/artweb/playwriting/seminar.html*

➤ John Vonhof at *http://www.footworkpub.com*

➤ Jim Watkins at *http://www2.fwi.com/~watkins/speak.htm*

➤ Terry Whalin at *http://www.terrywhalin.com*

➤ JoAnn Wray at *http://www.ilovejesus.com/lot/epistlewriter/TCWCpage.html*

ELECTRONIC PUBLICATIONS SITES

➤ Afterhours Inspirational Stories at *http://inspirationalstories.com*

➤ Chicken Soup for the Soul at *http://chickensoup.com*

➤ Heartwarmers4u at *http://www.heartwarmers4u.com*

➤ HollywoodJesus.com at *http://www.hollywoodjesus.com*

➤ January Magazine at *http://www.JanuaryMagazine.com*

Miscellaneous Resources
of Interest to Writers and Speakers

BOOKS *

1001 Ways to Market Your Book, by John Kremer (Fairfield, Iowa: Open Horizon, 1998).

The Complete Guide to Self-Publishing, by Tom and Marilyn Ross (Cincinnati, Ohio: Writers Digest Books, 1994).

Grassroots Marketing: Getting Noticed in a Noisy World, by Shel Horowitz (Springfield, Mass.: Chelsea Green, 2000).

Marketing Without Megabucks, by Shel Horowitz (New York: Fireside, 1991, 1993, 1998).

The Prepublishing Handbook, by Patricia Bell (Eden Prairie, Minn.: Cats Paw Press, 1992).

Christian Writer's Market Guide, by Sally Stuart (Harold Shaw, 1999).

Sally Stuart's Guide to Getting Published, by Sally Stuart (Wheaton, Ill.: Harold Shaw, 1999).

The Self-Publishing Manual, by Dan Poynter (Santa Barbara, Calif.: Para Publishing, 2000).

Smart Self-Publishing, by Linda Salisbury (Charlotte Harbor, Fla.: Tabby House, 1997).

COMPUTER AND SHOPPING SITES

➤ Consistent Computer Bargains at *http://www.1computerbargains.com*

* *All books may be ordered through http://www.writerspeaker.com/Bookstore.html.*

➤ MacMall at *http://www.macmall.com*
➤ PC Mall at *http://www.pcmall.com*
➤ uBid (online auctions) at *http://www.ubid.com*

E-BOOKS FOR WRITERS OF E-BOOKS

➤ How to Write, Publish and $ell eBooks at *http://www.booklocker.com*
➤ The Secrets of Our Success at *http://www.booklocker.com*
➤ U-Publish.com at *http://www.u-publish.com*

ONLINE COMPARISON SHOPPING SEARCH ENGINES

➤ Deal Time at *http://www.dealtime.com*
➤ mySimon at *http://www.mysimon.com*

ONLINE MAGAZINES

➤ *Contentious* at *http://www.contentious.com*
➤ *ForeWord Magazine* at *http://www.forewordmagazine.com*
➤ *Publishers Weekly* at *http://www.publishersweekly.com*
➤ *Self-Publishing Magazine* at *http://www.self-publishing.com/index.html*
➤ *Writer's Digest* at *http://www.writersdigest.com*

ONLINE MAPS

➤ MapQuest at *http://www.mapquest.com*
➤ Yahoo Maps at *http://maps.yahoo.com/py/maps.py*

PAPER AND MAILING MATERIALS

➤ Advanced Business Cards at *http://www.gapco.com*
➤ G&A Precycling at *http://www.gandaprecycling.com Packaging materials*
➤ Paper Direct at *http://www.paperdirect.com*
➤ Uline at *http://www.uline.com Packaging materials*

Twelve Things to Remember When Planning Your Web Site

by Teena Stewart

Careful planning can make the difference between a site with frequent visitors and one that is clicked on and quickly abandoned. Below are valuable tips to help organize and promote your site.

1. ORGANIZING YOUR SITE

Move from general to specific. Your home page represents the big picture and ought to clearly show the viewer your objective. Subsequent pages should lead the site visitor to more specific information listed on your home page. What is your Web site's purpose? Do you wish to inform people regarding a product or service? Do you wish to generate sales? Is it a member resource? Pinpointing the site's purpose gives a clearer direction when organizing the rest of the site. The next step is outlining major points or areas of interests. Subpoints connected to these main points can also become links. Each page should represent a different topic or sub area.

Keep it simple. The Internet offers millions of Web-surfing opportunities. If your site takes more than a few seconds to download, your site visitor may become frustrated and abandon your site. Why should he battle his way through your site when the next site is just a click away? Too many glitches and too much required effort practically guarantee the loss of your site visitor. Make navigation easy. Use a graphic or text at the top and bottom of each page so site visitors can quickly and easily return to previous pages or link from one page to the next. Everything should have a purpose. Make the site clean and simple and avoid clutter.

2 . DESIGNING YOUR SITE

Include nonlinear options. Your Web site can be built in both linear and non-linear format. Web site design novices frequently lay out their sites like links in a chain. They start with the home page, then create a link to a subtopic. From the subtopic they create another link. This isn't always the most efficient way of laying out Web pages since the site visitor has to back out of each page to get to the home page and choose another link. A good Web site allows non-linear movement. Visualize it as a family tree diagram with vertical and hori-zontal connections. Starting with the parent (home page), each generation branches out of the next. Imagine taking a family tree diagram and connecting each of its branches vertically and horizontally to other branches of the tree so that everyone is interconnected. (Scary thought.) That's a view of how a non-linear structure works.

Well-designed sites use both linear and nonlinear structure. For instance, your home page may list a variety of links. A site visitor clicks on one called "publication credits" and arrives at a separate page listing writing credits. The visitor clicks on one of the article titles and is taken to the article. From there he has a choice of backing out of the pages one click at a time, clicking on a link to the home page, or selecting one of several other links that will take him to other subpages. He doesn't necessarily have to return home to choose another page. This type of design takes more time, but in the end it simplifies movement for your viewer and makes the site more user-friendly.

Study other sites. What appeals to you about these sites? How's their layout? What colors did they use? How does their background look? Be careful not to duplicate copyrighted information and graphics.

Spend the most time and effort on your home page. It is the gateway to the rest of your Web pages. If a site visitor doesn't like the look of your home page, he won't bother to visit the rest of the site.

Use your organization's logo. A logo summarizes corporate identify. It assists the public with recognition of and identification with your organization and its purpose. You may allow it to dictate the colors and look of your home page.

Make it interactive. The more interactive your site is, the more popular it will be on the Web. Consider including a guest book, e-zine subscription information, contests, a thought for the day, etc.

3. BUILDING YOUR SITE

Build your web site in stages. Start with a simple design. Test your site frequently as you add new features so you can more easily detect and correct errors.

4. GETTING YOUR SITE NOTICED

Avoid the "if I build it, they will come" mentality. There are millions of sites competing for attention on the Internet. Having a Web site does not guarantee site visitors. You can increase your chances of getting noticed if you do the following:

Use "meta tags" in the Web page document head. These help search engines index your Web pages and make the best use of a search by providing specific information on your site. There are three types. The author meta tag is used to indicate who the author of the Web page is. The description meta tag is frequently used by search engines for a description that it can index. The keyword meta tag is used by robot search engines to index your site, and when someone does a word search, your site will be included in the output search results. Separate each keyword with a comma.

Include keywords as close to the top of your home page as possible so that your site appears high on the "hits list."

Use your Web site address on business cards, letterhead, and e-mail correspondence to help point people to your site.

Exchange links. You don't want your site visitor to wander off from your site to someone else's, nor do you want to lose your visitor to a competitor. Only link to sites that benefit you. Link your site to another in exchange for a link on theirs.

Creating a Web site takes time and patience, and with careful planning your site can become an invaluable promotional tool. Isn't it time you started one?

Teena Stewart is a writer and Web designer. She uses her Web site as a platform for both her writing and her graphics abilities. Her company, SmartWorks, specializes in creating projects where the graphics are as well done as the writing and vice versa. Her site is also an excellent example of using a Web site to feature samples of different styles of writing. Visit Stewart at http://www.smartwrks.com. This article used by kind permission.

Sixteen Ways for Speakers to Harness the Power of the Internet

by Andrea Reynolds

1. Exploit your e-mail address by revealing what you do: "ISpeak@aol.com" or what you're famous for: "brnstorm@GTE.net." Increase your name recognition by making your Web site domain name the same as your name: "www.AndreaReynolds.com."

2. Add your signature file at the bottom of every e-mail message. If you speak, say so, right after your name: "Andrea Reynolds, speaker, author." If you have a really topical lecture title, add the title to your sig file, and if you don't have a lengthy sig file, include the audience you want to address: "Build Your Million Dollar Advice Empire, for consultants and speakers."

3. Include additional promotion in your e-mail message. Take advantage of the Identity feature in your e-mail messages. Your message header can include the name of your speakers' bureau or agency in the line for organization.

4. Send a friendly e-mail to your family members and current friends (even your old college buddies). They, too, need to know you speak. We often assume the people closest to us should know what we do and offer, but often they are the ones who don't know. You might offer them a finder's fee for paid bookings that result from their referrals.

5. You can find discussion lists *(www.egroups.com)* and bulletin boards where you can post tips and advice, and let list/board members know you speak in the sig file at the bottom of your post.

6. Research current speaking fees by visiting Web sites of other speakers. You may decide to increase your daily rate of $150 for speaking in schools when you learn that some speakers charge a daily rate of $500.

7. Use some of the many search engines like Google to locate Web sites of conference and convention meeting planners and speakers' bureaus. These are the very people who are in a position to book you as a speaker for their clients' events.

8. Use the free Web space provided by your Internet service provider to create your first Web site. Having a presence on the Web really helps groups decide if you're the right speaker for their next meeting. Current browsers like Netscape 4.7 have included Composer features so that you can compose your own pages with greater ease.

9. Contribute a regular monthly column to an online magazine or newsletter (e-zine) in exchange for their putting up a Web page on their site that includes your speaker's bio, lecture topics, and how to contact you.

10. Start a monthly e-zine of your own on the topic that you speak on. Become the leading authority on your subject and let your subscribers know that you will travel if invited to speak in their community. Include your calendar of upcoming presentations in each issue. Your readers may come to your event or recommend you to their groups.

11. Generate book reviews in online publications by offering to send them a free review copy of your book. If you don't have a book, write a short tips booklet or package the notes from your seminar into a manual that can be purchased by mail. Be sure the review includes the price and a way to contact you.

12. Find audiences you'd like to address by using search engines to find local chapters of national organizations. Once you've spoken to one chapter, and assuming they liked you, ask for a letter of recommendation that can be distributed to other chapters.

13. Use the online bookstores like *www.amazon.com* to get ideas for upcoming speeches and seminars. Don't use the exact title—you're more creative than that—but look for phrases. I've seen a number of authors and speakers use the phrase "Jump Start Your..." (I'm one!)

14. List your books, e-books, or booklets from your Web page or Web site. Include a page in each publication, or a printed flier, that lists your speaking topics and how you can be booked for their next event.

15. Offer a freebie. On your Web page or at the bottom of an article you write for other people's sites, you can mention that readers can receive a tip sheet on "12 ways to…(whatever you speak about)" if they will send you an SASE (self-addressed, stamped envelope). If it's a one-page tip sheet, you can slip three to four more pages into the envelope without additional postage…but this will only work in your own country. I offer a two-page tip sheet "12 Steps to Becoming an Outstanding Speaker" for an SASE and include a flier for my $35 handbook, *The Speaker's Promotion Kit: How to Make Money As a Paid Speaker.*

16. Offer to review other people's books or e-books and offer to post the review online. Your blurb can discreetly mention that you're a speaker or you can identify yourself after your name as "Andrea Reynolds, author, lecturer."

Speaker and former speakers' agent Andrea Reynolds works as a marketing consultant and strategist for speakers, experts, and consultants through her business, Experts Who Speak. Reynolds has helped speakers and experts increase their visibility and income for over twenty years. She can be reached by e-mail at brnstorm@GTE.net or by calling 1-US-REYNOLDS. Visit her Web site at http://www. ExpertsWhoSpeak.org. This article used by kind permission.

NOTES

Chapter 1: Getting on the Road

1. Quoted in http://www.edmontonjournal.com/computers/010799c2.html
2. Quoted in http://www.uriel.net/~spunkie/morestory/stories/pcdata.html

Chapter 2: Exploring the Neighborhood

1. "Will Net stamps, email, hurt postal monopoly?" by Evan Hansen, CNET News.com, 25 October 1999, http://news.cnet.com/news//0-1005-200-1401751.html?tag=st.cn.sr.ne.2.

Chapter 5: Back to School

1. Sally Stuart, *Sally Stuart's Guide to Getting Published* (Colorado Springs, Colo.: Harold Shaw, 1999), 21-2.

Chapter 6: Business Calls

1. Extensive quotations in the following chapters are taken from e-mail correspondence. I appreciate the helpful insight from the editors and authors I contacted and their gracious permission to reproduce their words here.

Chapter 10: From the Ground Up

1. http://www.lawbuzz.com/justice/hurricane/lies_matter.htm
2. Quoted in "Watch Where You Put Your Property" by Amy Gahran, http://www.contentious.com/articles/V2/2-4/editorial2-4.html.

GLOSSARY

The majority of terms listed here are also featured in the text of *Writer-Speaker.com*. Additional terms have been included to help you in your time spent on the Internet.

attachment: A text, sound, or graphic file attached to and sent along with an e-mail message.

bookmark: Web-site addresses saved on a Netscape browser so you can quickly return to the same Web document without searching the Internet.

boolean: An "algebra of logic" developed by George Boole, which has become the basis for computer database searches.

browser: Software (program) that allows you to surf the Web. The most popular browsers are Netscape Navigator and Microsoft Internet Explorer.

buddy list: Software applications that, after registration, show you who you know online and lets you send messages to them.

chat: Real-time communication system with people typing their conversations over the Internet.

chat room: A place on the Internet where people go to "chat" with other people.

client: A software program, such as an e-mail or newsgroup program, that is used to contact and obtain data from a server software program on another computer.

cookies: A small text file that Web sites save on your computer to store information about you and your interaction on their site. In theory, cookies are there to make your surfing easier, faster, more personal, and more efficient. However, they are also used to collect your e-mail address so you can receive even more spam (junk mail). While you can set your browser to warn you before you accept cookies or not accept them at all, some sites (commerce) won't work if you don't accept their cookies.

cyberspace: Used to describe the Internet, the term was coined by science fiction novelist William Gibson in 1984 in his book *Neuromancer*.

domain name: The unique name that identifies an Internet site. This name takes the place of the specific Internet Proxie (IP) number given to each computer on the Internet and is much easier to remember than a string of numbers.

download: The transfer of information such as mail, graphics, sounds, or actual software programs from the Internet to your computer.

DSL (Digital Subscriber Line): A DSL circuit moves digital data over regular phone lines rather than converting the data into analog signals as does a modem. DSL is much faster than a regular phone connection but often more expensive and is not yet available in every area.

EAN Bookland Scanning Symbol: An international barcode used to identify books, videocassettes, audio cassettes, and software.

e-mail: Electronic mail. It allows you to send and receive mail (messages) over the Internet.

emoticon: A kind of emotional shorthand, composed of a few text characters that are used to add meaning to messages.

FAQs (Frequently Asked Questions): A FAQ file is a minihelp file consisting of common questions and answers on a specific topic.

favorites: Web-site addresses saved on a Microsoft Internet Explorer browser so you can quickly return to the same Web document without searching on the Internet.

flame: An angry or rude e-mail message, often posted as a public response on an e-mail or newsgroup discussion list.

freeware: Software provided by the creator for free.

FTP (File Transfer Protocol): Internet process for transferring files through the Internet from one computer to another.

GIF (Graphic Interchange Format): A common format for graphic files on the Web.

hierarchies: A method of organizing newsgroup categories.

home page: The main page of a Web site. Sometimes the entire site is erroneously called a home page.

host: The computer on which a Web site is physically located. Also called a server.

HTML (HyperText Markup Language): The language used to create Web pages.

HTTP (Hypertext Transfer Protocol): The protocol used to transfer Web documents across the Internet.

hypertext: Text on a Web page that links the user to another Web page. The hypertext or hyperlink will usually be a different color than the other text on the page.

instant messengers: Free software that allows Internet users to send and receive messages and chat via private text files.

IRC (Internet Relay Chat): Worldwide real-time chat on the Internet.

ISBN (International Standard Book Number): A standard identification system for books.

ISP (Internet Service Provider): A company that provides access to the Internet.

JPEG (Joint Photographic Experts Group): A compressed graphic format often found on the Web.

keyword: A word you might use to search for a Web site.

Library of Congress Card Number (LCCN): A unique title control number assigned by the Library of Congress to a given work.

link: Short for "hyperlink." Links can be text or graphic, and clicking on them allows you to jump from page to page.

listserv: The most common kind of Internet mailing list.

location: An Internet address.

lurk: Reading newsgroup or mailing-list messages without responding to them.

meta search engine: A search engine using several other search engines simultaneously with the results of all the engines presented in a unified format.

MIME (Multipurpose Internet Mail Extension): The most common method for encoding e-mail attachments over the Internet.

modem: Short for modulator-demodulator devices. Modems allow computers to connect with other computers over an analog phone line.

MOO (Multi-Object Oriented): Text-based chat option requiring special software. In some cases Moos are used to create multimedia virtual reality worlds.

navigate: Moving around the Web, using a browser to jump from link to link.

netiquette: Etiquette on the Internet.

newbie: A newcomer to the Internet or to a specific chat room, newsgroup, or mailing list.

newsgroups: Also called usenets, they are ongoing discussion groups among people on the Internet who share a mutual interest.

newsreader: A piece of software that you connect to your ISP's news servers to manage the messages in a newsgroup.

PDF (Portable Document Format): A special file format created by Adobe Systems, Inc. Documents in this format can be distributed electronically across the Web and on a variety of platforms, all the while retaining their original look.

PoP (Point of Presence): Usually means a city or location where a network can be connected to, often with dial-up phone lines.

POP (Post Office Protocol): The way e-mail clients (software) get mail from a mail server.

portal: A Web site that aims to be a "doorway" to the World Wide Web, typically offering a search engine, links to useful pages, free e-mail, news, or other services. Most portals exist to generate advertising income for their owners.

protocol: A set of rules that lets computers agree how to communicate over the Internet.

public domain software: Software that doesn't belong to anyone. It can be used for free.

search engine: A program that uses names and keywords to find pertinent Web pages.

server: A computer connected to the Internet to provide information and services to the Internet.

shareware: Software that is freely distributed without an up-front payment. After a trial period the user is expected to pay a fee.

signature: A short piece of text, usually at the bottom, transmitted with an e-mail message. Most signatures identify the sender's contact information, Web site, and often some marketing information.

snail mail: An Internet term for postal mail, because it's so slow compared to e-mail.

spam: The Internet version of junk mail. "Spamming" is sending the same unrequested message to a large number of users, usually to advertise something.

spider: A program that automatically retrieves Web pages. Spiders are used to feed pages to search engines. It's called a spider because it crawls over the Web.

surfing: The process of "looking around" the Internet.

thread: A topic of discussion in a newsgroup or mailing list.

upload: The process of transferring information from your computer to another computer through the Internet.

URL (Uniform Resource Locator): A Web-site address. It usually begins with "http://".

usenet: Ongoing discussion groups among people on the Internet who share a mutual interest. Also called newsgroups.

user ID: The unique identifier (like your log-on name) that you use to identify yourself on a computer.

Web: Short for the World Wide Web.

Web browser: The tool (program) that allows you to surf the Web. The most popular Web browsers are Netscape Navigator and Internet Explorer.

Webcasting: Using the World Wide Web specifically to broadcast information, using audio and video presentations.

WWW: An acronym for the World Wide Web.

WYSIWYG: Pronounced wiz-ee-wig, it is an abbreviation for "what you see is what you get." A WYSIWYG editor or program is one that allows you to create a Web page that lets you see what the end result will look like while the interface or document is being created.

INDEX

Carmen Leal is the author of *Faces of Huntington's,* a book for and about people with Huntington's Disease and others who care. With no distribution other than the Internet and her speaking engagements, Leal sold over forty-five hundred copies of this self-published book in the first year. Leal is also the co-author of *Pinches of Salt, Prisms of Light,* a collection of writings about ordinary people doing extraordinary things. Her stories and writings have appeared in books such as *The Gift of Miracles* (William Morrow), *Climb High, Climb Far* (Simon and Schuster), *Heart-Stirring Stories of Love* (Broadman & Holman), and *Ripples of Joy* (Harold Shaw Publishers), as well as in numerous other national and local publications.

A CLASS graduate (Christian Leaders, Authors, Speakers Services) and a member of Writers Information Network and Christian Writers Fellowship International, Leal is also a professional singer and speaker. A storyteller with a dramatic testimony, she is a popular presenter at conventions, conferences, and church groups throughout the United States. Leal is known for her down-to-earth style and common-sense approach to dealing with life, as well as her enthusiasm and sense of humor. In addition to her inspirational programs, she teaches workshops on topics such as "The Internet for Writers and Speakers," "Marketing for Writers and Speakers," "Self-Publishing," and "Writing for Publication" at national writers' conferences, churches, bookstores, and writers' groups.

Prior to relocating in Florida in 1996, Leal was a marketing consultant for ten years in Hawaii, providing promotional services to small businesses, churches, and nonprofit organizations. Leal is the mother of two teenage sons.